AD 381

Heretics, Pagans and the Christian State

CHARLES FREEMAN

PIMLICO

Published by Pimlico 2009

2 4 6 8 10 9 7 5 3 1

Copyright © Charles Freeman 2008

Charles Freeman has asserted his right under the Copyright, Designs
and Patents Act 1988 to be identified as the author of this work

First published in Great Britain in 2008 by Pimlico

Pimlico
Random House, 20 Vauxhall Bridge Road,
London SW1V 2SA

www.rbooks.co.uk

Addresses for companies within The Random House Group Limited can be found at:
www.randomhouse.co.uk/offices.htm

The Random House Group Limited Reg. No. 954009

A CIP catalogue record for this book
is available from the British Library

ISBN 9781845950071

The Random House Group Limited supports The Forest Stewardship
Council (FSC), the leading international forest certification organisation. All our titles that are
printed on Greenpeace approved FSC certified paper carry the FSC logo. Our paper procurement
policy can be found at www.rbooks.co.uk/environment

Typeset in Galliard by Palimpsest Book Production Limited,
Grangemouth, Stirlingshire

Printed and bound in Great Britain by
Clays Ltd, St Ives plc

For my children, Barney, Issie, Tom and Cordy,
in the knowledge that they will continue to think freely and
creatively about the things that enthuse them

CONTENTS

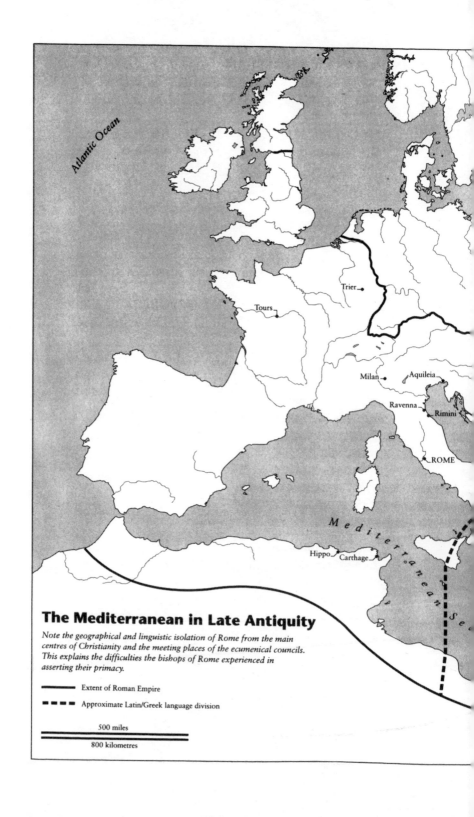

The Mediterranean in Late Antiquity

Note the geographical and linguistic isolation of Rome from the main centres of Christianity and the meeting places of the ecumenical councils. This explains the difficulties the bishops of Rome experienced in asserting their primacy.

—————— Extent of Roman Empire

▄▄ ▄▄ ▄▄ Approximate Latin/Greek language division

500 miles

800 kilometres

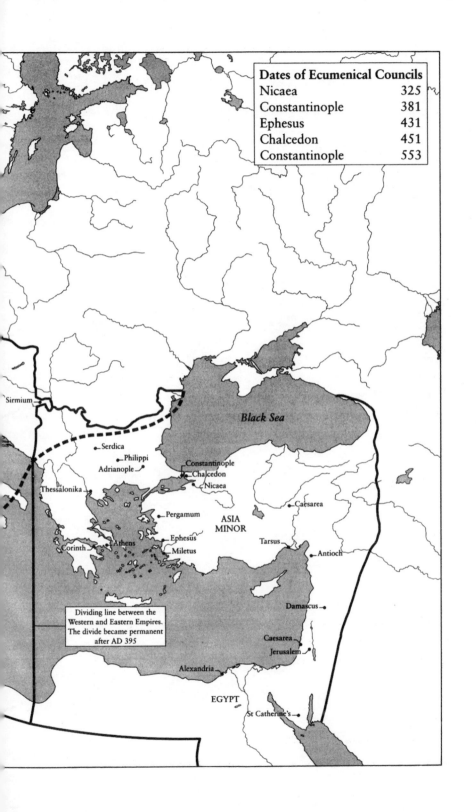

Dates of Ecumenical Councils	
Nicaea	325
Constantinople	381
Ephesus	431
Chalcedon	451
Constantinople	553

Sirmium

Black Sea

Serdica

Philippi

Adrianople

Constantinople

Chalcedon

Thessalonika

Nicaea

Caesarea

Pergamum

ASIA
MINOR

Ephesus

Athens

Tarsus

Corinth

Miletus

Antioch

Damascus

Dividing line between the
Western and Eastern Empires.
The divide became permanent
after AD 395

Caesarea

Jerusalem

Alexandria

EGYPT

St Catherine's

ACKNOWLEDGEMENTS

The number of books published each year has reached record levels but, paradoxically, it has become more difficult for a writer to get a book accepted. So I am thankful to my agent, Bill Hamilton, for placing *AD 381* with Will Sulkin at Pimlico. Will helped clarify the central themes of the book while, after it was completed, Jörg Hensgen offered effective guidance for tidying the text and tightening the argument. I am very grateful to them both. The text has been copy-edited with great care by Jane Selley and the index has been compiled by Oula Jones. My thanks are due to them both.

PREFACE

IN 1999 I signed a contract to write a book that was given the provisional title *The Triumph of Hellenism*. Its aim was to bring together some of the recent scholarship focusing on Greek culture under the Roman Empire. One of the benefits of Roman stability had been to allow the Greeks to consolidate their cultural dominance over the eastern empire while also maintaining a record of impressive intellectual achievement. Some of the finest minds of the Greek world, Plutarch, Ptolemy, Galen and Plotinus, were working in the early centuries AD and the quality of education for the elite remained extraordinarily high. An early-fifth-century philosopher, Synesius of Cyrene, gave a definition of a Hellene, by which he meant a pagan Greek, as one 'able to associate with men on the basis of a knowledge of all worthwhile literature'. Particularly impressive was the networking of this elite in the distribution to each other of copies of major works in almost every discipline. That literature circulated widely in the Christian as in the pagan world.

Having signed the contract and begun to work on the structure of the book, I had to provide a chapter or two on how the tradition of rational thought, which the Greeks had done so much to define, came to an end. For Edward Gibbon, in his *Decline and Fall of the Roman Empire*, intellectual life was already stagnant in the early Christian centuries, but this was clearly not the case. The rediscovery by modern scholarship of the cultural vitality of these centuries meant that new explanations were needed for its disappearance. In a Gibbonesque moment, sitting on the edge of the Roman forum, close to where Gibbon himself had been inspired to write his great work, I began looking at the spread of church buildings into the historic pagan centre. Just at a time when the empire was under severe pressure, close in fact to collapse in the west, resources were being shifted from the ancient temples and buildings to opulent churches. Did this reflect a similar shift of the ideology that underpinned the society of late antiquity? My research set off in a new and unexpected direction as I began realising the extent to which the Church had benefited from but had also been shaped by the patronage of the state. After the granting of toleration to Christians by Constantine in 313, an important new phase in Christian history began during which the Church became associated with massive buildings, support of the empire's objectives in war and a tightening up of authority as emperors such as Theodosius limited the freedom to discuss spiritual matters by both Christians and pagans. A new book rose from the contract of the old. It was later published as *The Closing of the Western Mind*.[1]

I was more than happy with the interest and discussion that the subject aroused. Despite some caricatures of my book as an attack on Christianity per se (and the criticism that I was reviving old, discredited arguments even though I was, in fact, responding to new research), most readers accepted the central premise that the Church had become politicised by the state, and the most thoughtful reviews saw the analogy between the fourth century, and the United States of the early twenty-first century where a similar relationship between Church and state appeared to be in the making. It was good to see the number of churches in the United States that chose *Closing* as one of their discussion books. I had protected my argument by adding a hundred pages of notes detailing the evidence for my argument, and there was no comprehensive attack on my thesis based on an analysis of this evidence. So I went on to other projects. Perhaps my temperament is to blame, but I needed a break from the abusive letters of Jerome, the posturings of Ambrose of Milan and the ever more gloomy prognostications of Augustine. This had never been intended to be my subject and there was no reason to stay with it.

One response, however, continued to bother me. It was the criticism that I had set out to oppose Christianity. I am not particularly drawn to organised religion but I enjoy many religious activities, especially listening and talking to those who have read widely in spiritual literature, Christian or otherwise. In fact, I believe that a spiritual dimension is part of any healthy mind. It is surely right to reflect on values that go

beyond the purely material, and I find the somewhat frenzied denunci-
ations of Richard Dawkins and his supporters simplistic. Human beings
have always organised themselves to participate in what can only be
called 'religious' activities and to speculate on what may or may not
lie beyond the material world. They have gained great comfort from
their shared involvement in these activities. How Professor Dawkins
imagines one can ringfence this aspect of human behaviour and
somehow eliminate it is not clear. (One thing I notice about Dawkins'
work is that he has no sense of the emotions that drive people to search
for religious meaning.) Where I have difficulty is being asked to believe
one dogma or another on grounds of 'faith' when there is no rational
underpinning for that dogma. One can surely combine a sense of the
spiritual, an understanding of the importance of ritual, without having
to express this in absolute statements of what God might or might not
be. Often, as in the case discussed in this book, one can, in fact, pinpoint
the specific historical and even political, rather than theological, context
in which an item of belief became privileged over alternatives and was
then transformed into dogma.

Ever since Christianity became deeply embedded in the structure of
secular societies, there has been a debate over the extent to which religion and civilisation reinforce each other. This debate seems to lead
nowhere largely because what is meant by 'civilisation' and 'Christianity'
has fluctuated so widely. There were Christian churches that supported
apartheid in South Africa, Christians who led the fight against it. Earlier
there were Christians who claimed that the Bible showed that God had
decreed the state of slavery. 'Slavery is God's punishment for sin', as
Augustine put it in his *City of God*. I am reminded of the nineteenth-
century bishop of Vermont who expressed his personal revulsion for
slavery but who acknowledged that his 'frail intellect' on the subject
had to be overruled by the authority of God on the matter as clearly
expressed in the scriptures. Despite this apparently divine support for
the institution, it was Christians who initiated the abolition of slavery.
Again, in the twelfth century Bernard of Clairvaux, the scourge of the
brilliant Abelard, was able to opine, 'Let him who has scanned the
heavens go down to the depths of Hell.' It is equally possible to conceive
of a (Christian) God who has created the world to run according to
stable natural laws and who exults in giving human beings reasoning
minds to discover and understand them. Newton was one of these, even
though he rejected the doctrine of the Trinity. So there are traditions

within Christianity (and other religions) that have opposed scientific investigation and others that have supported it. Similarly, while Francis of Assisi preached poverty, he was soon commemorated in his home town after his death by some of the most costly and beautiful buildings of the Middle Ages.

It seems, in fact, that the churches have been able to survive largely because Christianity has proved so astonishingly flexible. The early Church was Jewish, the 'Greek' Church of the second century often strongly anti-Jewish. In the third century there were campaigns of persecution of the Church so that, in the 250s and early fourth century, it operated as an underground organisation drawing strength from its martyrs. By 350, it was part of the structure of the empire, housed in opulent buildings and giving full support for the empire's wars. The sheer range of the texts that eventually came to make up the Bible has allowed theological and historical interpretations to shift with time. Fundamentalists claim to be returning to an original Christianity based on biblical texts, seemingly unaware that as early as the third century, Christian scholars such as Origen were arguing that the scriptures, at a time when the New Testament was still not in its final form, needed to be interpreted allegorically rather than literally. Who are the traditionalists here? The gospels have been interpreted to provide a Jesus for any occasion. Even in the past twenty years, there have been scholarly 'biographies' of the historical Jesus which have described him alternatively as a violent revolutionary ready to take up the sword against Roman oppression; an early feminist who elevated women to a higher status than traditional Jewish society allowed; an apocalyptic prophet ushering in God's reign on earth; a proto-Marxist social reformer urging an economic and social revolution; a Hasid, or Jewish holy man, of whom there were many other examples; and even a Greek-style Cynic philosopher who preached the renunciation of all worldly goods. Republicans in the United States have been able to find a proto-capitalist Christ, the gospel texts ingeniously reread in support of free enterprise. One of the most interesting transformations has been from the Jesus of whom Ernest Renan (1823–92) stated in his famous *Life* (1863) that 'fundamentally there was nothing Jewish', to the full acknowledged Jewishness of Jesus in recent scholarship. I was not surprised to hear from an Anglican vicar friend that the section of his library that dates most quickly is that on theology.

It is not only the interpretation of particular texts that has shifted with writer and period. In the fourth century, when Christianity became an integral part of the Roman state, attention shifted from the gospels to the Old Testament, which provided scriptural support for a ruler appointed by God whose status depended on success in war. By the end of the century Augustine is drawing heavily on the letters of Paul to provide intellectual backbone for his own theology, and his Christology, the study of the nature of Christ as revealed in the gospels, is relatively undeveloped in comparison. Any serious study of the history and present state of theology needs to include an analysis of which texts, from the wide variety available in the Bible, are being selected as most helpful in supporting the ideology of the day. One is reminded by Allen Dwight Callahan in *The Talking Book: African Americans and the Bible* that biblical texts that are unknown to white Christians have enormous potency among black communities, which are heirs to slavery and colonialism.[2]

So any argument that in general terms Christianity saved or destroyed civilisation, rational thought or whatever has to be qualified by a study of the specific historical and social context for which the statement is being made. When one reads that European civilisation is based on Christian values, one has to ask which of the enormously wide range of 'values' Christians have supported over the centuries are the relevant ones and whether some obviously important values, such as religious toleration, did not have to fight for survival against the attempts of the churches to suppress them. Too often specific values are proclaimed to be 'Christian' without any explanation of when or how the Church fostered or supported them. It is often asserted, for instance, that the churches promoted individualism and progress despite the evidence that Augustine's pessimism about the fallen, and thus helpless, nature of humankind was the prevalent ideology in Europe as late as the seventeenth century. I would argue instead that the historian should look closely at how specific manifestations of Christianity related to the wider dimensions of the society in which it found itself, and this is what I tried to do in *The Closing of the Western Mind*. I had no doubts, and still have none, that the Greek tradition of free-ranging intellectual thought was challenged by the specific ways in which Christianity manifested itself in the fourth and fifth centuries as the servant of an authoritarian state. After the collapse of the empire in the west, a very different Christianity emerged and faced a range of new challenges in the fragmented and often economically devastated societies of post-Roman Europe. So one starts a new chapter, a new analysis of how a Christianity that had flourished in the literate urban communities of late antiquity adapted to survival in rural societies in which literacy was almost nonexistent. Personally I find this approach to church history fruitful and absorbing.

In this book, I focus more closely on the important transitions that took place in the relationship between Church and state in the last thirty years of the fourth century. These seem to be crucial to the understanding of later developments in Christian thought and institutions. I stress the central role of the emperors, especially Theodosius I, AD 379–395, in defining Christian doctrine. The power of the emperor was such and the crises that faced his empire so immense that Theodosius chose to champion one faction of Christians, the supporters of Nicaea, over its rivals. He not only isolated what were now described in law as 'heretics' but attempted to suppress pagan thought as well. By doing so, he assaulted two important bastions of Greco-Roman civilisation. The first was a tradition of sophisticated debate that included both Christian and pagan thinkers, which retained its intellectual preeminence precisely because it could operate in comparative freedom. I argue, in particular, that the theological conflicts of the fourth century, before 381, may have been as erudite and penetrating, certainly as wide-ranging, as any that followed in the centuries to come. It is probably not until the thirteenth century, in the crucial debates over the place of reason in theology, that one finds anything as sophisticated – and that is largely because of the brilliance of Thomas Aquinas. The second was an understanding, matured over many centuries, of the importance of not only freedom of speech but also religious toleration. In the 360s, the court orator Themistius can be found arguing before the Christian emperor Jovian that religious belief could not be controlled by the state and that in fact 'God' *enjoyed* being worshipped in a variety of ways. It is one of the tragedies of western thought that this approach was, in effect, suppressed as a result of Theodosius' decrees against 'heretics' and pagans in the last quarter of that same century. So even Aquinas lived under continual threat of excommunication, with the promise of eternal punishment in hell (a concept unknown in the Greek world) that accompanied it. It is not until the seventeenth century that the concept of religious toleration is restated, and that was only after decades of debilitating religious wars showed, in the specific context of post-Reformation Europe, the moral and intellectual bankruptcy of institutional religion.

AD 381 is designed to be read independently of *The Closing of the Western Mind*. This does mean, of course, that there is some overlap in material between the two books. I have provided sources for quotes and given some suggestions for further reading but not the full panoply of references I provided in *Closing*. Those who want a fuller background to the suppression of the thought of the pagan world should return to *Closing*, where the background to the issues is presented in much fuller detail in the text and supporting notes.

I do not belong to an academic institution, although I have taught ancient history on the University of Cambridge's extramural programme. I believe that the best way to write with breadth and liveliness is to be involved in other activities that have little or nothing to do with the book I am writing so that I always return to it with vigour. The best ideas always come when one is least expecting them, often because a new situation challenges a conventional approach to an issue. So my thanks are not so much to academic comrades with whom I have discussed this book as to colleagues in other areas. There are those who come on my study tours to Italy (and who often look at great treasures in unexpected ways) and those with whom I work at the Blue Guides, where I serve as historical consultant. I revel in being asked why an eighth-century icon has ended up in a museum in Florence or to present a summary of Ruskin's views on Venice. Perhaps most stimulating of all has been my thirty-year involvement with the International Baccalaureate's Theory of Knowledge course, a student-centred introduction to critical thinking skills. Working with colleagues, now close friends, from all over the world and from a variety of disciplines, our debates are models of what intellectual enquiry should be. When I read of friends copying out and circulating manuscripts to each other across the fourth-century world, I feel at home with them for this very reason. The papyrus roll or parchment codex might have taken longer to arrive than an e-mail, but arrive it did with a degree of efficiency that was remarkable. It would be many, many centuries before literate elites would communicate again so easily across the Mediterranean world (and some would argue we have not yet recovered the freedom of debate enjoyed then). I hope that the traditions of toleration and free enquiry survive somewhat better in the twenty-first century than they did in the fourth.

Charles Freeman

NOTE ON SOURCES AND TERMINOLOGY

ALTHOUGH it is one of the arguments of this book that the story of AD 381 and the impact of Theodosius on the way Christianity came to be defined has been 'forgotten', this is not because there is a lack of original sources. My description of the Council of Constantinople of that year might appear shocking to those who have been brought up on the idea that it deserved the status of an ecumenical council or achieved a consensus on the Trinity. However, the contemporary accounts suggest otherwise. One of its own chairmen, Gregory of Nazianzus, has left a graphic, if self-pitying, account of the chaos, and the fact that the Council was not even able to publish its revised version of the Nicene creed in the hostile environment of Constantinople speaks volumes. In this book I have relied heavily on accounts by historians such as Socrates and Sozomen, who were writing shortly after the events described. Likewise the activities of the leading figures, such as Ambrose, Jerome, Augustine and Epiphanius, are well documented in their letters, sermons and standard biographies. I do not lay any claim to originality in setting out the events as they were recorded at the time or shortly afterwards. I have provided details in the Notes of the original sources I have used.

The legislation of Theodosius I and his successors also survives and is referred to when appropriate. All 'general' laws from 312 to 438 were collected in the law code drawn up by Theodosius II in 438, which was later used in the west and so remains intact. Although there is some argument as to how effectively laws were enforced (and some may have been no more than imperial propaganda), the Theodosian

Code shows just how widespread was the suppression of beliefs, both Christian and pagan, that conflicted with Nicene orthodoxy after 381. I remain totally unconvinced by those who argue that Christianity preserved reason and freedom of thought after 381, not least because such accounts usually make no attempt to confront or even recognise the mass of evidence, much of it unrelated to Theodosius' legislation, that contradicts them.

As regards terminology, the term 'Nicene Trinity' is a difficult one to define, but for reasons that will become clear as this book progresses, it came to provide the cornerstone of orthodox Christianity and so a workable definition is essential. The Trinity consists of three separate entities, God the Father, Jesus the Son, and the Holy Spirit. One approach (the 'Arian', although I prefer to use the term 'subordinationist' in this book) suggested that they were arranged in a hierarchy, the Father superior to the Son, whom He created, and both superior to the Holy Spirit. At the Council of Nicaea of 325, however, it was decreed that God the Father and Jesus the Son were 'of one substance'. They had each existed for eternity and there was no question of Son being subordinate to Father. Nicaea said little about the status of the Holy Spirit, but by the time of the Council of Constantinople of 381, many Christians were arguing that the Holy Spirit enjoyed equal status alongside the other two. One could talk therefore of one Godhead consisting of three personalities, Father, Son and Holy Spirit, even if it was to prove immensely difficult to find the terminology to define the relationship between them. This is what is normally referred to as the Nicene Trinity in this text. However, Nicaea was a Greek council, with virtually no participants from the Latin-speaking west of the empire. In the west, Christians tended to refer to the three members of the Trinity in rather general terms, such as 'of equal majesty'. As this formulation accepts their equal status, the term Nicene Trinity is extended here to include this western approach, which is also close to the terminology used by the (Spanish) Theodosius in his legislation even when he issued this in the east. Strictly speaking, however, eastern and western Trinities remained distinct. The most important western work on the Trinity, Augustine's *De Trinitate*, owed nothing to Greek theology.

'Paganism' is another term that is difficult to use. Historians normally talk of three distinct religious groups for this period – Christians, Jews and pagans. Paganism includes belief not only in the ancient gods of Greece and Rome and the plethora of other religious movements that are to be found in the late empire, but in all its major philosophies in so far as they were neither Jewish nor Christian. So the term 'pagan' includes much more than simply religious beliefs, and this should be borne in mind when it is used here.

As a study of the publication dates of books listed in the Bibliography shows, there is a mass of new research in this area which I have attempted to incorporate in my text.

INTRODUCTION

In January 381, the Christian Roman emperor Theodosius issued an *epistula*, a formal letter, to his prefect in the Danube provinces of Illyricum announcing that the only acceptable form of Christianity centred on a Trinity in which God the Father, Jesus the Son, and the Holy Spirit were seen as of equal majesty. Theodosius went on to condemn all other Christian beliefs as heresies that would be punished by both the state and the divine judgement of God. By July, the law had been extended across the whole of the eastern empire and then, in the 380s, to the west. Within a few years Theodosius had also moved to ban most forms of pagan worship, in effect challenging the religious and spiritual activities of the majority of his subjects.

It was a pivotal moment in classical and, indeed, European, history. Never before in the Greek or Roman world had there been such a sweeping imposition of a single religious belief alongside the active suppression of alternatives. The only precedent comes from ancient Egypt when the pharaoh Akhenaten replaced the mass of Egyptian deities with the single sun-god Aten in the fourteenth century BC – and even this policy was quickly reversed by his successors. Theodosius' decrees were especially startling because less than sixty years earlier, in 313, the emperor Constantine had issued, with his co-emperor Licinius, an Edict of Toleration in which he promised 'that no one whatsoever should be denied freedom to devote himself either to the cult of the Christians or to such religion as he deems best suited for himself'. As late as the 360s, the principle of freedom of speech and thought was being proclaimed by the court orators as essential to a healthy society.

Theodosius was not himself a fanatical Christian, and despite the harshness of the language in which his decrees were expressed, he showed some restraint and flexibility in the way he applied them. In a vast and administratively unwieldy empire, any law lost its impact as it filtered down into the provinces, and some may never have been systematically enforced.[1] However, this worked both ways – a law might be ignored, or it might be imposed with brutality by a local enthusiast. Several of Theodosius' Christian officials, particularly those he brought with him to the eastern empire from the west, acted with a ruthlessness that the emperor could not condone. Many launched violent attacks on pagan shrines and their occupants. Whatever the emperor had intended, the free discussion of spiritual matters was constrained in the Christian world for centuries to come. The Roman legal system was adapted so as to be able to target and remove dissidents, whether pagan or Christian. With the collapse of the empire in the west, the Church took over the powers of the state in which it had acquiesced under Theodosius, and by the twelfth century, Church and state were again united in suppressing freedom of religious thought. One has to wait until the seventeenth century before the principle of religious toleration, so deep-rooted a part of ancient society, was reasserted in Europe.

The story, as this book hopes to show, is well documented, but an alternative narrative, that the Church itself came to a consensus on the nature of the Godhead, is still the dominant one in histories of Christianity. The 'consensus' approach glosses over the violent antagonisms the debates over doctrine aroused and the pre-eminent role the emperors played in their resolution. Again there is seldom any mention, in this 'alternative narrative', of the other intellectual and spiritual traditions, many of which were rooted in the use of reason, that withered as a result of the emperors' interventions. The 380s were truly a turning point, and the story of how freedom of thought was suppressed needs to be brought back into the mainstream of the history of European thought. This is what this book aims to do.

I

DISASTER

THE Roman empire must rank as one of the most extraordinary political achievements history has recorded. The small city of Rome had expanded from a frontier city in a vulnerable position on the river Tiber in the centre of an open plain, to control of the entire Mediterranean world. Each of its victories gave the city the confidence and manpower to search for the next. Italy, of course, was the first territory to come under Roman rule, though the mountainous central core of the Apennines made control of the peninsula a formidable challenge. Then there was Sicily and the beginnings of a provincial empire. Spain and North Africa followed as the Carthaginian empire was defeated in the third century BC, then Greece in the second century and much of the Ancient Near East, including Egypt, in the first. In this same century Julius Caesar conquered Gaul and so extended the empire up to the Rhine and Germany, while in the first century AD much of Britain came under Roman rule.[1]

By now the relentless expansion of Roman power was beginning to falter. The republic, in which elected magistrates ruled the growing empire, had fragmented under the destructive ambitions of competing generals. The assassination of the last of these, Julius Caesar, in 44 BC led eventually to the emergence of his great-nephew Octavian as the emperor Augustus (27 BC), and republicanism never returned. Emperors continued to rule until the collapse of the western Latin-speaking empire in AD 476 and the fall of Constantinople in the east in 1453. (The eastern and western empires were divided administratively for the first time in the late third century, and permanently from 395.) Without the conflicting ambitions of commanders to drive it, conquest was more piecemeal, and emperors such as Hadrian (AD 117–138) favoured the consolidation of the empire within its existing borders over expansion. However, wherever the borders were drawn, there were always hostile outsiders, and by the second century these were gaining the confidence to attack.

By the late fourth century, the period that is the focus of this book, the empire had been under severe pressure for almost two hundred years. On the northern borders, which ran along the rivers Rhine and Danube, vital communication routes as well as boundaries, there was a mass of Germanic tribes whose internal tensions, shifting allegiances and hunger for resources coalesced in opportunistic raids on the empire. On their own these war bands were hardly a match for a Roman legion, but the border was long and often difficult to defend and raiders could strike deep into the empire before they were driven out. In the east, the Persian empire was a more stable opponent, but when wars broke out they tended to be major conflicts, with cities and large stretches of territory changing hands. In 363, the Persians gained an advantage when the Roman emperor Jovian's armies were trapped in Persian territory and he was forced into a humiliating peace treaty in which control over border provinces was surrendered by the Romans.[2]

Jovian died in 364, less than a year after his defeat, and, as often happened at times of crisis, his army declared one of its well-tested generals, Valentinian, as the new emperor. It was to prove a good choice. Valentinian had his dark side – a terrible temper and a propensity to deal brutally with subordinates – but he was effective. Revolts in Britain and North Africa were suppressed and Valentinian swept far into German territory, devastating the forest strongholds of the local tribes. Back on the Rhine and Danube borders he rebuilt forts and strengthened defences.

On Valentinian's elevation the army insisted that he appoint a co-emperor. Anxious to put in place an imperial dynasty, he delegated power over the eastern Greek-speaking provinces of the empire to his brother Valens. (The boundary was drawn so that, apart from Thrace, the whole of Europe remained under Valentinian.) There would have been better choices. Valens ruled conscientiously but he had none of the military flair of his brother. The historian Ammianus Marcellinus, one of the major sources for the period, describes Valens as 'better at choosing between different options than devising them' – a competent man but not one of initiative.[3] Like his brother, he campaigned across the northern border, among the Goths, a Germanic people settled north of the Danube and around the Black Sea, but any major victory eluded him. When eventually he signed a peace treaty with the Goths in 369, he trumpeted it as a success, awarding himself the title of Gothicus Maximus, but if he had been stronger he would have imposed clauses allowing him to recruit from the Goths the men he desperately needed to keep up his forces.

In 375 there was a fresh challenge to Valens from the Persian Empire. The empire's 'king of kings', Shapur, of the aggressive Sassanian dynasty, was threatening to take control of Armenia, a mountainous kingdom in eastern Anatolia (modern Turkey), which had traditionally been a buffer zone between the two empires. The Romans had themselves to blame for the confrontation as they had interfered in the kingdom's affairs, to the extent of killing the Armenian king, Pap, and installing their own nominee on the throne. To meet the threat, Valens moved his base to Antioch, an ancient and wealthy city that served as the administrative centre for Syria and the east, and began deploying troops across the eastern provinces. His problem was lack of manpower, and a revolt in the Roman province of Cilicia in 375 stretched his resources still further. However, overall he seemed in relatively good control of the situation and there were signs that the Persians, who faced unrest in their own eastern empire, were ready to back down. No one could deny the immense pressures the Roman Empire was under, but between them Valentinian and Valens could, by 375, be pleased with what they had achieved.[4]

Then devastating news arrived from the Balkans. In his determination to strengthen the Danube border, Valentinian had ordered a fort to be built north of the river in territory belonging to the Quadi, a German tribe. The Quadi were bitterly resentful at the intrusion, and when their king Gabanius was assassinated by the local Roman commander, they exploded in revolt and rampaged across the border into Roman territory.

Valentinian had been at the western headquarters of Trier on the Rhine but quickly marched eastwards along the border and into the provinces of Pannonia where the disorder was taking place. His reputation as a ruthless soldier travelled before him and the Quadi came to treat for peace. They explained that it was not they but 'bands of foreign brigands' who had been responsible for the unrest, and that they would happily submit and provide men and supplies to the Roman armies. Valentinian was not taken in by their grovelling. He lost his temper and furiously berated the Quadi envoys. Eventually he seemed to calm down, but then he had a major fit. His men rushed him off the scene but his powers were failing. Ammianus Marcellinus tells how he flailed about in desperation as he lost his speech. Nothing could be done to save him and he died soon afterwards.

In hindsight, Valentinian can be seen to have been the last Roman emperor to enjoy military dominance over Rome's enemies. The succession in the west was not secure and again rested on the elevation of Valentinian's own family. His son, Gratian, had already been declared of imperial status in 367 when only eight, and so he, still aged only sixteen, became senior emperor in the west. Valentinian's own commanders were determined to maintain their status against this inexperienced newcomer, so they declared Valentinian's youngest son, also Valentinian, as his fellow emperor, Valentinian II. Even though he was only four, they gave him nominal responsibility for the provinces of Italy, Africa and Illyricum, which they could then rule on his behalf. Ostensibly, it was a direct affront to the dignity of Gratian, but the atmosphere of crisis was such that Gratian had to condone the move. He did his best to reassert control by moving Valentinian into his court at Trier.

So Valens, in the east, suddenly found himself the senior of the three emperors, but he was now without the support of his formidable brother and with only two young nephews as his fellow rulers. It was unlucky that there were signs that the northern borders of his part of the empire were also troubled. At first it was not clear what was happening, but there were dispatches telling of masses of Goths migrating southwards towards the Danube. Shadowy reports suggested that beyond them a new people, the Huns, had been sweeping across the steppes from the east. 'This wild race, moving without encumbrances and consumed by a savage passion to pillage the property of others' was how Ammianus Marcellinus described them.[5] The Goths were refugees from the onslaught of the newcomers, and before long they were crowding along the banks of the Danube. The first that Valens may have heard of the crisis was in the autumn of 376, when envoys from the Goths arrived in Antioch, five hundred kilometres away from the border, pleading to be allowed into the empire.

Valens' response was probably dictated by his desperate need for manpower. He knew that here would be several thousand young men who would be glad of a place in the Roman armies, while other migrants could be settled as peasant farmers and then made subject to Roman taxation. This had happened before – it was one of the many strategies the Romans, who were always pragmatic in such things, had adopted in order to keep peace on the borders. It was essential, of course, that the migration should be orderly so that the newcomers could come under direct Roman influence and be found land where there was room. Accounts of earlier migrations – there was one of another tribe, the Sarmatians, in 359 – show that a contingent of Roman troops would supervise the movements of the incomers.

Valens learned that there were two tribal groups of Goths assembling on the banks of the Danube: the Tervingi, under their leader Fritigern; and the Greuthingi. In order to keep control of events, he ordered that the Tervingi should be allowed into the empire while the Greuthingi were to be kept out and patrol boats were to be stationed along the river so that they could not cross. The Tervingi appear to have asked for land in Thrace (the modern Bulgaria and European Turkey) to the south of where they were massed on the Danube. Valens agreed to this, a sign perhaps that he was already losing the initiative.

Things began to go wrong as soon as the migration began, sometime late in the autumn. The numbers may have been far greater than Valens realised: one estimate is that the Tervingi totalled some 200,000, a massive group to keep fed and under control. Certainly the reception was not well planned. Ammianus Marcellinus tells how the refugees swarmed across the Danube in boats, rafts and even hollowed-out tree trunks, with many drowning as they attempted to swim across. Those that did reach shore were met by unscrupulous Roman commanders who bartered dogs, as food, in return for taking the younger men as slaves for themselves. Disorder began to spread and the local Roman commander of Thrace, Lupicinius, penned the Goths into a camp near the town of Marcianople, the regional headquarters for the border area. When he clumsily tried to separate Fritigern and the other Goth leaders from their men, a major revolt broke out. Desperate to keep order, he now had to withdraw the troops policing the Danube, and the Geuthingi too poured across the river. The Geuthingi and Tervingi made contact, and Lupicinius' small force was overrun

The Goths, desperately in need of supplies, now swept over the Haemus mountains towards the city of Adrianople, where a Gothic contingent in the Roman garrison mutinied and joined them. Although the Goths were unable to take walled cities, they rampaged over the open plain of Thrace. 'All places were ablaze with slaughter and great fires; babies were torn from the very breasts of their mothers and slain, matrons and widows whose husbands had been killed before their eyes were carried off, boys of tender or adult age were dragged away over the dead bodies of their parents', wrote Ammianus Marcellinus.[6] Archaeologists have been able to date the destruction of luxurious Roman villas along the slopes of the Haemus mountains to this time.

Valens was now seriously worried. We know of a desperate mission by his court orator, Themistius, to Rome to ask Gratian to supply troops, while Valens sent some of his own men westwards from Armenia. These arrived in Thrace in the summer of 377 and had some success in pushing the Goths back across the Haemus mountains and holding them in battle at Ad Salices, 'the place by the willows'. It was a temporary respite. The Goths were now back in touch with the border tribes, and they even seem to have recruited some Huns with the promise of booty from further raiding. During the winter of 377 and 378 a fresh, larger enemy force moved back into Thrace.

It was essential that the Romans used the campaigning season of 378 to regain the initiative. By May, Valens had made concessions to the Persians and had returned from Antioch to his capital Constantinople, but a sullen welcome from the local population, who would have known of the devastation in neighbouring Thrace, must have brought home to him just how vulnerable he was. (The relationship between Valens and the inhabitants of Constantinople had never been good, and an attempted coup by one Procopius in 365 had found widespread support in the city.) The status of an emperor always depended heavily on his ability to defend the empire, and if Valens was to stay in power he had little option but to move quickly on into Thrace, where he began gathering his troops as they arrived from the Persian border. Gratian had also agreed to send men, but there had been a setback in his half of the empire. In February 378, one of the German tribes had crossed the Rhine while it was still frozen, and there were rumours that thousands more Germans, the Alamanni, were set to follow. Gratian could not leave his rear unprotected and the invasions took months to repel.

By July, Valens was beginning to panic. Gratian, though still very inexperienced, was proving an astute emperor. He made sure that his campaign on the Rhine was reported as a series of steady victories and this meant that Valens' own image was all the more fragile. Valens was torn between setting off on his own to secure a victory, and waiting until his nephew could arrive to support him. As it was, he was swayed by faulty intelligence. Reports suggested that the Goths had about 10,000 fighting men, but it was probably nearer 20,000. Even so, this number should have been easily containable by Valens' force of 30,000, many of whom were highly trained infantry. Fritigern, who had managed to remain in command of the Goths, certainly knew how vulnerable he was now that the Romans had assembled a proper army. He sent a priest to negotiate on his behalf (the Gothic tribes had been converted to Christianity in the middle years of the fourth century), in the hope that Valens would acknowledge him formally as leader of the Goths and help him keep order over his unwieldy band of followers, but Valens refused to meet the envoy. He had decided to upstage Gratian and go for battle.

On 9 August 378, the Roman army left its baggage outside the city of Adrianople and set off across the plain in the summer heat. It took them eight hours to reach the Goths, who were now drawn up in front of their wagons; even the toughest of the Roman infantry must have been exhausted. Once again Fritigern tried to sue for peace, but by now nerves were frayed. The Goths had added to the heat and confusion by lighting fires on the plain, and smoke drifted towards the Romans making them even more uncomfortable. Skirmishing broke out, which degenerated into full-scale fighting even before the Roman army had been properly deployed.

Despite this, the battle started well for the Romans. They advanced with their infantry in the centre and a combined force of cavalry and infantry on each wing. The left wing of the cavalry pushed the Goths back on to their wagons, and their line appeared to be about to break. Suddenly a large contingent of Gothic cavalry bore down on the Romans and to their horror they found themselves trapped between the wagons and the enemy cavalry. As the Roman cavalry disintegrated, the Goths were able to attack the infantry from the left. Roman legionaries were virtually unbeatable on open ground, where they could make use of their weapons, but in a restricted space they quickly lost the initiative.

Ammianus Marcellinus, writing a decade later, describes the battle:

The infantry was so closely huddled together that a man could hardly wield his sword or draw back his arm once he had stretched it out. Dust rose in such clouds as to hide the sky, which rang with frightful shouts. In consequence it was impossible to see the enemy's missiles in flight and dodge them; all found their mark and dealt death on every side. The barbarians poured on in huge columns, trampling down horse and man and crushing our route so as to make an orderly retreat impossible. Our men were too close-packed to have any hope of escape; so they resolved to die like heroes, faced the enemy's swords, and struck back at their assailants . . . In this mutual slaughter so many were laid low that the field was covered with the bodies of the slain, while the groans of the dying and the severely wounded filled all who heard them with abject fear . . . In the end the whole field was one dark pool of blood . . .[7]

As many as 20,000 of the best Roman troops may have died at the battle of Adrianople, and killed alongside them, some reports say burned to death in a house in which he was taken after being wounded, was Valens. His body was never recovered. It was an appalling disaster. The empire was left virtually unprotected, its borders open to further invasion, and if the Goths had been better organised and skilled in siege warfare they could easily have taken some of the major cities of the east. As it was, they advanced in some confusion, finally reaching the walls of Constantinople and looting its suburbs but unable to take the city itself. They could not destroy the empire but they had humiliated it. They had disrupted much of the administrative framework of the Balkans, and made its shortage of manpower even more acute, not least because the local Roman *magister militum* of the eastern provinces, one Julius, picked out the Goths serving in the Roman armies and had them all killed.

The focus was now on Gratian. He was still only nineteen, but rather than being overwhelmed by the situation, he and his leading commanders kept their heads. He had, at last, arrived in the Balkans and established his base on the Danube at Sirmium, an important imperial command centre. It was there that the remnants of Valens' shattered armies, together with displaced officials, made their way. It was essential that a strong man be found, one who, unlike Valens, was a hardened soldier, to take control and regroup them.

Gratian's choice was a tough Spanish general, Flavius Theodosius. Theodosius was the son of Valentinian I's Master of Cavalry, another Theodosius, who had played a crucial role in bringing the rebellions in Britain and Africa to an end. The elder Theodosius had taken his son on campaign with him, so Flavius Theodosius had spent his early life on the march. He had learnt fast, and already, at the age of twenty-seven, he had been made *dux*, military commander, of the frontier province of Moesia. Here he inflicted a defeat on the Sarmatians, one of the many tribes threatening the empire. All was going well in his career when Valentinian died, but in the turmoil of intrigue that swirled around the young Gratian, the elder Theodosius was arrested and executed. His son realised that he would be better off out of the lime-light and retired to the family's estates in Spain. He married one Aelia Flaccilla and the couple soon had two children, a daughter, Pulcheria, and a son, Arcadius. (Another son, Honorius, was born in 384.) By now, most of the Spanish aristocracy had converted to Christianity, and although Theodosius had not yet been baptised, he seems to have been a devout Christian. When his family's supporters regained the upper hand after a fresh bout of factional infighting at court, they petitioned Gratian that Theodosius deserved a new command. When Theodosius had proved his worth with another defeat of the Sarmatians, Gratian appointed him, in January 379, fellow emperor to replace Valens in the east. To strengthen his position he was also given responsibility for the strategically important area of Illyricum, which covered what is now Croatia northwards to the Danube border, for the duration of the Gothic wars. Theodosius was at thirty-three the oldest of the three emperors.[8]

II

THE DIVINE EMPEROR

In 363, the court orator, Themistius, had delivered a panegyric, or hymn of praise, in honour of Jovian, the emperor whose campaign against the Persians was to end in such humiliation. Despite the disastrous reality of Jovian's reign, the traditions of the panegyric required the adulation of the emperor as if he was divine. 'The emperor is the living law, divine law descended from on high, incarnation in time of the Eternal Good, emanation of its nature, Providence on earth, in constant contemplation of God, chosen to be his present reflection, in brief, true son of Zeus, raised up by Zeus, and sharing with Zeus his array of titles', as Themistius had put it.[1] Themistius proved to be a remarkable survivor, especially as he was a pagan in an increasingly Christianised empire. Eighteen years later he was still on hand in Theodosius' court to offer a new panegyric, which again stressed the divine imagery that surrounded the emperor. 'Mark well, exalted emperor, that neither beauty nor stature, neither speed nor prowess make a good ruler, if he does not bear in his soul some form of being like God.' Themistius then referred back to the poet Homer, who 'had taught us how a being walking on the earth and clothed in flesh can be thought to have the form of him who is enthroned above the highest vault of heaven and above everything that exists'. Theodosius was that 'being' and Themistius went on to argue that the fact that Theodosius had not usurped the imperial throne but had waited for it to be granted him by Gratian was a further sign of God's support for his promotion.[2]

The images that Themistius used to glorify Theodosius, with their references to Zeus (or Jupiter, as the Romans knew him – Themistius was speaking in Greek) and Homer, can be traced back to the adulation offered to the kings who succeeded Alexander the Great in the late fourth century BC. However, it had only been in the previous hundred years that they had been applied to Roman emperors. In the early empire the tradition had been that an emperor might be recognised by the senate in Rome as having acquired divinity only after his death. Julius Caesar, Augustus and Trajan were among those accepted as *divus* once their bodies had been burned. (A senator claimed to have seen Augustus' 'spirit' ascending intact to heaven through the smoke of the funeral pyre.) Any appropriation of divinity while the emperor was still alive was considered highly offensive and one of the reasons why the emperor Domitian, who had claimed to be 'lord god', was assassinated with senatorial approval in AD 96. However, by the end of the third century AD, when the empire was under severe pressure, emperors did begin to elevate themselves above the masses in order to enhance their credibility. Aurelian, emperor from 270 to 275, a man of immense energy and military talent, minted coins bearing the words *deo et domino nato*, 'born god and master'. He claimed to be the vice-regent of the god Sol Invictus, 'the Unconquered Sun', a popular cult with his soldiers. His successors, Diocletian and Constantine, also aligned themselves with favoured gods, Diocletian with Zeus/Jupiter, Constantine with Apollo and Sol. The honorific title *divus* was used of emperors in the east until the sixth century.

Although Constantine associated himself with Sol on coins as late as 320, he announced in 312 that his victory over his rival Maxentius at the Battle of the Milvian Bridge just outside Rome was due to the support of the god of the Christians. Following Constantine, all emperors, with the exception of Julian (361–363), were Christian and their 'divinity' had to be shaped so as not to conflict with the supremacy of the Christian God. This was not as difficult as it might seem, because most pagans accepted some form of supreme god (often presiding over lesser deities), and Themistius appears to have been able to use terminology that was acceptable to Christian and pagan alike without offence.

An ideology of Christian kingship had first been elaborated by the historian Eusebius, Bishop of Caesarea in Palestine, between 313 and 339, in his eulogistic *Life of Constantine*. Eusebius uses Constantine's vision of a cross inscribed 'Through this, conquer' in the sky before the Battle of the Milvian Bridge as unassailable evidence of God's support for his cause. It was God, Eusebius goes on, who drew

Constantine's rival Maxentius out of Rome into open ground where he could be more easily defeated. The ongoing support of God was shown in the success of Constantine in war and in the effective control of the empire for the rest of his reign: 'so God-beloved and Thrice-blessed that with utter ease he governed more nations than those before him and kept his dominion unimpaired to the very end'. In other words, God's will was shown through the ongoing victories of the emperor. In his sonorous *Oration in Praise of Constantine*, delivered at Constantinople in 336 to mark the end of Constantine's thirtieth year of rule, Eusebius develops the theme that Constantine is God's vice-regent on earth, mortal perhaps but enveloped in a supernatural aura as the result of the close friendship and support of his creator. In fact, he equates him with Christ: Christ leads the heavenly armies, Constantine the earthly ones; each is 'like a prefect of the great Emperor [God]'.[3] This is very much an Old Testament conception. In the Hebrew scriptures, the Messiah himself is envisaged as a warror king anointed as such by God.

Themistius was able to work within this tradition, and he developed the idea that the prosperity and good order of the empire under Theodosius were due to divine support. In his panegyric of 381 he stressed that rather than relying on the 'unchangeable and rigid letters' of the law books, Theodosius was able to transcend them with the help of God, producing justice and mercy to suit each individual case. The following year, 382, Themistius emphasised the prosperity brought by Theodosius' rule: 'Behold, how great is the power of [Theodosius'] just rule, the rewards of which extend not only to palaces and law courts, but to living beings and plants, and even to seeds and children yet in the womb.' The theme was taken up in Christian rhetoric. Christian and pagan writers might employ their rhetoric for different ends but they had 'in common a high level of shared vocabulary: the imagery of the ruler as good shepherd, God as father of all, man made in the image of God, the magnanimity of the good ruler – all are part of the common language of ruler theory since Plato – and available to Christians and pagans alike'.[4]

Themistius' panegyrics are echoed in the most famous surviving image of Theodosius, on a silver *missorium*, a large silver plate, dating from 388 and marking the beginning of the tenth year of his rule. The emperor is shown in the centre, larger than his co-emperor Valentinian II, who succeeded Gratian as sole emperor in the west in 383, and

Theodosius' son Arcadius, who are on either side of him. His face is ageless and he floats as if in a different sphere of existence from the material world. Behind him is the imperial palace. Subject to the emperors, and much smaller in size, is an official receiving his *codicilli*, a document case containing his appointment in the imperial service. Below the tableau, images of fertility stress the prosperity of Theodosius' rule, just as in the panegyric of 382. A personification of Tellus, the earth, is portrayed to show the extent of the emperors' domination of the whole earth, an image reinforced by including barbarians among the soldiers flanking the emperors.

The presentation of the emperor to his subjects had to match the rhetoric. In Trier, the imperial capital on the Rhine frontier, the fourth-century audience hall still stands, although it has long since been stripped of the fine marbles that once encased its walls. The emperor was enthroned behind a screen of curtains and there were elaborate conventions governing which of his subjects could approach him and how closely. Petitions would be relayed upwards through officials, and only those of the highest status had the right to kiss the emperor's purple robe. Any direct physical contact with the emperor's flesh was forbidden, and one can see on the *missorium* that the official's hands are veiled to preserve the separation. The emperor could not be referred to by name, and it was in these years that indirect methods of address such as 'Your Majesty' and 'Your Serenity', even 'Your Everlastingness', evolved. Through association with him, his palace was considered sacred, and the defacing of a statue of the emperor was treated as a direct assault on the quasi-divine ruler and subject to brutal punishment.

It was within this atmosphere and imagery that Theodosius suddenly found himself enveloped in January 379. It was a remarkable promotion. When Themistius stressed how God's approval had been shown through Theodosius receiving imperial status from Gratian (who, of course, was *divus* in his own right) rather than seizing it, he was making an important point. All Theodosius' immediate predecessors as emperor owed their promotion to the army or to family ties. Constantine had fought his way to power, but his father, Constantius, had been one of Diocletian's Caesars (deputy emperors). Constantine was succeeded by his three sons, the last of whom, Constantius II, died in 361 and was succeeded in his turn by his cousin, the pagan emperor Julian. Jovian was already a senior officer when he was proclaimed emperor by his troops on the death of Julian, as was Valentinian on Jovian's death. Valens, Gratian and Valentinian II were all, of course, members of the imperial family. In the circumstances, Theodosius' accession, from relative obscurity in Spain, must have seemed miraculous. While there is no direct record of what the Christian Theodosius felt, it seems likely he would have believed that he really was the chosen of God.

Yet an emperor was a human being on whom the demands were awesome. He could hardly sit impassively behind a curtain in the imperial audience chamber for long. Some of his public appearances, before the crowds in the hippodrome or when he entered a city in a ceremonial known as the *adventus,* might be stage-managed, but the image of mystique must have been hard to sustain. Ammianus Marcellinus provides a superb description of the entry of Constantius II into Rome in 357, the first time he had ever visited the city. 'The emperor was greeted with welcoming cheers, which were echoed from the hills and riverbanks, but in spite of the din he exhibited no emotion, but kept the same impassive air as he commonly wore before his subjects in the provinces ... he was like a dummy, gazing straight before him as if his head were in a vice and turning neither to right nor left. When a wheel jolted he did not nod, and at no point was he seen to spit or wipe or rub his face or nose or to move his hand.'[5] How long could such a stance be kept up, especially when outside the rarified atmosphere of the court the empire was in such disarray and only the emperor could galvanise a response to the chaos?

This was the crucial tension inherent in Roman imperial rule in late antiquity. Earlier emperors had remained close to the people. Hadrian, emperor from 117 to 138, was so easy to approach that there is a record of an old woman berating him for not listening to her petition, telling him that he had no right to be emperor if he did not respond. On campaign, the emperor was expected to share the hardships of his men; it was said that the emperor Augustus went so far as to sleep on a bed of straw. In complete contrast, the later Byzantine emperors in the east emphasised their imperial divinity and delegated their fighting to generals who would then offer the triumphs of any victories back to the emperor in a public ceremony in the hippodrome in Constantinople. Valentinian, Valens, Gratian and now Theodosius were in a transitional phase between these two extremes. They enjoyed the honour of imperial power, but they had also to plan strategies, raise resources and in the final resort win victories themselves. The fate of

Valens showed what disasters could follow if they cracked under the pressure.

Imperial rule was conditioned by the vastness of the empire. The northern border, from the mouth of the Rhine to that of the Danube on the Black Sea, was 2,000 kilometres long. The land route from the Black Sea to the Red Sea was 3,000 kilometres. In 376 Valens in Antioch was 500 kilometres from the Danube where the Goths were massing, and a message and its reply would have taken a month. The land routes were relatively secure; those across the Mediterranean less so as winds and currents varied. In the winter the weather was so unstable that shipping virtually came to a halt. As a result an emperor could never be sure when orders sent by sea might arrive, if at all. Studies of voyages between Rome and the wealthy province of Egypt show that they varied in length between 25 and 135 days. Very often an emperor could not have an accurate picture of an uprising or a raid over the border until it was over, and so he was very dependent on the initiative of his local officials. Yet their independence allowed them to build their local power bases outside the reach of the emperor. In theory, the emperor had absolute power embedded in his quasi-divine status and his role as supreme commander of the armies. In practice, policy-making could easily be confused by the immediate pressure of events and the strengths and weaknesses of the praetorian prefects, the senior administrative officials, and their subordinates. In remote areas the emperor might not even be known of at all. One of the most interesting intellectuals of late antiquity, Synesius of Cyrene, claimed that for his fellow Libyans 'the emperor, his close advisers, and the wheel of fortune . . . are just names that, like flames, have been kindled up to the height of splendour and then quenched'. For all they might know, he went on, the mythical king Agamemnon was on the throne and the Homeric Odysseus still alive as one of his advisers.[6]

It was, in fact, extraordinary that the Roman Empire had survived as a cohesive unit at all. The secret was the Roman openness to the integration of local peoples. In the short term, conquest could be exceptionally nasty. Often a city was taken and razed to the ground as an example to its neighbours. Revolts were brutally crushed, as the Jews found when three uprisings between AD 66 and 135 led to the destruction first of the Temple in Jerusalem and then of the whole city itself, which was later reconstituted as a Roman colony. Well might the historian Tacitus record (or perhaps make up) a British chieftain's cynical remark that the Romans created 'a wasteland' in conquered territory and called it 'peace'.[7] It was in the aftermath that local elites were drawn into Roman civilisation. The key was the city. In the east, cities had been the core of civilised life for centuries, and it was the imposition of the Pax Romana that allowed them to transfer their resources from defence into self-glorification. 'Under you all the Greek cities emerge ... all other competition between them has ceased, but a single rivalry obsesses every one, to appear as beautiful and attractive as possible' was how the Greek orator Aelius Aristides put it in a panegyric to Rome in AD 150.[8] In the west, among the Celtic peoples, urban life was rudimentary at first, but Tacitus, who maintained an ironic detachment from what his fellow Romans termed 'civilisation', tells of Britons speaking Latin, appearing in togas and being 'seduced' by bathhouses, arcades and banquets. Local gods would be merged into the Roman pantheon – a provincial god of thunder could simply be seen as Zeus or Jupiter in a different guise – with the result that a complex of interlocking rituals and sacred sites could sustain local cultures without undermining Roman supremacy. Over one or two generations of Roman rule, provincial elites, ancient or newly created, would come to recognise that it was in their interests to cooperate in the long-term survival of the empire.

As a result, the imperial administration was astonishingly light. The emperor ruled from Rome, although he could, of course, be called away on a campaign or to make a tour of the provinces. Some emperors actually preferred life on the move. Hadrian, for instance, was more interested in the Greek world than the Roman and was outside Rome for more than half his reign. Each province had its own governor, with a small staff, but much of the day-to-day administration rested with the local elites. There was, of course, a taxation system in place, a poll tax and property tax, the proceeds of which were sent to Rome to cover the costs of administration. It was always a tricky moment when Roman officials entered a new province to make the assessments, but once established, the system seems to have worked tolerably well. Its weaknesses were that the richer classes tended to pass demands down to the poorer, and that when there were unexpected pressures on the empire, as from a sudden attack, it was difficult to tap fresh resources quickly.

The borders of the empire were manned by so-called auxiliary troops who were drawn from the subject peoples of the empire and who often fought in their own units and with their own equipment. They were certainly well trained enough to deal with minor incursions, and are even recorded as winning battles in some campaigns, but when something more threatening was at hand, the legions, the crack infantry made up of Roman citizens, were called in. In times of peace the legions were strategically stationed along the more vulnerable borders – the Rhine, the Danube and the Persian – and could move into action when and where they were needed.

As has already been mentioned, it was the emperor Hadrian who had been shrewd enough to recognise in the early second century that continuous expansion meant there would be ever longer borders to defend and so was self-defeating. It was better to fortify the existing borders and focus on the existing prosperity of the empire. But any respite offered by this new policy was short-lived. Again, as has already been noted, there was major unrest on the northern frontiers as German tribes began raiding over the border from the 160s onwards. The causes of the unrest were varied. The empire was wealthy, its cities accessible to invaders along good roads, and the frontiers were too long to defend easily. Population pressures were causing realignments among the Germanic peoples, and the chance of victory and booty from the empire tempted the ambitions of many chieftains. There was essentially no way the Germans could be permanently defeated. The Romans developed a variety of tactics, in some cases allowing Germans into the empire for settlement, in others playing rival tribes against each other or just meeting them head on with a legion in the hope of warning off a particular grouping for ever. They could only be temporary solutions. The situation became more desperate in the third century with a revival of the Persian Empire under the Sassanians. Now the Romans often had to fight two very different kinds of enemies on two fronts. The difficulty was finding a stable leadership. If an emperor was defeated or killed, his successor was often an ambitious general, declared emperor by his troops, but this did not, of course, guarantee him any wider legitimacy across the empire as a whole. There were eighteen emperors between 234 and 284 and as much infighting among them as between them and Rome's enemies.

One of the great strengths of the Roman empire was its ability to reinvent itself to meet the new demands. Eventually the crisis threw up a succession of brilliant soldiers from the Balkans, many of them of surprisingly humble birth. There can have been no greater tribute to the loyalty the empire inspired. The most impressive of these new men was Diocletian, possibly the son of a freed slave, who seized power as emperor in 284. Diocletian had the political and administrative skills to put into action a comprehensive programme of reform. He realised that it was no longer possible for one emperor to control the vast extent of the empire, so he created a system by which four men, two senior emperors, the Augusti, and two junior ones, the Caesars, would share the responsibility. A Caesar would be promoted to an Augustus if there was a vacancy, with a new Caesar appointed to fill his place. This was a much more stable arrangement and the links between the four were strengthened by marriages between their families. Four frontier cities, Trier on the Rhine border, Milan for the central area, Sirmium on the Danube and Nicomedia in the east, were designated imperial capitals, from which campaigns could be planned. This was the moment when Rome ceased to be the active core of the empire.

The new system started well. A massive defeat of the Persians by Galerius, one of the Caesars, in 297 was so decisive that it brought peace on that frontier for decades to come and allowed Diocletian and his fellow rulers a breathing space in which the borders could be strengthened and other long-term reforms introduced. The provinces of the empire were now split into smaller units, the taxation system was reformed so that it was based on expected produce, and for the first time, a budget could be planned. Each of the new provinces had a separate military and civil administration. The military leader (*dux*) was in charge of its forces and responsible to more senior commanders, the *magistri militum*, the 'masters of the soldiers', and so ultimately to the emperor. The 114 provinces of the empire were grouped into fourteen dioceses, each under a *vicarius*, a deputy, while there were also proconsuls who might be given responsibility for a smaller number of provinces. The civilian governors reported to the praetorian prefects, men who held considerable power in their own right as the immediate subordinates of the emperor. Normally there were three of these 'regional prime ministers', one for the east, one for Italy, Africa and Illyricum, and one for Gaul, Spain and Britain. These reforms allowed resources to be grouped more effectively so as to provision and support the Roman forces, which were concentrated in the three most vulnerable areas, the Rhine, the Danube and the Persian frontier. There has been scholarly controversy over the total number of men under arms, with estimates ranging between 450,000 and 600,000.[9] This, then, was the administrative structure that Theodosius inherited in 379, with his own sphere of authority covering the whole of the eastern empire, under its own praetorian prefect, and, so long as the Gothic crisis lasted, Illyricum, again with its own prefect.[10]

So how was Theodosius able to exercise his own 'divine' power? Over the centuries the emperor had absorbed the traditional legal powers of the Roman senate and magistrates and so had become the focus of lawmaking in the empire. One way for an emperor to express his wishes was through an edict. In early Roman law, an edict had been a statement made by a magistrate when he assumed office of how he proposed to carry out his duties. It had no permanent effect and lapsed as soon as his appointment came to an end. The emperors used edicts as a way of announcing a new policy to the empire. One of the best-known examples is the edict of the emperor Caracalla, the so-called Antonine Constitution of 212, which gave citizenship to all free men and women of the empire. An edict might be addressed to the empire as a whole or to a particular city or province. In order to convert an edict into enforceable law, it had to be confirmed, normally in a letter (*epistula*) sent to a named official, a praetorian prefect or provincial governor perhaps, asking him to effect the specific policy or providing him with guidance for conduct in the courts. When the emperor or his jurists dealt with a case in person, their decisions might be issued as *decreta* or decrees, and these could be used as precedents in local courts. The majority of imperial lawmaking, however, was in the form of *rescripta*. These were the replies to petitions, many of which were requests for a clarification of a particular law.[11]

The implementation of laws and the administration of taxation and defence depended on the quality of the imperial civil service. The days when provincial governors and a small staff of a few hundred in total could run the empire were long over. From Diocletian onwards, a much larger civil service had grown up, with perhaps some 6,000 senior officials. Jobs were keenly fought over. As the emperor assumed the attributes of divinity, and even his palace and stables were regarded as sacred, so the status of his officials rose. There were many other perks to the job, including access to military rations, the chance to charge fees for services, and opportunities for corrupt activity. There was such a flow of eager young men towards the court that the emperors had to issue laws instructing them to remain in the cities, where they were needed for local administration. One result of the competition within the service was the proliferation of a mass of different grades. At the very highest level were the *illustres*, consuls, praetorian prefects and other chief ministers closest to the emperors; then came the *spectabiles*, a class including higher provincial governors, with both groups being part of the *clarissimi*, a status awarded to all those considered of senatorial rank, with other grades below these. Inevitably, preoccupation with maintaining status must have taken up a great deal of administrative energy. The sheer extent of the empire and the enormous pressures it was under made inefficiency and poor decision-making inevitable. It was remarkable that the system continued to operate as well as it did.

The challenges facing Theodosius when he became emperor of the eastern empire in 379 were immense. He had had experience as a successful commander and as *dux* in Moesia, a strategically important province on the lower Danube, but he had never been further east in the Greek-speaking world. He had not even visited his new capital, Constantinople. He was taking over a part of the empire where the Romans had lost the initiative. The borders along the Danube were breached and the Goths were moving freely through the Balkans, attracting other groups already settled there and ravaging the countryside. The Roman armies were demoralised and their manpower was diminished. The margins for success were very small – it would only need one more major defeat for the whole area to be lost to the empire.

The events of the next three years are poorly documented, but they appear to show Theodosius gradually strengthening his fragile position.[12] Various laws he promulgated during 379 insist, hardly surprisingly, that taxes and dues be paid in full and that only fit men, not slaves or riff-raff, be provided by landowners as their contribution to the army. These laws were issued from a number of small towns in the Balkans, suggesting that the emperor was on the move in campaigns that are otherwise unrecorded. His strategy appears to have been to strengthen the cities the Goths were unable to take and build up resources behind their walls. There is some evidence that he had a number of tactical successes against the Goths during 379, but there is no record of any major victory.

In the winter of 379, during which it would have been impossible to fight, Theodosius moved to Thessalonika, an important city on the Via Egnatia, which ran across the southern Balkans to Constantinople. Strategically this was a sensible choice, as the city could be provisioned from the sea and communications with the rest of the empire were good, but it was an admission that the northern Balkans were still not under his control. He stayed in the city well into the following year. A serious illness in February 380 was one reason for the delay; so close was Theodosius to death that he was baptised by the city's bishop, Acholius. (Baptism was often delayed, even by committed Christians, to shorten the period between its cleansing powers and death.) By the summer he was recovered, and boosted by the arrival of two legions from Egypt that had marched overland to the Balkans, he felt strong enough to risk a confrontation with the Goths, still under the leadership of Fritigern. It does not appear to have gone well, and his troops suffered further losses. Fresh demands for emergency taxes and pleas to Gratian for more troops are recorded. Later in the summer, Gratian and Theodosius met again, at Sirmium, to plan tactics, before Theodosius finally entered his capital, Constantinople in a stage-managed triumph in November 380 (see p.91). It seems largely to have been a propaganda show; there was little sign yet of any real progress in regaining control of the occupied provinces.

In these months, however, the emperor appears to have reassessed his position. He realised that it was unlikely he would ever defeat the Goths, and even if he did there would simply be new raids in the future. In 381, in fact, there are reports of Huns crossing the Danube border. But something had to be done as the continual ravaging of the Goths was causing immense hardship and local populations were beginning to collaborate with the invaders. A compromise peace was inevitable. In January 381, Theodosius reverted to a more conciliatory approach. One of the Gothic leaders, Athaneric, who had been out-manoeuvred by Fritigern and who was now seriously ill, approached Theodosius asking for formal settlement of his followers in the empire. Theodosius decided to make a show of the affair. He left Constantinople himself to meet Athaneric and his force and then welcomed him back into the city. The Goths were overawed by the opulence and grandeur of Constantinople, and when Athaneric died soon afterwards his troops joined Theodosius' forces. It was a small achievement but it showed the world at large that the Romans were prepared to offer some kind of settlement with the Goths.

Fritigern, however, was still on the move. For the next two years Theodosius appears to have delegated command of his campaigns to generals, some of them from the western empire. Possibly he had decided that he could not risk defeat in person and so kept himself away from the battlefields. The campaigns appear to have been successful in that they gradually pushed Fritigern's Goths out from the central Balkans into Thrace, in fact where Valens had originally agreed they would settle. By October 382, Theodosius was at last able to sign a treaty with the Goths.

The treaty reflected Theodosius' weakness. Normally such an agreement would have broken the Goths up into separate groups, which would then have been made subject to Roman control in the form of taxation and military recruitment as if they had been native peoples. Now, however, they were to be allowed to stay as one unit and were formally addressed as 'allies'. If the Romans wanted them to be recruited for future campaigns, they had to negotiate with them as a group. The ever-resourceful Themistius was on hand to trumpet the peace as a victory: 'Was it better to fill Thrace with corpses or with farmers? . . . To make it full of tombs or of living men? . . . I hear from those who have returned from there that they [the Goths] are now turning the metal of their swords and breastplates into hoes and pruning hooks . . .'[13] Everyone knew, however, that behind the rhetoric this was a form of surrender that normally would not have been tolerated. When four years later, in 386, a much smaller Gothic force crossed the border, they faced massacre and the survivors were drafted into the Roman armies or settled as unfree tenant farmers as far afield as Asia Minor. There can be little doubt that Theodosius would have liked to have done the same to the victors of Adrianople.

In short, the first three years of Theodosius' reign must have been deeply frustrating for him. He was still an outsider, a Latin-speaking Roman in a Greek world who had not yet succeeded in gaining the allegiance of his people. In the circumstances, Themistius' panegyrics were little more than rhetoric. Theodosius was beginning, however, to learn the importance of distancing himself from the disastrous legacy of Valens' defeat and establishing his own distinct image. One issue he could use was the controversy, to be explored in detail in the chapters to come, over the relationship between God the Father and Jesus the Son. While Theodosius supported the Nicene formula, that God the Father and Jesus were of equal majesty, even of one substance (see p.54), Valens supported the alternative 'Arian' view that Jesus was in some way subordinate to the Father. Theodosius now claimed that Valens had been defeated because he had forfeited divine approval as a result of his 'heretical' views. The Christian historian Theodoret, writing two generations later, recorded one of the stories that was put about. Valens had charged one of his defeated generals with cowardice. 'I have not been beaten, sir,' was the retort. 'It is thou who had abandoned the victory by fighting against God, and transferring His support to the barbarians.'[14] When Theodosius cleverly equated his Nicene beliefs with the promise of divine approval, he was not alone. At very much the same time, in the western empire, the Bishop of Milan, the formidable Ambrose, claimed that those areas of the empire where the Nicene faith was strong were stable while those where Arianism prevailed, notably along the Danube, were the most unsettled. He was building on the tradition that God expressed his support of the ruling emperor through bringing him victory.

Early in his reign, Gratian had followed in the footsteps of his father Valentinian in upholding toleration. The first signs that change was in the air came in August 379, when Theodosius and Gratian issued a joint edict proclaiming the Nicene faith. The edict is normally interpreted as the result of pressure placed by Bishop Ambrose on the young Gratian, and there is no evidence that Arian bishops were subsequently expelled from their sees. So the next edict, issued from Thessalonika in January 380 by Theodosius to the people of Constantinople, was rather startling:

It is Our will that all peoples ruled by the administration of Our Clemency shall practise that religion which the divine Peter the Apostle transmitted to the Romans . . . this is the religion followed by bishop Damasus of Rome and by Peter, bishop of Alexandria, a man of apostolic sanctity: that is, according to the apostolic discipline of the evangelical doctrine, we shall believe in the single deity of the Father, the Son and the Holy Ghost under the concept of equal majesty and of the Holy Trinity.

We command that persons who follow this rule shall embrace the name of catholic Christians. The rest, however, whom We judge demented and insane, shall carry the infamy of heretical dogmas. Their meeting places shall not receive the name of churches, and they shall be smitten first by Divine Vengeance, and secondly by the retribution of hostility which We shall assume in accordance with the Divine Judgement.'[15]

Theodosius had gone very much further than his previous legislation by actively condemning alternative beliefs and promising both divine vengeance and 'the retribution of hostility' to the 'demented and insane' heretics. As yet this was no more than an edict issued only to the people of one city of the empire, but the historian Sozomen notes that it would have 'quickly become known in the other cities, as if [proclaimed] from a kind of acropolis of the whole area subject to him'.[16] Why did Theodosius issue it? It is certain that the formula of 'the single deity of the Father, the Son and the Holy Ghost under the concept of equal majesty and of the Holy Trinity' was typical of the beliefs held by Spanish Christians, many of whom had joined the new court. There is evidence, from both texts and archaeological sites, that in Spain and Gaul the aristocratic class to which Theodosius belonged had already begun to enforce its Nicene views, often violently.[17] Theodosius must also have been encouraged by the Nicene Bishop of Acholius, who had links with the west. According to Ambrose, the Bishop of Milan, Acholius' prayers were so effective that they had resulted in the expulsion of a barbarian invasion in Macedonia and the spread of a plague among them! Thus Theodosius' adoption of the Nicene faith after he had come into close contact with such a miracle-worker was not remarkable in itself. It was his active and sustained condemnation of alternative views that was the innovation; in the years that followed, this was widened into an attempted suppression of all pagan thought. One can only imagine that, confronted by the unsettled atmosphere of his empire, Theodosius' immediate concern was to restore order through enforcing unity of belief. However, the uncompromising language of the edict suggests that he had no understanding of the diversity of spiritual life in the east and the long-standing tradition of freedom of speech that had sustained intellectual life there. This tradition needs to be explored.

III

FREE SPEECH IN THE CLASSICAL WORLD

IN January 364, the court orator Themistius addressed a panegyric to the Christian emperor Jovian congratulating him on his first consulship.[1] It was a tricky moment for both of them. Jovian's predecessor, the pagan emperor Julian, had removed Christians from teaching positions and abolished the tax exemptions they had enjoyed. Jovian was in the process of restoring them, and inevitably, many traditional Romans, still pagan, were resentful. They must also have been unsettled by the humiliating peace Jovian had made with the Persians. Themistius found himself in the position of being a mediator between the Christian court, and the pagan aristocracy. To preserve his own status in the court and also the peace of the empire, he realised how crucial it was for the new emperor not to try to impose a particular brand of Christianity or seek revenge on Julian's pagan advisers. So in his speech Themistius made a sophisticated case for religious toleration.

'It seems', he told Jovian, 'that you must be aware that a king cannot compel his subjects in everything ... there are some matters which have escaped compulsion ... for example the whole question of virtue, and above all, reverence for the divine. The impulse of the soul is unconstrained, and is both autonomous and voluntary.' There are areas of life, including the freedom of the soul, that even an emperor must not try to control; in fact, freedom to follow one's own way in spiritual matters is God-given. 'God made the favourable disposition towards piety a common attribute of nature, but lets the manner of worship depend on individual inclination.' (Though Themistius was a pagan, he was speaking at a time when even pagans talked of a supreme god.)

Showing off his knowledge of history, Themistius gives the cases of the pharaoh Cheops and the Persian ruler of Egypt Cambyses, who tried to impose religious uniformity on their subjects but whose laws collapsed after their deaths. In contrast, the law of God, which states that 'each man's soul is liberated for the path of piety that it wishes', can never be abrogated. 'Neither sequestration of property, nor scourges, nor burning has ever overturned this law by force. While you will persecute the body and kill it, the soul, however, shall escape, carrying its resolve free within it, in accordance with [God's] law even though it may have suffered constraint as far as the tongue is concerned.'

Themistius goes on to emphasise the political and social advantages of free speech. The clash of different views energises society. 'It is as if all the competitors in a race are hastening towards the same prize giver but not all on the same course, some going by this route, others by that . . . there is no one road . . . one is more difficult to travel, another more direct, one steep and another level. All, however, tend alike towards that one goal and our competition and our zealousness arise from no other reason than that we do not all travel by the same route.' Speaking in the city of Ancyra, where there had been open conflict between Christian groups, Themistius then touches on the religious disputes that have split the empire. These divisions, he claims, are even more dangerous to the empire than the Persian invasions. Finally he notes the importance of diversity. In an army, all kinds of troops are needed and different men bring their different skills to fighting (as infantrymen, sling-throwers or imperial bodyguards). In society as a whole there are farmers, public speakers, civil servants and philosophers. Each has his place. 'The creator of the universe also takes pleasure in such diversity.' He concludes that Jovian, as God's representative on earth, has the responsibility of upholding divine law.

Themistius was saying nothing new. Herodotus, the so-called 'father of history', who wrote his account of the Persian wars in the 440s and 430s BC, was a pious man who believed that the gods intervened in support of justice and good order. His beliefs, however, did not prevent him from showing an extraordinary tolerance towards the religions of non-Greek peoples, and he was quite happy to accept that the Greeks themselves had drawn on ancient Egypt for their own religious practices. What makes him a great historian is, in fact, this ability to empathise with the wide range of cultures he discusses. His successor, the historian Thucydides, who wrote in the last years of the same century of the new great conflict of the Greek world, the Peloponnesian War, acknowledges more explicitly the virtues of freedom of speech. One of the many speeches he quotes (or perhaps recreates) in his history of the war is placed in the mouth of one Diodotus. Diodotus had been appalled by an emotionally charged debate in the Athenian assembly that had resulted in a decision to kill all the male citizens of the island of Mytilene after the island had revolted against Athens in 427 BC. Haste and anger were always harmful in debate, Diodotus argued. 'Haste usually goes with folly, anger is the mark of primitive and narrow minds.' In this case it appeared to him that the hasty decision to deal ruthlessly with Mytilene would be counterproductive. Diodotus went on to outline the dangers of using emotional rhetoric to frighten or manipulate an audience into reacting rashly. Good citizenship depended on persuasion through fair and open argument, and 'a wise state, without giving special honours to its best counsellors, will certainly not deprive them of the honour they already enjoy; and when a man's advice is not taken, he should not even be disgraced, far less penalised'.[2] In other words, freedom of expression should be respected and even encouraged.

Where did this impulse to debate originate? The philosopher Aristotle saw the desire to question and discuss as intrinsic to being human. 'All men by nature desire to know', he wrote in his *Metaphysics*.[3] For Aristotle, the search for knowledge did not need to be encouraged; it was simply innate. But there was something unique about the argumentative atmosphere of Greek society, especially when one contrasts it with the comparative lack of original Roman philosophy. Recognition of the importance of freedom of speech seems to have originated in the sixth century BC, when the citizens of the emerging city states of Greece began to appreciate that argument rather than conflict was the best way of settling differences. It was in this century that assemblies and law courts developed as centres of debate. It must have been a tortuous process at first, but the pressure of debate appears to have forced an exploration of the nature of argument itself: what made a watertight argument, what was the role played by reason, and how could the validity of a logical explanation be tested?[4]

It was then appreciated that similar methods could be used to explore the natural world. The terms used by the first Greek scientists for 'proof' and 'evidence' are the same as those used by lawyers in the courts. This is not the place to describe the extraordinary achievements of Greek philosophy, but it thrived because no state or priesthood claimed a higher set of beliefs to which discussion had to conform. It was also intensely competitive. Philosophers had to live by their wits. It was common for there to be contests among orators at the public games, while teachers would compete to build up their own groups of pupils and supporters. It is not simply the quality of argument, it is the thinking about what makes a good argument that impresses.[5]

Fifth century BC Athens was the first public arena where competitive debate became deeply embedded in political and cultural life. Every male citizen had the right to speak in the Assembly, though the number actually able to dominate the raucous debates must have been very small. The major drama festival, the Great Dionysia, held every spring, attracted visitors from throughout the Greek world and challenged every kind of convention. The playwright Euripides, for instance, used the rewriting of ancient myths to disturb the complacencies of his audiences, while the dramas of Aristophanes mercilessly lampooned leading figures of the day, including the philosopher Socrates in *The Clouds*. After 431, this unabashed freedom of expression took place against the background of the Peloponnesian War between Athens and Sparta, when one would have expected free speech to be curtailed. The case of Socrates, who offended his fellow citizens through the alleged corruption of the young and attempts 'to introduce new gods', and was executed in 399, shows that Athenian tolerance had its limits. Yet it was this example that inspired Socrates' fellow Athenian Plato to develop his own antidemocratic philosophy, which, paradoxically, the tolerant atmosphere of Athens gave him the opportunity to do.

The Greeks were sophisticated enough to realise that the use of words can easily be coloured by emotion. The Sicilian orator Gorgias put it well in a speech on Helen of Troy he made in Athens in the 420s BC: 'The power of speech has the same relationship to the order of the soul as the order of drugs has to the nature of bodies. For just as different drugs expel different humours from the body and some put a stop to illness, others to life, so too some speeches cause pain, some pleasure, some fear, some induce confidence in the listeners, some drug and bewitch the soul with a certain bad persuasion.'[6] The response of the great teacher of rhetoric of the period, Isocrates (436–338 BC), to these fears of the 'bewitching of the soul' was that the speaker must be trained in moral goodness so as not to exploit the vulnerabilities of his audience.

However, Isocrates' contemporary Plato (*c.*429–347 BC) went further. Shocked by the way the mob had condemned his hero Socrates, he attempted to place philosophical discussion on a much more stable basis. Central to his own philosophy was the belief that a world of Ideas or Forms, which were much more 'real' than anything in the volatile world he saw around him, could be grasped by the reasoning mind. His was essentially an elitist philosophy; only a few, Plato said, had the intellectual capacity and discipline to reach an understanding of the other world, but once they had, they had the key to something vastly superior to anything that could be experienced in everyday life. The Forms were arranged in a hierarchy, with some easier to grasp than others but the lower Forms led on to the higher ones. So the Forms of Justice and Beauty would each contain something that could be termed 'Good', although the essence of this 'Good' would be different for each. However, they could each make up one strand of a higher Form, 'the Good', which would be at the summit of the Forms. Once they had understood the totality of the world of the Forms, the elite had the right to coerce the less disciplined masses into acceptance of what they, the elite, decreed was truly 'the Good', or Wisdom, Justice or Beauty. Later Platonists would equate 'the Good' with a supreme god and Platonism would provide Christianity with much of its intellectual backbone.

Plato's philosophy proved highly attractive, largely due to the coherence and depth with which he developed his arguments in his so-called *Dialogues*, in which Socrates was often given a leading part as a defender of Plato's views. Plato's belief that the soul existed independently of the body and carried with it memories of certainties of the world beyond that could be recovered through reasoning was enormously influential, while his distaste for emotion and sensual excess appealed to the more austere (and so, in later centuries, to ascetic Christians). The search to understand the nature of the Forms, such as Justice or Beauty, could appeal to anyone who felt that these were subject to abuse in their own society. However, the freedom with which Plato was able to develop his philosophy was in conflict with its end, which was to impose a minority's views on the majority. Moreover there was something joyless and ethereal in his ideal society, in which entertainment and good fun would have no place.

It says a great deal, however, for Plato's Academy, and Greek society in general, that his most brilliant pupil, Aristotle (384–322 BC), could reject this approach. Aristotle was suspicious of imaginary worlds outside the knowledge of the senses. While he was prepared to accept that there must be a supreme Unmoved Mover, whose existence could be supported by reason, he was not prepared to go further into the unknown. Instead he focused his brilliant mind on what could be grasped empirically in the natural world, and became the founder of the disciplines of botany and zoology. However, Aristotle went much further in exploring how one could assess and develop knowledge of the material world, and his researches took him into logic and an understanding of the underlying causes of physical change. He speculated on the nature of the universe, how to live an ethical life, and even on the purpose of tragedy and art. While he was prepared to accept that human beings did have a dimension that could be called the soul, he did not believe that this could exist independently of the human body (in another sphere of being, for instance). It was, he once said, like the image stamped on a coin, impossible to imagine apart from the coin itself.

This focus on empiricism underlies one of the most important differences between Plato and Aristotle. While Plato believed that only a tiny elite would reach true understanding, Aristotle had a much more democratic approach to knowledge. 'The investigation of truth', he wrote in his *Metaphysics*, 'is in one way hard, in another easy. An indication of this is found in the fact that no one is able to attain the truth adequately . . . everyone [*sic*] says something true about the nature of things, and, while individually they contribute little or nothing to the truth, by the union of all a considerable amount is amassed.'[7] In short, the contributions of all are needed to build up an understanding of truth.

The radically different approaches of Aristotle and Plato co-existed in the centuries to come, institutionalised to some extent, as with Plato's Academy (which survived in Athens for nearly nine hundred years) or Aristotle's Lycaeum. There were other philosophies where a central core of beliefs would provide argument for centuries. Stoicism is a good example. Founded in Athens by Zeno (*c.* 335–262 BC), Stoic philosophy was developed into a more formal system by Chrysippus at the end of the third century BC. The Stoics had an understanding of the *cosmos*, in other words the entire material world, encapsulated as the force of reason, *logos*, which moves inexorably onwards in a cycle. Within the *cosmos*, all beings – the divine, the natural world, human beings themselves – are linked to each other. Stoics held an essentially conservative view of society. A ruler is a ruler because his place in the *cosmos* determines that he is. Human beings cannot escape the fate that is decreed for them by the unfolding of the *cosmos*, but they can understand what that fate might be and how they can best deal with it. The Stoic accepted wealth if it came his way but affected to disdain it (even if he was not prepared to give it away!), and the ideal Stoic way of life was always restrained. The belief in the unity of the *cosmos* emphasised how all material things are joined to each other and how all depend on the reactions between them. So human life was linked to the survival of the natural world, and care of the environment fitted naturally within Stoic ideals. Stoicism appealed in particular to the Roman upper classes, and so debate was sustained in the intellectual circles of both Greece and Rome – the Roman emperor Marcus Aurelius wrote down his famous 'Stoic' meditations in Greek – and was still going strong in the third century AD. The interaction between the three main concerns of Stoic philosophy – ethics, logic and physics (the understanding of the material world and its relationship between its parts) – ensured that there was continuous discussion, especially about the boundaries of free will in a world whose future appeared to be determined. Stoicism provides an important example of how open debate could continue within a defined philosophical framework.[8]

Even though only a tiny proportion of the original written texts of the ancient world survive, we have enough evidence to know that there was a small but highly literate group of readers, and that a mass of different, and often sophisticated, approaches to knowledge continued into the Roman centuries. An analysis of the great papyrus heap at Oxyrynchus in Egypt, which has offered up 500,000 fragments of texts, shows how the classics such as Homer and Plato were read and reread over centuries, but it is the sheer variety, breadth and quality of intellectual life in other areas that impresses. The tools of reason formulated by Aristotle were used to stunning effect by mathematicians, astronomers and other scientists so that the leading schools of philosophy – those inspired by Plato, Aristotle or the Stoics – continued to evolve in original and unexpected directions. In the second and third centuries AD, the physician Galen, the spiritual thinker Plotinus, and the astronomer and geographer Ptolemy produced groundbreaking works that drew heavily on earlier thinkers – Plotinus on Plato; Galen on the father of scientific medicine, Hippocrates; Ptolemy on earlier workers in his field, including Aristotle. This sense of intellectual progress was typical of a society where rational argument was more valued than acquiescence in ancient authorities. The second century AD philosopher and historian Plutarch expected an educated man to be as much at home with the works of mathematicians and astronomers as with those of the great poets. The very longevity of this tradition, over 900 years between the philosophers of the sixth century BC and Themistius, is testimony to its vitality.

Texts were widely available for the literate minority, with libraries a feature of any self-respecting city or cultured household. That in Alexandria, the greatest, is recorded as having 490,000 rolls of papyrus – the catalogue drawn up by the scholar Callimachus filled 120 of them. In the second or third century AD one scholar, Diogenes Laertes, was able to compile a list of some 350 works of philosophy with 250 named authors. The so-called Villa of the Papyri in Herculaneum held around 1,100 rolls, many still surviving, though charred by the eruption of Vesuvius that buried them in AD 79. A first century AD poet, Perseus, is recorded as having 700 rolls of the works of the Stoic Chrysippus in his collection. (Sadly, not one full work by Chrysippus now survives intact.) The library of another poet, the third-century Serenus Sammonicus, contained 62,000 papyrus rolls when he bequeathed it to the emperor Gordian. The Stoic philosopher Seneca complained of social climbers who filled their houses so full of rolls that it would have taken them a lifetime just to read the titles.

It was comparatively easy for searchers after knowledge to join the 'school' of a favourite philosopher and move from one to another scholarly community in a lifetime of learning. Plato was studied not only for himself but for the veneer of culture he imparted. 'Everyone, even those who do not accept their teachings or are not enthusiastic disciples, reads Plato and the rest of the Socratic school', wrote Cicero in the first century BC.[9] There were even study guides of the philosopher produced for aspiring intellectuals. One by the Egyptian philosopher Thrasyllus (died AD 36) arranged thirty-six of Plato's works into nine groups of four related texts. Those who joined other schools faced different challenges. Aristotle's texts were notoriously difficult to master – in origin they were often little more than lecture notes – and so they needed a teacher or commentaries to expound them. The Stoics are recorded as refusing to be bound too closely to the master texts, preferring to develop their own ideas in their discussion groups. It was an important feature of most schools that they used the foundation texts as a springboard for further study. The library of the Villa of the Papyri contained the seminal works of the philosopher Epicurus, but also extensive development of his thoughts by one Philodemus (it may have been the library of his patron). Many teachers transcended any one philosophical school.

Christianity was derided by some for its lack of intellectual rigour and the credulity of its adherents, but this was not true of many educated Christians in the Greek-speaking empire. Christians inherited from Judaism a respect for the written text, and by the second century there were many sacred writings available for study. Although there was a trend towards establishing central authority in the Church (to be discussed in the next chapter), it was not until the fourth century that the texts included in the New Testament were finalised as a canon, nor was there any firm definition of the heretical, so Christians could range freely within Greek philosophy and use it to develop insights for their own work.[10] It was likewise an important feature of second- and third-century Christianity that individual teachers could explore Christian belief in their own schools with their own pupils. Clement of Alexandria (c.160–c.215) is a good example. He set up a school in Alexandria in which he taught a fusion of Greek philosophy, notably *logos*, the power of reason, and Christianity – Jesus is the *logos*, the Word, incarnate, as John had already stated in the introduction to his gospel. The most important Christian theologian of the third century, Origen of Caesarea in Palestine, another with his own school and devoted pupils, worked within a Platonic framework, like many of his fellow theologians, but he also borrowed from Aristotle and the Stoics and embedded his ideas in the thought and imagery of the Bible. He was remarkable for a Christian of his time in being able to read Hebrew and thus the Old Testament in its original language. He kept an extraordinarily open mind. His pupil, Gregory of Thaumaturgus, recorded that 'Origen saw fit for us to study philosophy by reading with our entire energies all the writings of the ancients, both philosophers and poets, rejecting nothing and refusing nothing. He excepted only the works of the atheists [by whom he would have meant the Epicureans, who believed that the gods did not exist].'[11] (I will discuss Origen more fully in Chapter Ten.)

Yet the mid third century was a time of persecution for Christians. It was stimulated by their rejection of the traditional gods of the Roman Empire, especially by their refusal to carry out the sacrifices that were at the core of ritual. When the empire was under pressure, as it was in the the third and early fourth centuries, it was easy to believe that this refusal to sacrifice had offended the gods, who had then withdrawn their support from the empire. Persecution of Christians was as much about their refusal to sacrifice as about their actual beliefs, yet there were also deep-rooted prejudices against them. Christian services were ridiculed as occasions for cannibalism (the eating of the body of Christ) or sexual debauchery (a misinterpretation of Christian 'love'). Christianity was seen as an upstart religion, and its growth and vitality appeared to threaten traditional worship.

So here was a contradiction – a society that normally tolerated free debate was persecuting one of its minorities. A few thoughtful pagans spotted the problem. The matter was raised, for instance, by the philosopher Porphyry in a work called *Philosophy from Oracles,* which survives only in fragments.[12] Porphyry had been born in 234 in Tyre. He provides an excellent example of how a scholar could exploit the intellectual resources of the empire. As a young man he had studied with Origen in nearby Caesarea. However, he never converted to Christianity and progressed to Athens, the centre of pagan philosophy, before moving west to Rome, where he studied with the distinguished Neoplatonist philosopher Plotinus. It was Porphyry who published Plotinus' famous *Enneads* after the great philosopher's death. The *Philosophy from Oracles* is probably a work of Porphyry's old age. (It is first mentioned in 305 and may have been completed just before then.) Porphyry accepts the importance of tolerance of religious belief and is one of the first to talk of there being different paths to the truth, a view echoed by Themistius sixty years later. Among these paths are those of the philosophers and those of traditional religious cults, all of which provide acceptable ways of understanding the supreme reality or God. He even sees Judaism as important in this respect. On the other hand, he argues that there must be limits to toleration and he singles out the Christianity of his day. Porphyry agrees that Jesus was an important spiritual leader, so important, in fact, that he, like the Jews, could provide one of the paths to the understanding of God. However, Christians have erred in making Jesus divine, as in doing so, they have broken with tradition and have defied the teachings of philosophers, lawgivers and emperors (and, by implication, Jews) who have established that a human being cannot be divine. The persecution of Christians is therefore justified. However,

Porphyry does go on to suggest that if Christians could reject the idea that Jesus was divine then they could be integrated within Roman tradition and tolerated. In short, he appears to be reluctant to exclude Christians and would prefer to find a means of including them within an open society. Even so, Christians were bound to feel angry with this justification for their persecution, and the *Philosophy from Oracles* soon provoked a response from a Christian writer, Lactantius.

Lactantius had been born in North Africa around 250, and some time before his conversion to Christianity had been appointed by the emperor Diocletian as a teacher of rhetoric in the important imperial city of Nicomedia. He had then converted, and had lost his post during Diocletian's persecution of Christians in 303. The experience of persecution made Lactantius determined to refute Porphyry and show that Christianity deserved to be offered toleration. Lactantius was remarkable in that he did not deny toleration to other religions, and his *Divine Institutes* (c.308–309) provides a Christian rationale for the toleration of all religious beliefs.

As someone who had been brought up with a traditional Roman education, Lactantius knew his classical authors, and he cites the Roman orator and statesman Cicero for his view that one should approach the gods with piety but that it must be for God/the gods, not human beings, to decide the nature of appropriate worship. Lactantius goes on to argue that to use force to impose religious belief pollutes the very nature of religion. God values devotion, faith and love, and an act of force contradicts exactly what He most requires; in fact, it diminishes the deity in whose name persecution is effected. Those who persecuted Christians had actually discredited their own gods by doing so. He makes another point, which reappears in later writers, that belief imposed from outside is meaningless to God, who places greater value on conviction from within. On the other hand, it is justified to use reasoned argument to persuade others of one's own beliefs, and Lactantius says even of the pagans that 'We are ready to listen, if they should teach.' Lactantius counters Porphyry's accusations that Christianity is outside the bounds of Roman tradition by arguing that there is nothing in Christianity that conflicts with Roman law or with traditional religious practice.[13]

How far Constantine knew of and was influenced by the *Divine Institutes* is unclear, although Lactantius joined the imperial court in 317, when he was made tutor to the emperor's son Crispus. The emperor's Edict of Toleration of 313, issued a year after his victory over Maxentius at the Battle of the Milvian Bridge, certainly accords with the policy of the *Divine Institutes*. 'With salutary and most upright reasoning,' the Edict proclaims, 'we resolved on adopting this policy, namely that we should consider that no one whatsoever should be denied freedom to devote himself either to the cult of the Christians or to such religion as he deem best suited to himself, so that the highest divinity, to whose worship we pay allegiance with free minds, may grant us in all things his wonted favour and benevolence.'[14] When, later in his reign, Constantine became ruler of the whole empire, he sustained this policy of toleration. In a letter issued to the eastern provinces in 324, he emphasised his own adherence to Christianity but promised that 'those who still rejoice in erring' should receive 'the same kind of peace and quiet' as believers. Everyone 'should follow what his soul prefers'. He appears to have assumed that with time and open argument all would become Christians. Other aspects of his policy appear to support this approach. Constantine did not try to abolish the temple cults – in fact he set one up in honour of his family at the city of Hispellum on the Flaminian Way in Umbria. While he was willing to punish Jews if they tried to convert or circumcise Christians, he gave the same exemptions from official duties to Jewish priests as he did to the Christian clergy. His imperial panegyrics after 321 were, in the words of one authority, 'written in terms of a neutral monotheism which would be acceptable to Christians and pagans alike'.[15]

In proclaiming toleration for Christians as well as all others, Constantine was bringing Christianity into the mainstream. This was emphasised by the short reign of the pagan emperor Julian (361–363). Despite being brought up as a Christian, Julian reverted to paganism partly because of his distaste for destructive debates over doctrine and partly because his imperial 'Christian' relations, the sons of Constantine, had murdered the closest members of his family. Julian did not persecute Christians and they were able to keep preaching, but he attempted to diminish the public role of the bishops, fostering traditional cults instead. Julian argued that it was important for cultures to worship gods who reflected their own specific values, and he went so far as to support this ideal by paying for the restoration of the Temple in Jerusalem, destroyed by the Romans in AD 70. Not everyone shared this active response to religious diversity. When the building was brought to a halt by a major fire, Christians were seen to rejoice. Were they simply exploiting the freedom they had been given by Constantine so as to threaten the rights of others? To answer this question we need to explore how the relationship between Christianity and the state had begun.

IV

THE COMING OF THE CHRISTIAN STATE

UNTIL the Edict of Toleration, the early Christian communities had been isolated and largely confined to the Greek-speaking cities of the empire. Even as late as AD 300 Christians made up only a tiny minority, 2 per cent at best, of the Latin-speaking west. This 'Church' was much more diverse and unstructured than the word suggests to modern readers. While the first Christians had been Jewish, the movement soon spread among Gentiles but manifested itself in a surprising variety of ways as Christian beliefs interacted with those of other cults. There had to be a continuous process of self-definition through which emerged a mainstream Church that was not only distinct from other spiritual movements but from the Jews and the plethora of pagan deities.

The early Church was held together in the first instance by the commitment to Jesus Christ, a commitment that had been spelled out in Jesus' own teachings and in the letters of Paul. Most Christian communities had an initiation ceremony, baptism, which was referred to as 'putting on Christ', 'an enlightenment' or 'a rebirth'. This gave access to the Eucharist, a shared meal in memory of Christ. Intrinsic to the process of initiation was a period of preparation centred on not only what should be believed but how the Christian should behave.[1] The result was exclusive communities, meeting in secret but vulnerable for this reason to accusations that they indulged in cannibalism or sexual free-for-alls.

It is hard to know, with any religious movement, what gives it its impulse. For Christianity, the hope of salvation promised by Christ, the belief in a benevolent God who will care for all, the shared values of the Christian communities, which appeared to care well for their own, specific rituals that gave a meaning and purpose to life, all must have played their part. So must a common defensiveness against their prejudiced opponents. The growth in numbers of these communities is largely undocumented, but studies of third-century Anatolia, for instance, show a patchwork of Christian communities, strong in some cities, nonexistent in others.

Overseeing these developments were the bishops. These had emerged as early as the first century as leaders of Christian communities, and gradually grew in status. At the beginning of the second century, Ignatius, Bishop of Antioch, the city where the word 'Christian' is first recorded, told his congregation, 'You are clearly obliged to look upon the bishop as the Lord himself'.[2] The authority of the bishop derived from his succession to the apostles, who had received theirs from Jesus Christ himself.[3] A bishop of a city such as Antioch, where tradition recorded that Peter was the first bishop, had special significance. Peter was also credited with moving on to lead the Christian church in Rome, and the tradition of his martyrdom there gave that city a status above that of Antioch. The direct apostolic succession asserted by the bishops of Rome was boosted by the claim (in Matthew 16:18) that Jesus had proclaimed Peter to be the rock on which he would build his Church. A third major bishopric emerged in Alexandria where the first bishop, the evangelist Mark, was believed to have been a disciple of Peter. There was a sense of common purpose among the bishops, although the sheer size of the empire and the difficulties of communication across it meant inevitably that links between them were tenuous. 'Separated from you by great stretches of land and the sea, yet I am bound to you in my heart', wrote Gregory, Bishop of Rome, across the Mediterranean to his fellow bishops of Antioch and Alexandria in the late sixth century.[4] There needed to be something more substantial to bind the bishops together if one was to talk with any meaning of a unified Church.

The earliest Christian traditions were oral ones. Jesus did not leave any written texts of his preachings – we are dependent on what memories were passed down to the gospel writers – and it seems clear that an oral tradition, passed on within the emerging Christian communities, was resilient at least until AD 130. The problem lay in the fragility of memories and the tendency for oral traditions to evolve with time. They could also be threatened by self-appointed Christian prophets. In the late second century a group known as the Montanists (after their leader, Montanus) caused a stir with their claims that they had direct contact with God and that the end of the world was at hand. A 'New Jerusalem' would descend from heaven to a small town, Pepuza, in Phrygia. It did not, but the fervour of the Montanists, who had women among their leaders, appears to have been the catalyst that turned the bishops back to a more secure footing of written texts. There never could be any stability in the emerging Church if its teachings could be subverted by those claiming to be in direct touch with God. Perhaps the most important figure in the tightening up of Christian authority was Irenaeus, bishop of the (Greek-speaking) community in Lyons, who insisted on defining the Church through its adherence to a canon of texts, approval of which could, he claimed, be traced back to the early Church. While, as we have seen, Christian doctrine was still fluid and intellectual debate lively and wide-ranging, Irenaeus set the trend towards establishing central authority.

The difficulty lay in formulating this canon of fundamental texts, partly because there was such a variety of early Christian writings.[5] The oral traditions about Jesus' life and teachings had been written down in several, perhaps as many as twenty, gospels, but gradually four of these, the gospels of Matthew, Mark, Luke and John, had emerged as the most authoritative, partly because they were the earliest to have been written. Then there were a few letters, survivors of probably many more now lost, from the apostle Paul to the early Christian communities. Manuscripts of the Acts of the Apostles, written by tradition by Luke, the author of the third gospel, which covers the mission of the Church from Jesus' Ascension to Paul's arrival in Rome (*c.* AD 62), were also in circulation. All these books had been composed in Greek, which explains why in the early centuries Christianity was essentially a Greek-speaking religion. The very earliest fragment of a Latin Christian text is dated to as late as 180. By AD 200 a selection of these writings can be found listed together as a canon, an agreed set of core texts, in what is now called the New Testament. Other texts such as the epistle to the Hebrews and the Book of Revelation were added later, and the first reference to the complete New Testament as we know it today dates from as late as 367.

These were not the only canonical texts. Jesus and his disciples had been Jews and were familiar with the Tanakh, the Hebrew scriptures.[6] For centuries Jews had been migrating from Israel into the Greek-speaking Mediterranean (the diaspora), and gradually they began losing touch with their language and culture. The moment came when if Judaism was to survive at all in the Greek world, the Tanakh would have to be translated from Hebrew into Greek, and this was done in the third century BC. Although there is a legend that the translation of the Tanakh from Hebrew to Greek was ordered by King Ptolemy Philadelphus of Egypt to fill a gap in the library at Alexandria, it is likely that the impetus for the translation came from within Judaism itself. The translation is always known as the Septuagint, following the legend that seventy-two Jewish scholars worked on it, being led by divine guidance to come up with identical versions.

In the middle of the second century AD, as Christians began to turn away from oral tradition towards a faith incorporated in written texts, they were faced with the momentous decision as to whether they should adopt the Septuagint, which was, after all, a purely Jewish text, as one of their own sacred writings. The issue was given focus by one Marcion, who was born on the shores of the Black Sea about AD 100 and who came to Rome in about 139.[7] Marcion had read widely in Jewish and Christian literature and had become a champion of the letters of Paul. Taking on board Paul's teaching that Christ had transcended the Jewish law, Marcion now argued that the Tanakh no longer had any relevance for Christians. He elaborated his argument by claiming that God as portrayed in the Tanakh was stern, vengeful and 'lustful in war', precisely because he had to enforce the law against its enemies. Jesus had brought with him a completely new God who had not made any previous appearance until the moment Jesus had come to earth. This new God of Jesus (Marcion called him 'the Stranger God') had come into the world to save people from the forbidding God of the Tanakh. Jesus himself, said Marcion, was fully divine and only appeared to be human – a view known as docetism, after the Greek *dokeo*, 'I seem'. Marcion suggested a canon that would include the letters of Paul and Luke's gospel, but that would definitely exclude the whole of the Tanakh. This idea of the two gods was, of course, revolutionary, and a council of Christians in Rome condemned it. Marcion was forced to leave Rome, but he was such an inspiring preacher that in parts of the eastern empire he attracted more followers than did the conventional Christian churches. Marcionites were still strong at the time of Augustine in the early fifth century.

With the rejection of Marcion's theology, the Septuagint became part of the Christian canon of texts. Marcion's argument remained

unresolved, in that there was an obvious contrast between the God of
the Old Testament (as the Septuagint became known among Christians
in contrast to the New Testament of the gospels and epistles) and the
more gentle God preached by Jesus in the New. However, the two sets
of writings were given an overall coherence by the claim that the Old
Testament provided a foretelling of the coming of Christ. Old Testament
texts, such as 'Behold a virgin will conceive' (Isaiah 7:14), were interpreted as prophecies of Christ's birth. Isaiah provided another important
image. One of the difficulties in accepting Jesus as *christos*, the Greek
for messiah, had been that in Judaism, messiahs were portrayed as
wholly human, never divine, figures of power. Jesus had been shown
to be powerless when confronted by the Roman and Jewish authorities, his death through crucifixion the most humiliating the empire
could devise. The prophet Isaiah appeared to put forward an alternative tradition of a messiah who suffered (Isaiah 53), and this provided
a much more appropriate model. Less happily, the adoption of the
Septuagint meant that Christians had to justify their appropriation of
the sacred texts of the Jewish religion, which they claimed to have
superseded. Some Christians, such as the writer of the epistle of
'Barnabas' (Barnabas was the companion of Paul, but this work dates
probably from the early second century), were virulent in their denun-
ciation of the Jews. The author of the epistle even claimed that the
Tanakh had never been a Jewish scripture in the first place. More
moderate Christians argued that it had been but that the Jews had
proved themselves unworthy of it through their complicity in the death
of Jesus. The long and difficult relationship between Christianity and
Judaism was rooted in these early tensions.

By the third century, a loosely organised Church, whose bishops
based their authority on succession from the apostles and their faith
on a large and varied collection of sacred writings (far wider than the
present New Testament suggests), was in place. It was becoming increasingly visible. By 200 the fiery Christian writer Tertullian from Carthage
was able to proclaim to the pagans that Christians 'live together with
you in this world, including the forum, including the meat market,
baths, shops, workrooms, inns, fairs, and the rest of commercial intercourse, and we sail along with you and serve in the army and are active
in agriculture and trade', although his own version of Christianity
was austere and deeply misogynist.[8] The bishops were also enhancing
their status. Cyprian, Bishop of Carthage (248–258), showed how fully

integrated into Roman society the institution was when he described the authority of the bishop in very similar terms to that of a Roman provincial governor. 'Does anyone who acts against the bishops of Christ think that he is with Christ . . . he carries arms against the Church . . . he fights against the will of God . . . he is an enemy of the altar, a rebel against Christ's sacrifice', as Cyprian wrote in his *On the Unity of the Church*.[9] Yet it was just this uncompromising position that brought the bishops into increasing danger in a society whose gods they openly rejected. Christians had always been vulnerable to persecution – the crucifixion of Christ by Roman soldiers provided, after all, a paradigm for the faith – and some seem to have seen martyrdom as a mark of their commitment. 'Allow me to be bread for the wild beasts; through them I am able to attain to God. I am the wheat of God and am ground by the teeth of the wild beasts, that I may be found to be the pure bread of Christ' was how Ignatius of Antioch put it when he was taken off to Rome to his death in 107.[10]

In the third century, when the pressures on the empire were immense, there was increasing concern by the imperial authorities that the support of the pagan gods of Rome was being lost through the refusal of the growing number of Christians to sacrifice to them. In the 250s, all were required to participate in public acts of sacrifice, which would be acknowledged by a signed certificate from a state official. Many Christians acquiesced – in Carthage, Cyprian was shocked by the way in which his congregation capitulated – but others held out and Cyprian himself was martyred in 258. Another major persecution took place fifty years later, in the reign of Diocletian. Diocletian himself appears to have been reluctant to waste resources on rounding up Christians, but Galerius, his Caesar in the east, was more vindictive. At first, only Christian property was affected, and many bishops surrendered this without feeling they had compromised on their faith. Then the imprisonment of clergy was ordered, and finally, in April 304, all Christians were condemned to die if they failed to sacrifice. As with all such proclaimed laws, local officials differed considerably in the vigour with which they enforced them. In some areas Christians were rounded up en masse; in others governors continued to turn a blind eye to Christian worship. Constantius, the father of Constantine and another of Diocletian's Caesars, based on the Rhine frontier at Trier, was said to have actually favoured the Christians of his household who refused to betray their faith, on the grounds that this showed an admirable strength of character.

In 305, Diocletian did something hitherto unprecedented for a Roman emperor: he abdicated, together with his fellow Augustus Maximian. The system of government that Diocletian had introduced required that the Caesars be promoted to Augusti to fill the vacancies, and Constantius became emperor of the west, with one Severus appointed as the new Caesar. When Constantius died the very next year in York, he should have been succeeded by Severus, but instead, in a gesture that had become common in the previous century, Constantius' troops proclaimed his son, Constantine, emperor. Diocletian's system had broken down and Galerius, who had been promoted legitimately from Caesar to Augustus of the eastern empire on Diocletian's abdication, had no option but to acquiesce in Constantine's promotion. Things were made more complicated when Maxentius, the son of Diocletian's co-emperor Maximian, seized power in Italy and in 307 was proclaimed Augustus by the Senate in Rome.

Galerius remained Augustus in the eastern empire, delegating power over the important provinces of Egypt and Syria to his Caesar, Maximinus, and over Pannonia, the vital Balkans area, to Licinius. When Galerius died in agony from bowel cancer in May 311– Lactantius is recorded as saying that it was the retribution of God for his persecutions – Maximinus emerged as Augustus in the far eastern provinces of the empire but claimed that he should be emperor of the whole east. Licinius, however, hung on to the European provinces of the eastern empire, notably those in the Balkans. Far from the ordered transferral of power that Diocletian had hoped and planned for, each part of the empire was now in contention, between Constantine and Maxentius in the west and between Licinius and Maximinus in the east.

Constantine was ambitious and ruthless: he was after absolute power in the empire. There was no pretence that he owed his position to Diocletian's system. Rather he proclaimed that his father Constantius was the descendant of an earlier emperor, Claudius Gothicus (268–270), so he, Constantine, was emperor through legitimate descent. The court panegyrists were ordered to embellish the myth that the heavens were opened to Constantius on his death and Jupiter, father of the gods, stood there holding out his right hand to the ascending emperor. The support of the gods was always essential, and Constantine himself told of a vision of Apollo who, accompanied by the goddess Victoria, promised him a reign of thirty years. Apollo was represented by images of the sun, and this underpinned Constantine's association with the cult of Sol Invictus, the Unconquered Sun. On a coin minted in 313, Constantine is shown alongside Apollo with the latter wearing a solar wreath.

If Constantine was to fulfil the destiny that he claimed the gods had predicted for him, a showdown with Maxentius was inevitable. It came in 312 after Constantine had marched into Italy. Maxentius left Rome and met him where the Via Flaminia, the ancient road that led north from the city, crossed the Tiber. The Milvian Bridge there had been cut and replaced by a bridge of boats that Maxentius and his men crossed to meet Constantine. The battle was nasty and decisive. When Maxentius' men were forced to retreat back over the provisional bridge, it broke up and thousands, including Maxentius, were drowned. Later Constantine told of the cross he had seen in the sky and claimed the support of the Christian God for his success. A separate account told how he had had a dream in which he was commanded to put a sign of Christ on his soldiers' shields. The next year, after a meeting with Licinius in Milan at which Licinius married one of Constantine's half-sisters, Constantia, the two emperors issued the so-called Edict of Milan, or Edict of Toleration, in which Christians were given freedom to worship and the right to have their property returned. As we have already seen, the Edict also reaffirmed the right of all to follow their own religion.

Few moments in history have been more endlessly discussed. There is no evidence that Constantine became any more pious or less brutal in either his public or private life after his victory, so was this a genuine conversion, and if so what did Constantine mean by it? How did his adoption of Christianity affect his relationship with the other gods he had shown allegiance to? The ambiguity became clear when a new triumphal arch decreed by the Roman Senate in Constantine's honour was unveiled in 315; in its surmounting inscription, it attributed the victory of the Milvian Bridge to 'divine inspiration' and to Constantine's 'own great spirit'. Alongside a relief of Constantine entering Rome in triumph after his victory is a roundel showing the sun god Sol ascending to heaven in a four-horse chariot. In public monuments in such a sensitive arena as the ancient ceremonial centre of Rome, Constantine had little option but to sustain pagan symbols; it may even be that he was unaware that his commitment to Christianity required that he reject other gods. It was quite acceptable in the pagan world to hold a variety of spiritual allegiances simultaneously or in succession, so it is difficult to know the extent to which, behind this façade, he was personally committed to his new faith.

The one consistent theme in Constantine's policy towards Christians is that he, rather than the Church, defined the relationship. He was, after all, offering a persecuted minority full membership of Roman society and he knew it would be dependent on him. More than this, he proclaimed that the clergy would now be exempt from taxation and civic duties so that 'they shall not be drawn away by any deviation and sacrifice from worship due to the divinity . . . for it seems that, rendering the greatest possible service to the deity, they most benefit the state'. This is Constantine not so much humbling himself before God, as using the power of the Church to sustain his own rule. 'The primary duty of the [Christian] clergy', noted the scholar J.H.W.G. Liebeschuetz, 'always was to maintain the divine cult [of the emperor], and by their prayers to ensure that God would support the emperor and his subjects.'[11] Constantine fostered the process by granting immense patronage to the Church in the shape of buildings, in Rome with the church of Christ the Redeemer (later St John Lateran), Santa Croce delle Gerusaleme (named after the *titulus*, name board, of Christ's cross brought from Jerusalem by Constantine's mother Helena) and the first basilica of St Peter's over the supposed burial place of the martyred apostle on the Vatican Hill. These buildings were plain on the exterior (presumably so as not to offend pagans) but glittering with gold and mosaic inside. In this way a pagan custom, the worship of gods through impressive buildings, was transferred successfully into Christianity. Such display was completely alien to the Christian tradition, and the ascetic scholar Jerome must have spoken for many traditionalists when he complained that 'parchments are dyed purple, gold is melted into lettering, manuscripts are dressed up in jewels, while Christ lies at the door naked and dying'. Now opulence became central to Christianity's public identity. It was one of the most important architectural and economic revolutions in European history. Walk through any city with a medieval past and note the extensive space and resources given to churches. In the early fourteenth century the poet Dante himself lamented:

> Ah, Constantine, that was indeed a curse,
> not thy conversion, but thy dower which
> first filled the Holy Father's purse![12]

These developments were extraordinary in themselves but masked something just as fundamental. When Christianity became Constantine's religion as the result of the apparent support shown for him by the Christian God at the Milvian Bridge, it meant accepting that God willed the rise to power of the emperor by means of bloody warfare. Constantine's biographer, Eusebius of Caesarea, had no difficulty in finding relevant texts from the Old Testament to explain the victory. Exodus 15:4, 'Pharaoh's chariots and his force he [God] cast into the sea, and picked rider-captains he overwhelmed in the Red Sea', clearly referred to the similar fate suffered by Maxentius and his men in the waters of the Tiber. According to Eusebius, Psalm 7:15–16, 'he dug a hole and excavated it, and will fall into the pit he made', certainly told of the consequences for Maxentius of having broken down the original Milvian Bridge![13] Thus the Hebrew scriptures, which had been adopted by Christians as foretelling the coming of Christ, were now used to foretell the victory of a Roman emperor over his adversaries. But not everyone felt so comfortable about this use of the Old Testament. When the Christian missionary Ulfilas, working among the Goths, translated the Bible into Gothic, he deliberately left out the two books of Kings on the grounds that the Goths were warlike enough already and did not need any further encouragement. On the other hand, as we will see, bishops such as the formidable Ambrose of Milan followed Constantine's precedent by equating God's support with the coming of imperial victory. The consequences of this relationship between Christianity, war and imperial conquest still resonate today.

The Church centred on the bishops, and it was essential for Constantine to forge some kind of stable relationship with them. Bishops had not supplanted the secular authorities, the local governors and prefects, in the cities, but they had often built up impressive networks through their congregations. While a provincial governor might stay in post for three or four years, bishops could be in office for twenty, even thirty, years. They met their congregations on a weekly basis, and many were talented orators. Congregations were growing as persecution ceased and resources were targeted to the Church. (Eusebius bemoaned the hypocrisy of these new 'Christians' who joined the faith only now that the going was good.) A bishop with popular support could be a formidable figure, even able to challenge the will of an emperor. It has been argued that Constantine's prime motive for his conversion was the desire to integrate these important figures into the

Roman state.[14] It is certainly true that he used them for public purposes: from Constantine onwards emperors encouraged bishops to use their courts for solving local disputes and for overseeing poor relief. We know of Constantine channelling corn and oil to the poor of Alexandria through the city's bishop and so effectively merging the Christian duty to help the poor with the political need to prevent unrest by feeding the volatile population. In Constantinople, the Church was ordered to organise free funerals for the poor. Bishops were given the same rights as secular magistrates to free slaves. So the status of the bishop rose steadily.

Within this framework, however, tensions between and within local Christian communities suddenly became important in a different way. There had been local meetings of bishops in the past to sort out disputes, but the Church as a whole had no means of coming to any coherent conclusions on its organisation or doctrine. In a sense this was its strength, as local communities could create their own interpretation of Christianity and elect a bishop who suited their own needs. But now there might be two or more rival Christian communities in a city, each claiming the tax exemptions and patronage of the emperor. Who were the 'real' Christians, and who decided this in any case?

This issue first arose in North Africa, where the aftermath of Diocletian's persecutions had caused divisions within the Christian communities. Clergy who surrendered precious vessels and sacred texts were now called *traditores*, 'the traitors', by those who had stood firm, and the question arose whether consecrations of clergy or sacraments administered by the *traditores* had any legitimacy. Rigorous Christians insisted that anyone baptised by a *traditor* after his 'betrayal' would have to be baptised again; the retort was that baptism as a sacrament was valid in itself irrespective of the cleric who administered the rite. The dispute became so intractable that it caused a schism in North Africa. The hardliners, known as the Donatists, followed their charismatic bishop Donatus, while the rival group elected one Caecilian as their bishop.

At first Constantine appears to have been happy to let the Church deal with the problem, and he asked the Bishop of Rome, Miltiades, to preside over a small gathering of bishops, mostly from Italy, to decide the issue. But after appeals and counter-appeals from both parties – Constantine was always ready to listen to petitioners, often giving them personal audiences – he gradually, over three or four years, tended towards the Caecilianists. Donatus' refusal to compromise with the imperial authorities led to the isolation of himself and his followers from state patronage, which was now channelled towards the Caecilianists. It was a moment of immense symbolic importance, because Constantine was in fact shaping the form and structure of what became the Roman Catholic Church. By supporting those bishops who were prepared to acquiesce in his rule, he created an alliance between Church and state that was to persist, if often uneasily, in western Europe for centuries to come. The precedent had now been set that the emperor might intervene not only to strengthen the Church but to influence doctrine. (There does seem to have been some initial state persecution of the Donatists, but in 321 Constantine ordered the *vicarius* of Africa to relent, and despite their lack of patronage, the Donatists flourished and became the largest Christian community in Africa.)

These pragmatic moves went hand in hand with Constantine's rise to domination over the empire. Licinius had eliminated his rival Maximinus in 313 and became Constantine's sole rival for power. Over the coming years the relationship corroded, and the records suggest that Constantine gradually took more decisions without reference to Licinius. In 323 Constantine crossed into Licinius' half of the empire, establishing a cause for war that his rival could not ignore. In two major battles in 324, one near the city of Adrianople, Licinius was defeated. Constantine now ruled the entire Roman empire, east and west, and to celebrate he set in hand a new imperial capital, strategically placed on the site of ancient Byzantium between Europe and Asia. The 'new Rome', Constantinople, was to be capital first of the eastern empire, and later of the Byzantine empire until its fall to the Ottoman Turks in 1453.

In the eastern empire Constantine encountered a Christian church that was much more deeply rooted than anything he had found in the west. While only sixteen bishops are known for the whole of Gaul for 314, there were perhaps seven or eight hundred in the eastern empire. Furthermore, it was a culture that buzzed with speculation on theological issues. At first, like many Roman leaders before him, Constantine could not grasp the importance of debate to the Greek mind and how seriously doctrinal issues were taken. With the Donatists there had been a separate group of bishops who were alienated from their fellows by a distinctive policy over the admittance of those who had given in during the persecutions. However difficult it was to resolve, it was a relatively cut-and-dried issue. In the Greek world there was, as there had been for centuries, a mass of different interpretations of Christianity. Did it matter? At one level for Constantine it did not, simply because he could not see how anyone could take seriously all the hours spent nit-picking over words. He seems to have envisaged God as the heavenly equivalent of a Roman emperor who like him had to manage different power groups and interests in the higher cause of unity. To his annoyance, however, he soon discovered that some disputes were getting so fierce and so entangled in issues of authority and personality that they actually threatened the peace of the territories he had just won.

The greatest turbulence centred on a confrontation between Alexander, the Bishop of Alexandria, the richest and most prestigious city of the Greek east and the setting of some of the finest achievements of the Greek mind in science and mathematics, and one of his priests by the name of Arius.[15] There were a number of undercurrents to the dispute – how far did a priest, however learned, have the right to develop ideas different from those of his bishop, for instance – but the particular debate focused on defining the relationship between God the Father and Jesus the Son. This had become one of the most challenging issues in Christian theology. If Jesus was divine, how could that divinity relate to that of God? Had Jesus always been in existence alongside God in some way, or had he been a later creation? The debates took on an extraordinary emotional intensity, as most of the participants believed that their salvation depended on finding the correct answer. Alexander and Arius took opposing positions along this fault line; Alexander arguing for the eternal co-existence of Father and Son, Arius for Jesus as a separate creation, albeit at the beginning of time.

This debate and those on the nature of Christ that followed in the eastern Church in the next two hundred years were bound to be intractable. Inevitably the scriptures, both the Old and New Testament, would be combed for support by both sides. Yet the Bible as it was being formed in these years (there was still debate in different parts of the empire over which texts should or should not be included) is a collection of a very wide variety of different types of literature – poems, stories, letters, histories, biographies, lists of ritual requirements, meditations on the meaning of life, and so on. Any writing that had been incorporated into the canon was seen by Christians as the inspired word of God, but there was no systematic theology that could easily be drawn from the texts. If one took the gospels, it was quite clear that Jesus abhorred violence, yet the God of the Old Testament often seemed to revel in it. As seen above, it was verses from the Old Testament that were produced to justify the Christian emperors' assault on their enemies. So where did this leave those who wished to focus their beliefs on the teachings of Jesus?

Many Christians were learned in Greek philosophy, and inevitably they used it as a tool for achieving systematic statements about Christian theology. In any debate, however, there proved to be little stable ground on which any argument could be based. Quite apart from the difficulties in interpreting the broad spectrum of scripture, there were too many varied sources and too many philosophical traditions, some very sophisticated and always in a state of development. This was the nature of the Greek intellectual world. It proved extraordinarily difficult to define the parameters of a theological issue and find ways of resolving it. Consensus was always unlikely. The bitterness, mutual recriminations and nit-picking that was so often a feature of fourth- and fifth-century theology arose not because Christians were any less intelligent or more disputatious than their pagan counterparts but because the central debate over the divinity of Christ was, as one contemporary historian, Socrates, noted, 'a battle fought at night, for neither party appeared to understand distinctly the grounds on which they calumniated one another'.[16]

Such was the background to the 'Arian' debate. Although he was about sixty in 325, Arius had proved himself a determined man. Summoned before Alexander, he had stood up for himself in person and continued to recruit supporters in the city even after he had been excommunicated by his bishop. He was adept at suggesting that he was only drawing on the wisdom of his predecessors and was prepared to suffer in its defence 'for the glory of God'. More ominously for Alexander, Arius had then gone off to seek support, notably from the bishop of the important imperial city of Nicomedia, Eusebius, a well-respected scholar and supporter of similar ideas to those of Arius. Eusebius sensibly advised Arius to clarify his views and then arranged to have them endorsed by a council of local bishops. Arius found further support from another Eusebius, Bishop of Caesarea in Palestine, the future biographer of Constantine. Alexander counterattacked by getting signatures of support from some two hundred bishops, many of them from his own diocese of Egypt. It was in this atmosphere of escalating tension that Constantine sent his closest adviser, the Spanish Ossius, Bishop of Cordova, to carry out an investigation of the unrest. Ossius' own sympathies were clearly with Alexander (and the episcopal authority of this ancient see), but he realised that the only way to solve the issue was to call a larger council under the auspices of the emperor himself.

So a debate that might well have been smoothed over by a compromise now drew in bishops from across the eastern Mediterranean. Attention turned to the coming council. Never had there been such a chance for so many bishops to meet together to decide on an issue. Constantine chose his palace at Nicaea as the venue, and some 250 bishops, most of them from the east, began assembling there for the first session. It was an extraordinary moment. Many of the bishops still carried the marks of the persecution the imperial officials had inflicted on their bodies – now they were meeting face to face with the emperor himself. Constantine flaunted his own status by wearing a purple robe studded with gold and diamonds. Eusebius of Caesarea describes how the bishops reacted to the dazzling sight with the incredulity of children.[17]

Constantine had already met Eusebius of Caesarea, his biographer-to-be, and had been impressed by him. Even though Eusebius had recently been condemned as heretical by a council of 'Alexandrian' bishops meeting in Antioch, the emperor was not going to deprive him of the privilege of making a speech. The bishop put forward a formula that might be acceptable to both sides. Jesus Christ was 'the Word of God, God from God, light from light, Son only begotten, first-begotten of all creation, begotten before all ages from the Father . . .' This was a sensible compromise because it accepted the full divinity of Christ, which Arius' supporters were prepared to do, but it said nothing that implied Jesus was subordinate to the Father. Its success was probably the cause of its own weakness. Alexander and his supporters realised that Arius (who was actually in attendance, although, not being a bishop, he was unable to speak) could endorse the statement and return to Alexandria to go on preaching as he always had done. It seems to have been Ossius, probably with Constantine's support, who suggested that there needed to be something added to the statement. The word suggested was *homoousios*, 'of the same substance' – Jesus was to be proclaimed 'of the same substance' as the Father, a formulation that would place him unequivocally on Alexander's side of the argument.

The bishops must have been taken aback. *Homoousios* was a term taken from Greek philosophy, not from scripture. It had been used by pagan writers such as Plotinus to describe the relationship between the soul and the divine. Even the most ingenious biblical scholars combing their way through the Old and New Testaments could find no Christian equivalent. Quite apart from this the word had actually been condemned by a council of bishops meeting in Antioch in 268 on the grounds that it failed to provide sufficient distinction between Father and Son, and users of the term risked being associated with a view that had already been condemned in the third century, Sabellianism. Sabellius, who had taught in Rome, had argued that Jesus appeared on earth simply as a temporary manifestation of God. The word 'substance' also suggested some kind of physical material, yet could one talk of God as in any way material? Furthermore, how had Jesus become distinct from his Father – had there been, for instance, an original *ousios* that was somehow split into two? One of the arguments against the term put by Arius and Eusebius was that if Jesus came from the same substance as God, then his creation, by detracting from the 'substance' of God, must have diminished the deity. Cumulatively these arguments made it formidably difficult for the *homoousion* to be accepted in the wider Church.

It is always hard for historians to recreate the mood of a meeting in which high drama, the grand surroundings and the sheer unfamiliarity of the occasion must have swept events along. The emperor issued his own warning of the perils of continuing disagreement. 'For to me,' the emperor told his audience, 'internal division in the Church of God is graver than any war or secular battle, and these things appear to cause more pain than secular affairs.' This must have had its own effect in achieving a consensus. One catalyst for the change in mood may have been a document mentioned in one account of the council as having been put forward by Eusebius of Nicomedia, the supporter of Arius, which was considered so blasphemous as to evoke a reaction against its author and his views. There was now a groundswell of opinion against Arius, and the Nicene statement specifically condemned some of his beliefs, notably that there had been a time when Christ had not existed. Arius and two of his closest supporters were excommunicated by Constantine himself when they refused to sign the document. Later, Eusebius of Nicomedia, who had refused to endorse the specific condemnations of Arius, was also banished from his see. While it is clear that many of the bishops were uneasy about the use of *homoousios*, a consensus of sorts appeared to have been achieved. The council ended with the remaining bishops summoned to a great victory feast by the emperor.

The Nicene statement was to form the core of the Nicene Creed, which forms the basis of faith in the Catholic, Orthodox and many Protestant Churches today. Yet no one at the time would have expected it to fulfil this function. It was shaped by the concern to deal with the immediate issue of the relationship between Son and Father; it said nothing about the Trinity, for instance – the only reference to the Holy Spirit was 'And I believe in the Holy Spirit'. The word *homoousios* was clearly an embarrassment and was to be condemned in the years to come. As Richard Hanson, whose *The Search for the Christian Doctrine of God* is one of the fullest and most balanced studies of the issue, comments, 'the Creed was a mine of potential confusion and consequently most unlikely to be a means of ending the Arian controversy'.[18] No positive mention of it is found in any text until the Bishop of Alexandria, Athanasius, who had attended the council as Alexander's deacon, revived it in the 350s. Yet Nicaea had produced a written text that could become a talisman in a debate with few clear boundaries. This was to prove its abiding strength.

It is to Constantine's credit that once he realised how little support the *homoousios* formula and the condemnation of Arius had in the wider Greek world, he backtracked in the hope of finding a broader consensus. He actually received the elderly Arius personally and ordered that he be reinstated to his position in Alexandria. (It appears that Arius made some sort of recantation of his ideas, which Constantine was prepared to accept.) Alexander refused to admit him – it would have been too humiliating for the bishop to give way on the issue – and when Alexander died in 328, his successor as bishop, Athanasius, also refused. Athanasius soon found himself in more trouble with the emperor after a flurry of accusations that he had asserted his authority in Alexandria with violence and intimidation. Constantine, who put good order and the reconciliation of factions above everything, exiled this intransigent man from his see to Gaul and now asked the Bishop of Constantinople to admit Arius back into the Church. However, in the procession to the ceremony Arius was taken ill. He struggled off to a nearby latrine and was found there dead. His enemies spoke of the will of God destroying a heretic; his supporters suspected poison.

It may simply have been the impact of the drama of the moment on an elderly man. (Later, after the Nicene cause triumphed, the latrine was shown to visitors as evidence of God's punishment of heretics.) The death did not deflect Constantine from his policy of maintaining an open mind to the debate. When he was eventually baptised, in the closing months of his life in 337, the emperor called on Arius' old supporter, the 'blasphemous' Eusebius of Nicomedia, whom he had reinstated in his bishopric in 327, to administer the sacrament.

In his *Life of Constantine*, Eusebius of Caesarea openly acknowledges the independence of the emperor from the Church. He even quotes Constantine as saying he was the bishop for those outside the Church and portrays him as the direct representative of God. Constantine thrived in this role, but he clearly found the bishops more troublesome than he had hoped. 'You, the bishops, do nothing but that which encourages discord and hatred and, to speak frankly, which leads to the destruction of the human race,' he exploded at one point.[19] This was unfair, as Constantine was trying to mould a Church of his own making and in doing so he had broken with much of Christian tradition. He bequeathed lasting tensions to the Church in the form of debates over the correct use of wealth (how much, for instance, should be diverted into showcase buildings), the relationship of Christians to war and imperial authority, and the nature of the Godhead itself. There is no significant evidence that Constantine was prepared to compromise with what had already been established as Christian teaching, and he kept himself clear of the institution of the Church itself. It has even been argued that the founding of Constantinople, an expansion of Byzantium, a city with no Christian heritage, was a means of distancing himself from those cities where Christianity was deeply rooted. He had been, after all, the chosen of God, and blasphemous though it might appear, his mausoleum in Constantinople was dedicated to the Holy Apostles of whom he considered himself number thirteen! The context within which the Church operated had been changed for ever. 'The master narrative of Christianity would become so deeply implicated in the narrative of imperial power that Christianity and government would become inextricably linked.'[20]

V

TRUE GOD FROM TRUE GOD?

ON the death of Constantine in 337, the debate between Arius and Alexander remained unresolved. There were two rival conceptions of Jesus' divinity embedded in the Christian communities. Alexander had argued that Jesus was always fully God and had existed eternally alongside God the Father. This view had been accepted at Nicaea with the addition of the term *homoousios*, 'of the same substance', to describe their shared status. Arius, on the other hand, argued that Jesus had been created as a subordinate god within time, the Son of the Father who became Father only at the moment of Jesus' creation. The evidence seems to suggest that after Nicaea, Constantine was shrewd enough to accept that the debate was impossible to resolve. His policy was to be tolerant of differing beliefs while remaining intolerant of any bishops, such as Athanasius of Alexandria, who caused or intensified unrest in their communities. For Constantine, as with most emperors, good order was more important than correct doctrine.

The original conception of Jesus in the context of the Jewish world in which he lived and taught was that he was fully human. It was impossible to conceive, in fact blasphemous for a Jew to believe, as it would later be for Muslims, that he could be divine. This possibility could not even be considered until Christianity spread from the Jewish into the Greek world where the boundaries between human and divine were less clearly defined. Even here there were many Christians who continued to see Jesus as no more than a man, though one of great spiritual qualities. One Theodotus, a cobbler from Constantinople who came to Rome about 190 and gathered his own congregation in the relatively fluid Christian world of the period, used logical analysis derived from Aristotle and the mathematician Euclid to conclude that, while the Holy Spirit was involved in the conception of Jesus, this did not give Jesus divine status – he was always 'a mere man'. Theodotus was excommunicated by Victor, the Bishop of Rome, but his congregation seems to have still been alive in the 260s, though by this time some of them believed that Jesus had finally become divine, at the resurrection.

However, mainstream Christian teaching soon came to accept that Jesus was divine. In retrospect, this was perhaps the most significant development ever to take place in Christian theology. It further distanced Christianity from Judaism and, in so far as any empirical evidence for a divine presence is difficult to discern, it meant that there would be acute speculation about the nature of that divinity, especially in an intellectual tradition as sophisticated as that of the Greeks. In his *Voting about God in Early Christian Councils*, Ramsay MacMullen lists fifty key theological issues raised in the debates of the following years. They include the more philosophical, such as 'Does "like" mean "identical"?'; the theological, 'Was Christ a man indwelt by God?'; the quasi-scientific, 'Is God's substance increased or divided in begetting?'; and the more esoteric, 'Did Christ's existence begin in the womb or at birth?'[1] As we have seen, the Greek philosophical tradition was as alive in the Christian world as it was within paganism.

It was not only Jesus' relationship to God the Father that was difficult to define. Any attempt to relate Jesus' divinity to his humanity was similarly fraught with difficulty. The great third-century theologian Origen recognised the intractability of the problem: 'Of all the marvellous and splendid things about him [Jesus], there is one that utterly transcends the capacity of our weak mortal intelligence to think of or understand, namely how this mighty power of the divine majesty, the very Word of the Father, and the very Wisdom of God ... can be believed to have existed within the compass of that man who appeared in Judaea ... When we see him in some things so human that he appears in no way to differ from the common frailty of mortals, and in some things so divine that they are appropriate to nothing else but the primal and ineffable nature of deity, the human understanding with its narrow limits is baffled.'[2] In the fourth century, asceticism became increasingly important, and with it a denigration of the human body. This made it even more difficult to imagine why Jesus should have adopted flesh. As the theologian Gregory of Nyssa put it in one of his

Catechetical Orations of the 380s: 'Why did the divine descend to such humiliation? Our faith staggers at the thought that God, the infinite, inconceivable and ineffable deity, who transcends all glory and majesty, should be clothed with the defiled nature of man, so that his sublime activities are abased through being united with what is so degraded.'[3] Equally baffling was the issue raised in the Arius and Alexander debate, the moment and context in which Jesus was, or was not, created by God the Father.

Despite the assertion of the Nicene Creed that Jesus was one in substance with the Father, the most persistent belief – persistent in that it had deep roots in the Christian tradition – was subordinationism. Subordinationism was a broad movement that included Arius as well as many others who had developed their ideas independently of him, among them earlier scholars such as Origen. They believed that Jesus was a later creation by God the Father, of lesser divinity and thus subordinate to him in some way. The subordinationists drew their strength from a mass of biblical texts that appeared to support their case. From the Old Testament there was a verse from Proverbs (8:22) – 'God created me, Wisdom, at the beginning of time' – which, if Wisdom could be seen as an allegory for Christ, seemed to make clear that Jesus was a later, if early, creation of God. In the New Testament, the gospels of Matthew, Mark and Luke (the so-called synoptic gospels) were rich in subordinationist texts. So when Jesus says, 'Of that day and hour knoweth no man, neither the angel in heaven, nor the Son, but only the Father' (Mark 13:32), 'My God, my God, why hast thou forsaken me?'(Matthew 27:46), or 'The Father is greater than I' (John 14:28), he is clearly attributing some form of superiority to God the Father. Peter's statement in Acts 2:36 that 'God has made [sic] him both Lord and Christ, this Jesus whom you crucified' was another important subordinationist text, as were a host of others that appeared to show Jesus as anguished, ignorant, hungry or tired.[4] As will be seen, anyone who wished to argue that Jesus was equal in divine majesty to God the Father would need to exercise considerable literary ingenuity to find alternative explanations of these texts. To the subordination-ists they seemed incontrovertible, and this helps to explain why the gulf between them and the followers of the Nicene Creed, with their insistence on 'one substance', became so wide.

Subordinationism was also supported by Platonism, especially in the way that Plato was interpreted by the first century AD Jewish philosopher Philo. Increasingly Platonists talked of the supreme Good, the apex at the top of the hierarchy of Ideas or Forms. Philo, who had never heard of Jesus and was concerned only with the Hebrew scriptures, claimed that Plato's Forms had been known to the prophets. As Plato had argued that the Forms existed eternally, Philo concluded that they could have been understood before Plato, for instance by someone supremely wise like Moses. 'Who is Plato but Moses speaking Greek?' he asked. The question then was how the Forms might reveal themselves in the material world. In his philosophy, Philo gave central importance to *logos*, reasoned thought, as a Platonic Form that existed somewhere between God and the material world. 'The *Logos* is an ambassador and suppliant, neither unbegotten nor begotten as are sensible things.'⁵ One of the roles of the *logos*, Philo suggested, was that of God's architect, who put God's creative power into action in the material world. For instance, the voice from the Burning Bush (in Exodus 3) might be that of *logos* revealing itself. Obviously, *logos* was subordinate to the Good. When Philo's ideas filtered through into the Christian world, the evangelist John saw how Jesus could be conceptualised as *logos* become flesh (the English translation 'Word' gives nothing of the richness and breadth of the Greek original). Although John's approach to the relationship between God and Jesus is ambiguous – both Nicenes and subordinationists have been able to use him in their cause – the concept of Word becoming flesh could be interpreted to support the *logos*/Jesus as subordinate to God, sent by him to mankind.

In addition to support from scripture and Platonism, a major strength of the subordinationist position was that subordinationists did not have to define Christ's divinity rigidly (as it had been, for instance, by a term such as *homoousios*), and so space was left for the humanity of Jesus. There was general agreement that Christ brought salvation to the human race by undergoing suffering for the sins of mankind. This would make no sense if he was incapable of feeling his scourging and the hammering in of the nails. So if his suffering was central to Christian belief, one could argue that his divinity, even if it was not easy to define, did not prevent him undergoing the human suffering essential for the salvation of mankind. His was therefore a lesser form of divinity to that of God, who was above all suffering.

The subordinationist argument was set out with some clarity in a creed drawn up by a small group of bishops at Sirmium in 357. It deserves to be quoted in full:

It is agreed that there is one almighty God and Father, as is believed throughout the whole world, and his only Son, Jesus Christ the Lord, our Saviour: but there cannot be two gods nor should that be preached, as the text [from John's gospel] runs. Therefore there is one God of all, as the apostles taught, and the rest agrees and can contain no ambiguity. But as for the fact that some, or many, are concerned with substance (which is called *ousia* in Greek), that is to speak more explicitly, *homoousion* as it is called – there should be no mention of it whatever, nor should anyone preach it. And this is the cause and reason, that it is not included in the divine Scriptures, and it is beyond man's knowledge nor can anyone declare the birth of the Son ... for it is clear that only the Father knows how he begot his Son and his Son how he was begotten by the Father. There is no uncertainty about the Father being greater; it cannot be doubted by anyone that the Father is greater in honour, in dignity, in glory, in majesty, in the very name of 'Father', for he himself witnesses. And nobody is unaware that this is Catholic [i.e. universal] doctrine, that there are two persons of the Father and the Son, and that the Father is greater, and the Son is subjected in common with all the things which the Father subjected to him; that the Father has no beginning, is invisible, immortal and impassible [i.e unable to suffer]; but that the Son is born from the Father, God from God, Light from Light, whose generation as Son, as has been said already, no one knows except the Father; and that the Son of God himself, our Lord and God, as it is said, assumed flesh or body; that is man from the womb of the Virgin Mary, as the angel foretold. As all the Scriptures teach, and especially the teacher of the Gentiles himself, the apostle [Paul], he took human nature from the Virgin Mary, and it was through this that he suffered. But that is the summary of the whole faith and the confirmation of it that the Trinity should always be preserved, as we read in the gospel.[6]

One of the attractions of this creed is that, in the spirit of Origen, it does not try to go where it cannot understand. 'It is clear that only the Father knows how he begot his Son and his Son how he was begotten by the Father' is a neat way of avoiding what might otherwise be a dead-end debate. It rejects the term *homoousios*, not only because it is incompatible with the distinction made between Father and Son, but because, as has already been mentioned, it had no support from scripture. It also accepts the human suffering of Jesus. As Richard

Hanson puts it in his own commentary on the creed: 'It is the Son who suffers through his body. The Father is incapable of suffering. This is a doctrine of God suffering, and the suffering is done by a lower god [Jesus] who can endure such experiences.'[7] There remains the problem that although the creed gives Jesus the status of Lord and Saviour and describes him as 'God from God', it also tries to maintain that there are not two gods. The challenge of insisting that Jesus (and in later debates, the Holy Spirit) is divine and distinct without there being two (or three) gods was one of the main conceptual difficulties in the whole debate, and remains so today.

This creed accepts the Trinity, of Father, Son and Holy Spirit. The Latin term itself, *trinitas*, was first put forward by Tertullian, writing in Carthage around AD 200. In Tertullian's Trinity, Jesus is envisaged as being generated from the Father as *logos*, the Word, in different stages in the course of the creation, revelation and redemption, and so at least in part is a later creation. The concept of a Trinity presented no problem to the subordinationists. Arius had suggested a strong distinction between Father, Son and Holy Spirit and set them within a hierarchy. 'Certainly there is a Trinity,' he had written, '. . . but their individual realities do not mix with each other and they possess glories of different levels.' Each of the three persons of the Trinity has his own function, but the Father is 'infinitely more splendid in his glories' and is distinct from the Son because He has no beginning.[8] But there had been no mention of the Trinity in the Nicene Creed. The assertion 'And I believe in the Holy Spirit' had been included, but nothing was said of the Spirit having any divine status or being related to Father and Son in any way.

One important school of subordinationism was that of Aetius, a man born humbly, possibly in Cilicia, about 295. After a training as a goldsmith, he somehow acquired an impressive education (centring on the works of Aristotle) and then converted to Christianity. He is found teaching in the two great Christian cities of the east, Antioch and Alexandria, and in the latter he acquired a secretary, one Eunomius, from Cappadocia. Eunomius developed Aetius' ideas, and as only his works have survived, the school is often known as Eunomian.[9] While many subordinationists were happy to accept some similarity between Father and Son, Aetius and Eunomius stressed the ways in which they were *unlike* each other. For instance, God the Father was 'unbegotten' – he had existed without cause from the beginning of time – while

Jesus the Son was 'begotten'. Surely, Eunomius argued, the distinction
between an 'unbegotten' and a 'begotten' being is such that one cannot
possibly argue that the two are of the same substance. The Eunomians
thus strongly rejected *homoousios*. Eunomius prided himself on his
akribeia, precision in the use of language, and his relentless logic made
him a formidable player in the debate. Consequently he was accused
by his opponents of relying too heavily on Greek philosophy, and even
taunted for having Aristotle as his bishop.

Eunomius' confidence in the power of logic was such that he asserted
that it was possible to know God as well as one did oneself. Naturally
this was shocking to some, but it illustrates well the intellectual confidence of a trained Greek mind. Eunomius' opponents claimed that, on
the contrary, the Godhead was beyond reasoned understanding and its
essence could be grasped only through faith. This was a fundamental
disagreement, which went to the core of the whole debate. Could the
issue of whether Jesus had existed eternally or been created in time be
solved by the reasoning mind, as Eunomius suggested it could, or was
it beyond reason? If it was beyond it, was it a debate at all, or could
a resolution only be achieved by other means – a direct revelation of
God, for instance? A belief sustained by faith or received as a revelation is of a completely different status from a belief sustained by reason
or empirical evidence. The first becomes bound up with the authority
that proposes it and thus must be challenged through that authority,
the second is freestanding and can always be modified as new evidence
or ways of thinking appear. The Eunomians represented the rationalist
approach, and the number of named tracts – usually entitled *Contra
Eunomium*, 'Against Eunomius' – targeted at them shows how unsettling
they were to their opponents.

The debate might have continued if Constantine's son, Constantius,
had not attempted to bring some order to the Church by seeking agreement on a new creed. Constantius had gained control of the whole
empire through the elimination of his two brothers and other rival
claimants by 351. His own sympathies were towards a subordinationist
belief, such as that outlined in the Sirmium Creed quoted above. In
other words, Nicaea and the tradition of Alexander would be rejected,
along with the term *homoousios*. On the other hand, however,
Constantius and the bishops who supported him did not want to make
the distinction between God the Father and Jesus the Son too great,
so they proposed a different term: *homoios*, 'like': Jesus is 'like' the

Father. This would isolate the Eunomians with their stress on 'unlikeness' and leave the Homoians, as they came to be known, occupying the centre ground, as subordinationists between the Nicenes and the Eunomians.

There was no doubt of Constantius' determination to sort out the problem. In 359 he summoned two councils. One, representing the bishops from the Greek-speaking east, was to meet at Seleucia in Cilicia; the other, with bishops from the Latin-speaking west, would meet at Ariminum on the Adriatic coast of Italy. Both were presented with Constantius' creed, known as the Dated Creed, the name referring to its date, which was specifically included in its prologue. It was a complex statement of belief, though clearly subordinationist in content. In the east, where the issues had been debated most vigorously, there was no real consensus on a response, although the Egyptian participants, loyal as they were to the tradition of Alexander, insisted on inserting the word *homoousios*. The remainder of the bishops got hopelessly bogged down in hair-splitting discussions about the way in which the Son might be like the Father without sharing a substance with him. In the west, there is very little surviving evidence of the debate, but many of the western bishops appeared happy to accept the text of the creed formulated at Nicaea, apparently as a reaction to the vagueness of the Homoian creed Constantius was trying to impose.[10] This was a setback for the emperor. He could hardly have the majority of Greek Christians rejecting *homoousios* and the Roman Christians retaining it! When the westerners sent a delegation to report to him, Constantius forced it to accept an Homoian creed. Eventually it was possible for there to be a joint declaration by both councils of a creed in which Jesus was 'the one only begotten God who before all ages and before all beginning and before all conceivable time and before all conceivable substance was begotten impassably through God' (in other words, created, but at the beginning of time) and 'like to the Father who begot him', which, it was claimed, was 'as the scriptures taught'. It ended, 'The word *ousia* [substance] because it was naïvely inserted by the fathers [at Nicaea], though not familiar to the masses, caused disturbance, and because the scriptures do not contain it, we have decided that it should be removed.'[11]

As with any conceivable formulation, the creed had its critics. The supporters of Nicaea felt bullied and manipulated. The Eunomians went so far as to set up their own group of bishops covering territory

in a sweep from Constantinople around the eastern Mediterranean and
as far west as Libya. Within the Homoian community, those who had
accepted Constantius' formula, there was a mass of different interpretations of 'like the Father'. Some suggested that he was *homoiousios*,
not 'of the same substance'; but 'like in substance'; others saw a likeness in the 'image' rather than the 'substance' of the two. The theologian Gregory of Nazianzus, whose sermons on the Nicene Trinity will
be discussed later, complained that '*homoios* was a figure seeming to
look in the direction of all who passed by, a boot fitting either foot,
a winnowing with every wind'.[12]

A long-term settlement would have required Constantius to enforce
commitment to the *homoios* formula for several years until it was
accepted as the norm. Yet he died the very next year, 361, and was
succeeded by the pagan Julian, who, as we have suggested, expressed
himself horrified by the infighting between Christian groups, believing,
according to Ammianus Marcellinus, that if left to themselves the
bishops would tear the Church apart: 'No wild beasts are such enemies
to mankind as are most of the Christians in their deadly hatred of each
other.'[13] Julian's early death meant that Christianity was soon restored,
by his successor Jovian.

As if the debate was not already one of mind-boggling philosophical
complexity, it was made more bitter and intense by ecclesiastical politics. A bishopric provided status as well as access to patronage and
resources, not least from the surrendered wealth of the ascetics, who
were becoming an increasingly powerful force in Christianity. Of course,
bishops could exercise some control over how money was spent, and
many focused on the poor. Basil, Bishop of Caesarea in Cappadocia,
created a complex of leper colonies, taking on the Christian injunction
to work among the most distressed and using his own inheritance to
do so. Others, however, saw the chance of going on a building spree.
Ambrose of Milan ringed the city with his basilicas. The bishops of
Rome, reported Ammianus Marcellinus, 'enriched by the gifts of
matrons, ride in carriages, dress splendidly and outdo kings in the
lavishness of their table'. Separate sources suggest that the Bishop of
Rome's income was equal to all that of his other clergy put together
– and equal to the sum laid aside for the poor. With such opportunities at hand, it is hardly surprising that when Liberius, the Bishop of
Rome, died in 366 there were conflicts between rival factions in which

a hundred are believed to have died before Damasus emerged as the new bishop. The high level of religious violence in this period has been largely ignored by historians, but a close reading of the sources shows that almost every vacant bishopric gave rise to murder and intimidation as rival candidates fought for the position.[14] Unrest of this sort was so threatening to the authorities that there are at least two instances where men who had a reputation for being able to keep order, Ambrose in Milan in 374 and Nectarius in Constantinople in 381, were appointed bishops even before they had been baptised!

It was during this troubled time that there was a revival of Nicene orthodoxy, the Alexandrian concept of Jesus as fully God for all eternity, one in substance with the Father. This was partly a reaction against the imposition of the Homoian formula by Constantius, but it also reflected the wider social and political context in which the Church now functioned. Jesus had been executed as a rebel by the Roman Empire. The centuries of persecution before Constantine's victory in 312 had reinforced Christianity as a religion of outsiders, and Tertullian even suggested that martyrdom acted as the seed of the Church. Jesus' humanity and vulnerability could be accepted within this framework. In complete contrast, in the fourth century, Christianity had become linked to the empire and its success in war. Housed in great churches and enjoying the patronage of the state, the Church was now firmly embedded within traditional society. The outsiders had become insiders. Jesus, the all-too-human rebel against the empire, now seemed an inappropriate role model, and the response was to elevate his divinity. This meant a shift away from the gospel texts, which stressed his humanity and supported a subordinationist position, and towards the Old Testament and the letters of Paul. The God of the Old Testament appeared a better support for an authoritarian empire, while in Paul's letters Jesus' crucifixion and resurrection were transformed into cosmic events, isolated from the political context in which they actually took place. (This development will be discussed further in Chapter XII.)

It was one thing for the changing mood to support a Jesus whose divinity was stressed at the expense of his humanity. There remained immense problems in formulating this in any coherent way. There were a few biblical quotations, such as John's 'I am in the Father and the Father is in me' (14:9–11), that supported a unity of the Godhead, but as seen above, there were many texts from the gospels that rejected this idea of unity in favour of subordinationism. Even the most committed Nicene knew that he was vulnerable to counterattack on this ground, and this explains the enormous energy the supporters of Nicaea expended in finding alternative interpretations of key subordinationist texts. Another difficult issue for the Nicenes was that of Jesus' 'begetting'. The Nicene Creed referred to 'Lord Jesus Christ the Son of God, begotten as only-begotten of the Father'. This presented no problem for the subordinationists, as the 'begetting' simply referred to the method of creation of Jesus, the subordinate Son, by his Father. Yet the Nicenes wished to argue that Father and Son had co-existed for all eternity – so when could the 'begetting' have taken place if there was never a time when the Son did not exist as begotten? The problem simply took the debate on to a new level of intractability. (It has to be remembered that these debates were taking place in both Greek and Latin and there was great potential for confusion when translating complex philosophical terms from one language to the other.)

There were two other major problems for the Nicenes. The first was that if Jesus was fully God from eternity, then how did his human existence fit alongside his divinity? The greater the degree of divinity – and one could go no higher than that posited by the Nicenes, in which Jesus was actually 'of the same substance' as God the Father – the more difficult it was to give Jesus a meaningful human existence in which he actually suffered. Then, as already mentioned, there was the problem of the Trinity. The subordinationists had no difficulty in accepting the concept of a Trinity in which there was a hierarchy of God the Father, Jesus and the Holy Spirit, but, as already noted, the Nicene Creed of 325 had nowhere referred to a Trinity, and the strict interpretation of the text would seem to exclude one. There was, in fact, a group called the Macedonians, after Macedonius, Bishop of Constantinople, who argued that their support for the text agreed at Nicaea, and thus a consubstantial Father and Son, left the Holy Spirit as a subordinate extra. If one was going to accept a Nicene Trinity in which the three persons of the Trinity were of equal status, then the creed passed at Nicaea would have to be rewritten to give the Spirit a suitable divine role. The main problem here was that the scriptural basis for such a formulation of the three as of equal divine status seemed particularly weak. Furthermore, when discussions of the nature and purpose of the Spirit did get under way, it was clear that there was no agreement on what that nature might be.

The key figure in initiating a revival of Nicene theology was

Athanasius, Bishop of Alexandria from 328. Athanasius had emerged from the shadow of Alexander, the champion of anti-Arianism, and he clung resolutely to the formula at Nicaea, including *homoousios*. However, his life at Alexandria was continually troubled by the tensions of the city and his readiness to exert his authority with violence. Constantine had already exiled him once, and he continued to offend emperors (who could hardly turn a blind eye to unrest in so important a city) and his fellow bishops, particularly his subordinationist opponents, with the result that in his forty-five years of office, he was forced into exile a further three times, a total of over fifteen years.

Athanasius was not an intellectual. He does not seem to have experienced a 'classical' education, and the sources of his theology are largely biblical. 'His thought is not wide ranging or considered in its use of philosophical distinctions and concepts' is the verdict of David Brakke, an authority on the bishop. 'Instead,' Brakke goes on, 'Athanasius focused with laser-beam intensity on a single idea: the fully divine Word of God became incarnate in human flesh to save humanity from sin and death'.[15] From the 350s, Athanasius insisted that the creed of Nicaea represented orthodoxy. In a debate in which more educated minds were able to dissect each nuance ad infinitum, this clear message was certainly an advantage, and it appealed to those who liked the authority of the imperial document of 325. Yet the creed had hardly been a coherent theological statement, and defending its assertions, especially the *homoousios*, proved difficult. Athanasius drew an impenetrable barrier between the Creator and the created, with Jesus as 'one in substance' with his Father on the side of the Creator. The incarnation of this fully divine Jesus was essential, said Athanasius, because human beings had sunk so deeply into sin that they had to be saved. Athanasius' critics noted, however, that he failed to define the distinction between Father and Son with any clarity, or, indeed, how Jesus' divinity could co-exist with his humanity. Athanasius created an elaborate portrayal of the divine *logos*, Jesus the Son, somehow keeping a divine mind in a human body, leaving it uncertain whether he could suffer psychologically – as presumably he needed to if he were to bring about salvation. One can hardly complain that Athanasius was unable to solve a problem that might have been, in any philosophically coherent sense, insoluble, but his intellectual clumsiness was exposed by the issue, and more sophisticated minds did not take him seriously.

Nevertheless Athanasius was an important figure. First, he appealed to theologians in the west, perhaps the last Greek theologian to do so. His emphasis on the unity of the Godhead, even if not explained in any coherent way, meshed well with western thinking and so strengthened the Nicene cause there. Second, he did appreciate the importance of bringing the Holy Spirit, marginalised at Nicaea, into the debate, and one of his pamphlets dealt with the issue of the Spirit's divinity. However, there was a darker side to this tempestuous if determined man. He had the propagandist's trick of creating a fixed enemy, in this case the Arians, on whom he poured his venom. Not the least of their iniquities, he argued, was their power to reinvent themselves whenever they appeared on the verge of defeat. 'An Arian', Athanasius blustered, 'is a wicked thing in truth and in every respect his heart is depraved and irreligious. For behold, though convicted on all points and shown to be utterly bereft of understanding, heretics show no shame, but as the Hydra of Gentile fable, when its former serpents were destroyed, gave birth to fresh ones, contending against the slayer of the old by the production of the new, so also are they hostile and hateful to God . . .' All manner of subordinationists, many of whom had probably never read Arius, were thrust into this writhing snakepit of heresy, with such lasting effect that the debate is still often referred to as 'the Arian controversy'.[16] Athanasius may have heralded a new departure in the complex history of fourth-century theology, but at the cost, through his intransigent invective, of lowering the intellectual tone of the debate.

A much more sophisticated attempt at finding a settlement based on Nicene principles was proposed by the so-called Cappadocian Fathers: Basil, Bishop of Caesarea, his brother, Gregory of Nyssa, and Gregory of Nazianzus. The Cappadocians were men of great learning. Gregory of Nazianzus, for instance, had arrived in 348 from his native Cappadocia at the age of eighteen or nineteen to study in Athens, a city he called 'truly of gold and patroness of all that is good'.[17] He stayed there for ten years, during which time he became absorbed in classical authors, often accumulating his own copies on papyrus rolls that he took around with him as he moved. Far from rejecting pagan texts, he, like Origen a century before him, considered them an essential part of a full education. His friend Basil, who studied alongside him in Athens, argued in an important work, *Address to Young Men on the Right Use of Greek Literature*, that 'profane writings' are a stepping stone to the deeper truths of the 'Holy Scriptures'.

Into the life eternal the Holy Scriptures lead us, which teach us through divine words. But so long as our immaturity forbids our understanding their deep thought, we exercise our spiritual perceptions upon profane writings, which are not altogether different [*sic*], and in which we perceive the truth as it were in shadows and in mirrors. Consequently we must be conversant with poets, with historians, with orators, indeed with all men who may further our soul's salvation. Just as dyers prepare the cloth before they apply the dye, be it purple or any other colour, so indeed must we also, if we would preserve indelible the idea of the true virtue, become first initiated in the pagan lore, then at length give special heed to the sacred and divine teachings, even as we first accustom ourselves to the sun's reflection in the water, and then become able to turn our eyes upon the very sun itself.[18]

Just how broad this reading was can be seen from an analysis of Gregory of Nazianzus' writings, which illustrates the sources he drew on. He provides another example of just how wide a variety of texts was available for those ready to search for them, and his stretch back over a thousand years. There was Homer, of course, certainly the most widely read ancient author even at this date, and Hesiod (*c*.700 BC), who wrote a mythical account of the creation, the *Theogeny*, as well as *Works and Days*, which bemoans the breaking down of ethical standards in his day. The philosopher Heraclitus from Ephesus, fluent about 500 BC, would have challenged Gregory with his study of contradictions and the problems associated with natural change – if one stands in the same river on two separate occasions, is it the same river? – although Gregory may have been more interested in Heraclitus' view of the human soul, which Heraclitus connects to *logos*, the power of reason. There was a wide choice of poets: Sappho, Theognis of Megara, Simonides, and Pindar, author of victory hymns to the winners of the Olympics and other games. The two great historians of the fifth century, Herodotus and Thucydides, were both cited, and Gregory also drew, inevitably, on the works of Socrates, Plato and Aristotle. Plato was perhaps the single most important classical influence on Gregory, and it is clear that he also read widely in the Neoplatonism of his own day. There were examples of the great rhetoricians such as Isocrates and Demosthenes, whose speeches rallied the Athenians against the looming power of Philip of Macedon. From the first century AD, Gregory had read the works of the Jewish philosopher Philo, and from the second, Plutarch, whose *Lives* of famous Greek and Romans was one among a mass of works on moral philosophy and history. (By Gregory's time, Plutarch had become a classic, and one list of his works includes 227 items, the vast majority now lost to us.) In addition to all these 'pagan' authors, Gregory was also well versed in the Bible, and in the works of Origen, his theological mentor.[19]

This impressive education, in both pagan and Christian texts, gave the Cappadocian Fathers the intellectual capacity to devise a formula to express the distinction between God the Father and Jesus the Son within a single Godhead. Basil, for instance, argued that there was a divine essence shared by God the Father and Jesus that could be adequately described by the word *homoousios* and understood through an analogy with light. As he put it in a letter of *circa* 370, 'Since therefore the Father is light without beginning, and the Son is begotten light, yet one is light and the other is light, they [the fathers of Nicaea] rightly declared them *homoousios*.'[20] To strengthen his argument, he drew on an Aristotelian idea of distinguishing between the substance of a thing and its individual properties. You might divide a single piece of wood into two and paint one part red and the other blue. The two pieces would share the same substance, the wood, but would appear differently due to their paint; so God the Father and Jesus the begotten Son could share a substance while being different in appearance. To give added sophistication to his argument, Basil adapted a terminology, probably originated in the works of the great Neoplatonist philosopher Plotinus, in which he used the word *homoousios* to describe the single Godhead, in which he included the Holy Spirit (developing his thoughts on the divinity of the Spirit in his *On the Holy Spirit* of 375), and *hypostasis*, personality, to express the distinct identity of each of the three within this single Godhead. None of this offered any kind of rational proof for the Nicene view. In fact, it added a new element to the debate, in that it was hard to see how the three members of the Trinity could each be fully God yet have a distinct personality without there being three gods. Gregory of Nyssa, who many scholars see as the finest theologian of the three Cappadocian Fathers, produced a work of great erudition, *On Not Three Gods*, to counter his opponents.[21] Yet whatever their protestations that the three divine personalities are co-equal, the Cappadocians often refer to the Father as the source or fountainhead of the Trinity, which suggests that they retained a subordinationist instinct.[22]

In short, by the 370s one can see a debate that, in the east at least, was still lively (for the west in this same period, see Chapter Eight) and, thanks to the input of the Eunomians and the Cappadocian Fathers, who acted as stimulants to each other, impressively sophisticated, but which remained by its very nature no closer to philosophical resolution. There were too many plausible solutions, each of which could draw on some support from scripture or terminology adapted to the purpose. Even if some form of philosophical consensus had been found, other rivalries and different factions within the Church would probably have undermined it. In Antioch, for instance, there were two opposing Nicene bishops: Meletius, appointed in 360, and Paulinus, who was elected by rivals in 362 on the grounds that Meletius, despite an outward adherence to Nicaea, had leanings toward the Homoian cause. Meletius was supported by Basil of Caesarea, Paulinus by Athanasius and Damasus, the Bishop of Rome. The disagreement was so bitter, it was still corroding church politics in the 380s. It was hard to see how the church could possibly come to a consensus on a theological question so deeply embedded in the philosophical problems and the personal rivalries that infused the debate.

Nor did the emperors seem an appropriate means of resolving the issues at stake. They could hardly compete on a theological basis with the likes of the Cappadocian Fathers or Eunomius, and if they made their personal views known, their immense influence, which was enhanced by their own 'divine' status, could all too easily be used by one faction or another in the Church's internal struggles. If they were to remain figureheads of the whole empire, above its controversies, their duty was to maintain good order, suppress outbreaks of violence between the opposing factions and, if they accepted Themistius' arguments, support freedom of speech.

This is precisely what happened in the western empire during the rule of Valentinian I (364–375). Although Valentinian is normally seen as sympathetic to the Nicenes, he kept his personal beliefs to himself. According to Ammianus Marcellinus, 'He took a neutral position between opposing faiths and never troubled anyone by ordering him to adopt this or that mode of "worship".'[23] When a group of bishops came to ask for permission to hold a council, he told them: 'I am but one of the laity and have therefore no right to interfere in these transactions: let the priests, to whom such matters appertain, assemble where they please.'[24] His senior appointments show that he was as likely to favour pagans as Christians. His desire to put good order first is shown in his treatment of the bishopric of Milan. The incumbent, Auxentius, was a subordinationist but was challenged by the Nicene Hilary of Poitiers, who hoped that a Nicene emperor would support him. Valentinian sent Hilary packing as a troublemaker. When Auxentius died in 374, Valentinian acquiesced in the process by which Ambrose emerged as the man most likely to keep good order among the factions in the diocese. In the bitter conflicts over the bishopric of Rome in 366 and 367, Valentinian once again put the need for peace over the support of either side. His city prefect stood aside while the fighting between the henchmen of the rival candidates was going on, and then backed the victor, Damasus. Brutal though he may have been in his military campaigns, Valentinian deserves recognition as the man who kept Constantine's policy of tolerance intact.

Valens also maintained a tradition of broad tolerance in the east but in a much more unsettled atmosphere. Constantius' Homoian settlement of 360 was still predominant, and Valens chose to uphold it as the status quo. This seemed the most sensible way of keeping overall good order. However, there were important Nicene bishops, the irrepressible Athanasius in Alexandria and Basil in Caesarea, for instance, who had powerful local followings. The emperor allowed both of them to stay in their posts. Other Nicene bishops were removed, but in many cases this seems to have been related to breaches of discipline that Valens could not condone. Some Nicene supporters seem to have returned to their sees as a result of a deliberate policy of reconciliation he initiated in 375. Although later Nicene historians rewrote the events of these years to suggest that Valens persecuted the Nicenes, there is very little evidence for this, and one might sum up his policy as one of pragmatic tolerance.[25]

By 380, the debate had progressed considerably. Christian intellectuals of the period had shown themselves to be well read and highly sophisticated and ingenious in argument. It is true that some participants, such as Athanasius, used invective rather than reason in their dealing with rivals, and both sides felt able to threaten their opponents with the certainty of eternal hell fire. However, this was not the first, or certainly the last, academic debate in history where personal emotions have transcended reflective argument. Just as interesting was the efficiency by which new ideas, arguments and ripostes were being spread through the circulation of texts. Many of the participants must have employed an army of scribes in order to keep up with the demand for copies of their works. An equivalent circulation of ideas of such complexity, across such a wide region, would probably not be seen until the invention of printing in the late fifteenth century.

As the controversy continued, the issues became more closely defined and fresh insights were added, particularly in the works of the Cappadocian Fathers. According to Ramsay MacMullen: 'How they [the questions] multiplied! And as they did so they imposed sharper choices of belief to be made at a deeper level of understanding and with more complex consequences in logic.'[26] This was, of course, a reflection on the relative freedom within which the discussion took place. However, the chances of the theologians themselves coming to a consensus on the Nicene issue were very slim. Participants had the scriptures and the legacy of Greek philosophy at their disposal, but these could not be used to provide incontrovertible evidence either way for an 'event' – the creation or non-creation of Jesus – that was clearly beyond the reach of human understanding. Left to itself, the controversy might eventually have fizzled out as the participants realised that further discussion would never lead to a resolution.

Yet it was just at this moment that Theodosius' edict reached Constantinople. No one knew at this stage whether its condemnation of the subordinationist side of the debate as heretical would be translated into law. For the time being the freedom to discuss the issues was preserved, but all this would be threatened if the emperor used his coercive powers to enforce the edict.

VI

THE SWANSONG OF FREE SPEECH: THE THEOLOGICAL ORATIONS OF GREGORY OF NAZIANZUS

THEODOSIUS' edict reached Constantinople in January or February 380. By then the city had enjoyed the status of an imperial capital for fifty years, although its history, as the Greek city Byzantium, went back a thousand years earlier. Situated at the end of a peninsula at the extreme eastern edge of Thrace, surrounded on three sides by the sea and defensible from land attacks by its great walls, it was virtually impregnable. Even if the land routes were blocked, it could be supplied by sea. In the AD 190s the emperor Septimius Severus took two years to subdue a rival who held it, and it was to be another thousand years, in the Fourth Crusade of 1204, before it fell to invaders again.

There was much more to Constantinople than its impregnability. It overlooked the Bosporus, the shortest sea crossing between Europe and Asia, through which flowed an ancient and always busy trade route between the Aegean and the Black Sea. It was also comparatively close to the Danube and Euphrates borders, a vital consideration now that the Roman Empire was under such threat. Major land routes ran west – the Via Egnatia to Thessalonica and then across Greece, from where a sea route led to Italy and Rome – and east through Asia Minor towards the Persian frontier or southwards towards Syria and Egypt. Constantinople was, in short, the linchpin of the eastern empire.

The founding of Constantinople illustrates how Constantine, whatever his personal commitment to Christianity, distanced himself from the Church. The emperor himself inaugurated the building programme by marking the new limits of the city with a spear as in traditional Greek ritual. An imperial palace and hippodrome followed Roman models; the hippodrome was a smaller copy of the Circus Maximus in Rome. Among the ceremonies of the official foundation on 11 May 330, a chariot bearing a statue of Constantine, which itself carried a statue of Tyche, 'good fortune' personified as a goddess, was paraded in the hippodrome, watched by the bejewelled emperor himself from the imperial box he had installed at the edge of the palace. Every year the ceremony was repeated on the anniversary of the city's foundation.

Septimius Severus had rebuilt Byzantium after his capture of the old city. Constantine appears to have left Severus' foundation intact and constructed, just outside its walls, an oval forum with a statue of himself in the guise of the sun god, Helios, placed on a column in the centre. (The column still survives, although in a very battered state.) Arched passageways led from the forum into the Severan city and its main procession route, the Regia, and westwards along a new processional route, the Mese (the Middle Street) to Constantine's own set of walls, which were situated 400 metres beyond those of Severus. Statues were collected from all over the empire to embellish the ceremonial ways and the forum. This was another tradition that, in Rome, had stretched back for many centuries during which the booty of war had been brought back to the city in triumph. Churches were also built, but their dedications to Wisdom (Sophia), Peace (Eirene) and 'the Sacred Power' suggest that Constantine was working with an imagery that was as much pagan as Christian. Certainly several pagan temples were allowed to stand in the old city while only one church was completed before Constantine's death in 337: his mausoleum, the Church of the Holy Apostles. Constantine was stressing the ancient tradition of the supreme deity supporting the emperor – even if his own behaviour left it unclear whether this was Jupiter (or Apollo), an abstract Platonic principle, Helios (or Sol Invictus) or the Christian God. It was only after Constantine's death that Constantinople became an unambiguously Christian city. The city's cult of the ancient virgin goddess Rhea, left untouched by Constantine, gradually became transformed into that of the Virgin Mary.[1] Constantinople soon acquired a reputation for the passion and intensity with which its Christians discussed theological issues.

The vast building programme and the designation of Constantinople

as the 'new Rome' brought a large influx of immigrants. One estimate
is that the population already numbered some 90,000 by 340. The
orator Libanius, whose native Antioch was among those affected by
the migration, complained that the sweat of other cities was being
transformed into the fat of the capital. Constantinople had its own
senate and its own consul, and Constantine set in hand the building
of a residential district of grand mansions so that the city's administrative elite could be suitably housed. Latin was the language of the
administration (and remained so until the sixth century), Greek that
of the mass of the population – an *epistula* from the emperor to an
official would be sent out in Latin and then translated into Greek if
it was published by him. Settlement was further encouraged by the
grant of a permanent grain ration from Egypt. Each year in April the
grain ships would arrive from Alexandria and dock at a port constructed
by Constantine on the southern edge of the city, and then return two
or three times during the summer. As the population grew, the original
water supply was supplemented by new aqueducts, one built by
Constantine, another by Valens. Whatever the provision for the poor
in the shape of grain, water, and the chariot races for which
Constantinople became famous, the division between rich and poor
was absolute. John Chrysostom, bishop of the city from 398 to 404,
contrasted the extravagance of the elite's lifestyle – their chamber pots
made of silver, their horses' chewing bits cast in gold – with that of
the poor, who froze in the winter cold and even blinded their own
children to gain alms.

While there is little record of Constantinople's Christian history
before Constantine's foundation, the bishop of this imperial city had
the chance of direct access to the emperor and so the see had come to
enjoy a high status. The city had followed the Homoian creed of
Constantius (see p.64), and Demophilus, the bishop at the time of
Theodosius' edict, who had been in office since 370, was himself a
Homoian. Understandably, any bishop of Constantinople faced the
resentment of the bishops of those cities with a more authentic Christian
past. Those of Rome and Alexandria, in particular, were furious that
an upstart bishopric could have so much influence in imperial politics,
and as both bishops were Nicene supporters in 380, they were ready
to conspire to impose a Nicene bishop on the city.

In 380 the Nicene community in Constantinople was very small and
made up largely of administrators and city officials. This is a rare case

where we know the social composition of a Nicene congregation, and it suggests a link between Nicene beliefs and the upper echelons of the civil service. The congregation was without its own priest until the arrival in 379 of the Cappadocian Father, the scholarly Gregory of Nazianzus. Gregory's appointment had been the suggestion of an assembly of 150 Nicene bishops organised in 379 by Bishop Meletius of Antioch. The main issue in the assembly of 379 was how to resolve the dispute between Meletius and Paulinus. Meletius forced a conciliatory settlement that allowed Paulinus some form of status as co-bishop with a right of succession when Meletius died. Discussion then turned to the Nicene cause in Constantinople. It seemed important to send a sound man to rally the believers in his capital before Theodosius himself arrived. Gregory was known to be a fine orator who had been favoured by the well-respected Basil. Little notice was taken of the fact that, technically, he was still bishop of the obscure see of Sasima, partly because he had been so reluctant to take up residence in such a remote area of Cappadocia that, since 374, he had been living in a monastery in southern Asia Minor. It was from there that he set out to Constantinople in the autumn of 379, full of misgivings about his new role.[2]

When Gregory arrived in Constantinople, the city was still in fear of the rampaging Goths who had swarmed into its suburbs and even swept up to its walls in the aftermath of the Battle of Adrianople. No one yet knew whether Theodosius would be able to restore order to Thrace. Gregory himself reported that 'what is seen and heard now is terrible, devastated homelands, thousands of victims, the ground covered with blood and ruins, people speaking like barbarians'.[3] Within the city, Gregory's own congregation proved to be an arrogant and elitist group who ridiculed this shabbily dressed newcomer whose body was withered from fasting. In his long (and somewhat self-pitying) poem on his own life, De Vita Sua, Gregory tells how he was mocked for his refusal to enjoy fine food and bask in imperial glamour.[4] As courtiers, his congregation had learned the art of flattery and a readiness to change their colours when the political climate shifted from emperor to emperor, and they were critical of the rigidity with which he expounded his Nicene beliefs.

When Gregory arrived, the Nicenes did not even have a church, and it was lucky that a cousin of his, Theodosia, who had married one of the city's senators, owned a villa in the residential part of the city. It was large enough for Gregory to set aside a room for his eucharistic services for those baptised, while he would preach to a larger audience in the open courtyard. He called his church Anastasia, 'resurrection', in recognition of the fact that he was 'resurrecting' the Nicene cause after forty years of subordinationist bishops in the city. With remarkable energy for a man of fifty who had known many periods of ill health, he set himself a punishing schedule of orations.

Fundamental to Gregory's preaching was the belief that only a few, very committed, thinkers were able to tackle theological issues, and that they alone could discern and preach what was the unassailable truth (which Gregory believed, of course, was the Nicene faith). Here were shades of his mentor Plato: the select few ascend to a deeper understanding of the immaterial world, whose 'reality' they alone have the right to interpret for others. It was not an easy message to sustain. Gregory's own congregation found his lack of social graces unsettling, while the wider population of the city, who had, in any case, heard only subordinationist teaching, were hardly likely to relish being told that they had no contribution to make to theology. Everyone had become used to talking about the issues openly – when Gregory of Nyssa arrived in Constantinople in 381, he recorded that even the bath attendants were ready to debate the relationship of Father to Son!

Gregory's task was made more difficult by the split between Meletius and Paulinus at Antioch. Its impact resonated even in Constantinople. Gregory was loyal to Meletius and supported his generous resolution of the crisis. He was deeply upset to find that many of his own congregation rejected Paulinus (who never seems to have had much of a following) and so sustained the scandal of a divided Church. He told them that the damage done to a faith whose relationships should be based on love was greater than that posed by the barbarians, not least because it gave the pagans a reason to ridicule Christianity. There were some who disagreed so strongly with him on the issue that they stormed out of church in the middle of one of his sermons.

Nevertheless Gregory persisted in preaching a coherent theology. He argued that his Nicene faith represented a Golden Mean – a concept that ran deep in Greek philosophy and so would have been recognisable to his more educated listeners – between the view of Sabellius that Jesus was only a way in which God manifested himself for the specific purpose of salvation, and the subordinationists, who believed that Father, Son and Holy Spirit were fully separated from each other. In such a wide-ranging debate, virtually every belief could be placed as a Golden Mean (the Homoians could be seen as a Mean between the Eunomians and the Nicenes, for instance), but the continual repetition of Gregory's central message, of a Godhead united by substance (*ousia*) but divided by the personality (*hypostasis*) of Father, Son and Holy Spirit, must have had some impact. Gregory soon reported a growing audience for his outdoor sermons.

Theodosius' edict was only an announcement of the emperor's proposed policy and did not, as such, have the force of law so long as it contained no instructions for its implementation. Demophilus remained as bishop, despite being included in the edict's category of 'demented and insane' for his Homoian beliefs. Yet inevitably the edict brought a new tension into the city. Theodosius was not merely challenging the beliefs of the majority of his capital's inhabitants; imposition of the edict as law would mean that the Homoian clergy and their churches would be deprived of all their privileges and tax exemptions. There would be losses either way. If Theodosius triumphed over the Goths, he would enter his capital and the majority of the clergy would lose their churches; if he did not, presumably the city would remain under threat from the Goths. Constantinople was full of apprehension.

At Easter 380, the tensions erupted into violence. Gregory was determined to use the feast to baptise those of his congregation who were ready for the sacrament, yet traditionally only a bishop could carry out baptisms. In effect, Gregory was challenging the authority of Demophilus. The services of the Easter Vigil at the Anastasia were interrupted by a crowd of monks, nuns and hangers-on who stoned the building and then got inside and ransacked the altar and smashed up the liturgical vessels. Gregory himself was even hauled off before a magistrate but was later released. Doubtless the magistrate realised that things would not look good if Theodosius did eventually arrive in the capital and heard that such a prominent supporter of his own faith had been imprisoned. Shortly afterwards, Gregory fell ill. Among the 'well-wishers' who came to his bedside was a young man sent to assassinate him. Luckily the 'assassin' broke down in tears and confessed when alone with his intended victim.

Gregory's congregation needed protection, and help now arrived from an unexpected source – the city of Alexandria. The first grain ships of the year arrived from Egypt, and the Bishop of Alexandria, Peter, who had succeeded his brother Athanasius and who was, like him, a supporter of the Nicene cause, had ordered some of the sailors to remain behind in Constantinople as a bodyguard for Gregory. Among the newcomers was one Maximus, a tall and striking figure dressed in a philosopher's robe who quickly established a rapport with the isolated Gregory. Gregory welcomed his new supporters by dedicating a full sermon to their former bishop Athanasius, whom he proclaimed as the bastion of the true Nicene faith. The sermon concentrated on Athanasius' life, rather than his writings, which were barely mentioned.[5] Presumably, even if Gregory had seen copies of these, he would have regarded them, as later commentators have, as much less sophisticated than his own work. Yet simply talking about Athanasius seems to have given Gregory new confidence, and he soon declared that he would preach a series of sermons setting out the Nicene faith in detail.

The five so-called Theological Orations were preached between July and August 380. They are normally seen as the fullest exposition of the Nicene position and were treated as such for centuries to come, earning their creator the accolade of 'The Theologian'. In view of the disasters that were to overwhelm Gregory the following year, they stand out as his finest achievement, not least for the courage he shows in proclaiming a minority belief so openly in a largely hostile and volatile city. The Orations are particularly remarkable in that Gregory sets out all the objections to his beliefs and attempts to answer them. John McGluckin suggests that Gregory may, in the final oration at least, have been answering interventions from opponents in the audience. If so, here was the ancient tradition of open and free debate at its best. Gregory was not alone in preaching freely. Eunomius himself was now resident in Chalcedon, just across the Bosporus, where he was reported to be reading his works aloud to admiring crowds.[6]

The first of the orations (Oration 27 in the accepted enumeration of Gregory's works) was entitled 'Against the Eunomians'.[7] Gregory was rather disingenuous here. The Eunomians, with their central belief that the Father and the Son were 'unlike' each other, were opposed to the Homoians, who argued that they were 'like' each other. Yet Gregory tended to merge the two groups, something he must have known would infuriate Demophilus, especially when Eunomius was preaching so close by. He started the sermon with his usual theme: that only those who have purified their body and soul and undergone disciplined study are capable of discussing theology. Even then the theologian has to choose his time, his audience and the themes it is appropriate to discuss. In a

challenge to the loquacious inhabitants of Constantinople, Gregory
derides those for whom theological discussion is a social pastime, like
'wrestling bouts . . . stage-managed to give the uncritical spectators
visual sensations and compel their applause'. He seems to be intimating
that he is of good birth, while his opponents are upstarts playing to
the populace. (It was indeed true that Eunomius and Aetius came from
relatively humble backgrounds.)

There is much knockabout rhetoric in this oration. One could hardly
accuse Aetius and Eunomius of lack of thoughtful analysis or learning,
but Gregory's point that theology requires reflection and study is a
perfectly valid one. In the second oration (Oration 28), he goes on to
examine what it is possible for the trained theologian to say about the
nature of God. He challenges Eunomius' view that through the application of rational thought to the scriptures it is possible to know God.
Using the analogy of the reflection of the sun shining on water, Gregory
argues that it is impossible to look at the sun (for which read God)
directly but that we gain some understanding of it by seeing the way
its light is reflected off the water. It is a particularly apt analogy for
Constantinople, where water surrounds the city on three sides and the
sun on the sea must often have dazzled onlookers. But anyone who
had read Plato's parable of the cave would also recognise the approach.
Those who live in the darkness of Plato's cave, where the only light is
the reflection of fire on the walls, are dazzled by the sunlight when
they first come out into the open air, and have to find temporary ways
of dealing with it, looking at reflections or coming to terms with moon-
light before experiencing the full glare of the sun. Gregory uses other
analogies taken from the mysteries of everyday life. One of these is the
nature of the mind. 'What makes the mind both confined and bound-
less, both at home in us and touring the universe in flowing rapid
course? In what way is mind conveyed and communicated by speech?
What makes it share in sense-perception, while isolating itself from
self-perception?' What is it that draws parents and children to each
other? How is sound produced by the vocal organs and received by
the ears? How are 'sounds and ears knit together by the imprinted
impulse transmitted by the intervening air?' If there are such mysteries
that cannot be perceived by the reasoning mind in the material world,
how much more difficult is it to grasp the mystery of God? All one
can expect is 'a slight glimmer, a small beam from the Great Light',
but ultimately God is 'incomprehensible to the human mind and of an

unimaginably glorious grandeur'. By believing that they could understand God, Gregory argued, his opponents would invariably get a false
and limited perception of the Almighty, and it was not surprising, therefore, that they came up with false doctrines – such as that Jesus is not
fully God but a later creation.

This is powerful rhetoric and a fine demonstration of the breadth
of Gregory's mind. In the next three orations, Gregory defended the
Nicene interpretation of the Trinity as he perceived it. It was a daunting
task because the issues seemed far beyond human grasp. Understandably,
the Sirmium Creed of 357 had declared that the *homoousion* (the 'one
in substance' of the Nicene Creed) 'is beyond man's knowledge nor
can anyone declare the birth of the Son . . . for it is clear that only the
Father knows how he begot his Son and his Son how he was begotten
by the Father'. In the third of the orations (Oration 29), Gregory dealt
with the common substance of Father and Son and the co-eternity they
enjoy. He bravely set out ten objections to the Nicene formulation,
each of which he attempted to answer. A central issue was that if one
describes the Son as begotten from the Father, this must imply a moment
when he was not begotten. The subordinationists argued that the act
of begetting must have involved the will of the Father and the formulation of that will must have preceded the act itself. In other words,
the pre-existence of the Father to the Son must be assumed. Gregory
tries hard to combat this, but in the end he has to accept that the
begetting is a mystery. He describes how even the act of *human* begetting, 'the principles involved from conception through formation to
birth and the linking of soul to body, of intellect to soul and of reason
to intellect', as well as the way a human body works after birth, are
hard enough to discover. How much harder is it to understand God's
begetting of Jesus? He also accuses the subordinationists of treating
'begetting' as if it were a corporeal event as it would be between human
beings. On the contrary, everything to do with with the begetting of
Jesus takes place on an incorporeal plane and so cannot be explored
by analogy with human begetting. The 'begetting' of Jesus is like no
other begetting; for a start, one can hardly imagine God having sex.

However, a major problem with this approach had been noticed by
the Eunomians. They had always argued that scripture should be interpreted in its plain sense, without the use of allegory. If the Old Testament
talked of a piece of wood, that was what it meant, not necessarily a
symbol prefiguring the cross. Similarly one could not use the word

'begotten' and then expect it to be used in a completely different way when talking of God. The Nicenes, the Eunomians argued, were being disingenuous if, when presented with objections to their use of terminology, they avoided the issue by claiming that the words they used had a different meaning in a theological context. In other words, they could not use 'begotten' in a sense where it was clearly inappropriate and then claim a special meaning for it when challenged. If there was not a definable act of 'begetting' in the normal sense of the word, then surely the word should not be used at all.[8]

Gregory must have known the strength of these arguments, and one senses the rise of tension in his voice. To the reasonable assertion of the subordinationists that one cannot describe Jesus as both 'begotten' and 'uncreated', if there was not a time when he was not begotten, he testily replies that this is 'logical drivel'. He also had to contend with the assertion, which formed the core of the Eunomian position, that if the Father is described as 'unbegotten' and the Son as 'begotten', then surely it is enough to show that they are different kinds of beings. Gregory argued in response that being 'unbegotten' and 'begotten' are only different qualities of the same substance and do not provide an essential difference between Father and Son. Moreover, 'unbegotten' is only one negative statement about God, while there are so many more positive things one can say about him. But Gregory failed to explain why, if it is a mere quality, the begotten nature of the Son is given so much prominence in the Nicene Creed of 325.

Turning to the many biblical texts that had sustained subordinationism, Gregory argued that his opponents had failed to distinguish between the sayings of Jesus that were spoken in his human capacity and those spoken in his divine capacity. When, in John 11:34, Jesus asks where Lazarus has been buried and weeps and sighs over his death, he is acting according to his human nature; when he raises Lazarus from the dead, he is acting according to his divine nature. The concept of a Jesus alternating between one nature and another is not a very convincing one, but it seemed the only way that even such an erudite theologian as Gregory was able to reply to his critics.

There is little in Oration 29 that gives a convincing exposition of the Nicene case. The overwhelming impression is of Gregory on the defensive, doing his best to find ways round the plausible arguments of the subordinationists. It is interesting to speculate why he chose this approach. After all, he could have ignored his opponents' case and simply argued his own as if there were no significant points against it. Why did he choose to expose himself by presenting their best arguments? He was surely intelligent enough to realise that many would not be convinced by his counter-arguments. This readiness to place himself in difficult situations, almost as if he wanted to be humiliated, seems to have been rooted in his complex personality. It was to prove his undoing in the year to come.

In his fourth Theological Oration (Oration 30), Gregory selected ten texts from scripture used by the subordinationists to defend their beliefs, among them: 'The Lord created me [Wisdom] as the beginning of his ways for his works' (Proverbs 8:22); 'The Son can do nothing of himself but only what he sees the Father doing' (John 5:19); 'None is good save only one, God' (Jesus' own words in Luke 18:19); 'No one except the Father knows the last day or hour, not even the Son himself' (also Jesus' words, in Mark 13:32). Again, no one can accuse Gregory of not presenting his opponents' case at its strongest. Yet his own interpretations of the texts are often so convoluted as to appear no more than special pleading. Take Mark 13:32, for instance, 'No one except the Father knows the last day or hour, not even the Son himself.' The text seems to suggest that Jesus accepts the Father has knowledge that he himself does not, a reading that would seem to preclude their being of the same substance. Gregory argued that Jesus is here speaking in his human capacity, while in his divine capacity he would of course know 'the last day or hour'. If this is not convincing enough, Gregory told his listeners that Jesus is ostensibly claiming ignorance because the knowledge of 'the last day' has to be placed off limits to the human mind! As Frederick Norris notes in his commentary on this oration, the ambiguous terms used by Gregory – 'cause', 'essence', 'impassible', 'passible' – 'probably represent the greatest unresolved philosophical difficulties in the Theologian's Christology'.[9] The problem of giving a clear definition to a human nature of Jesus that suffers alongside a divine nature that cannot suffer (as a Jesus who is fully part of the Godhead cannot) appears to be insoluble.

In the fifth and final oration (Oration 31), Gregory returned to one of the most intractable issues of the whole debate: the nature and purpose of the Holy Spirit. Here he faced opposition from within the Nicene camp, from those 'Macedonians' who preferred to keep to the original Nicene Creed of 325 in which the Holy Spirit is given no special status. Gregory had to accept that 'amongst our own [Christian]

experts, some took the Holy Spirit as an active process, some as a crea-
ture, some as God. Others were agnostic on this point.' He accepted
too that the great theologian Origen believed that the Spirit was limited
in power. He thus had a hard task proving that the Spirit is not only
fully divine but consubstantial with the Father. At this point a number
of objections were raised, possibly directly from his audience. What is
the biblical evidence for the divinity of the Spirit? Where is the evidence
that it has been worshipped as divine in the past? Does divinity auto-
matically imply consubstantiality? If God the Father is 'unbegotten'
and Jesus is his 'begotten' Son, then how does the Holy Spirit relate
to them both?

In answer to the last question, Gregory introduces the idea of
'procession', as in John 15:26, 'The Holy Spirit which proceeds from
the Father'. Irritated by an interjection from the congregation
enquiring how he can explain 'procession', he retorts: 'You explain
the unbegotten nature of the Father and I will give you a biological
account of the Son's begetting and the Spirit's proceeding – and let
us go mad the pair of us for prying into God's secrets.' In effect, he
was opting out of the argument. Dealing with another objection –
that if one adds the Spirit to the Father and Son, then one risks
having three gods – he became entangled in explaining why mathematics is not an appropriate way of dealing with the Trinity. Everyone
knew this was the most challenging of the theological problems
presented by the Nicene Trinity. It was to be explored, perhaps with
greater subtlety, by Gregory of Nyssa, who preached on the subject
in Constantinople the following year.

Gregory then addressed the question of why the Spirit has not been
recognised as God in the gospels. His answer was that the doctrine of
the Trinity has been subject to progressive revelation. First, God the
Father has to be revealed, in the Old Testament; then, through the
gospels, Jesus the Son; and finally the Holy Spirit, who appears to
enthuse the disciples after the Passion and through the fiery tongues
at Pentecost. 'God meant it to be by piecemeal additions . . . by progress
and advance from glory to glory, that the light of the Trinity should
shine upon more illustrious souls.' During Jesus' time on earth there
had simply been too much for the disciples to take in, and the Godhead
of the Spirit was retained until they were able to absorb it. Gregory
brought the oration to a close with a meditation on the difficulty of
expressing the nature of the Divine through analogies such as water

flowing in a stream from a spring or light emanating from the sun. None is adequate, and Gregory resolved to take the Spirit as his guide 'as I strike out a path through this world'.

The overwhelming impression one receives from these orations is the difficulty of saying anything of certainty about the nature of the Godhead, a difficulty Gregory fully acknowledges. The problems are fairly laid out in the orations, but the proposed solutions are often incomplete or fail to convince. The most important legacy of the Theological Orations is as a high-quality exploration of a theological problem that seems essentially insoluble. However much one may fail to be convinced by some of Gregory's arguments, one has to admit that this is a rhetorical and theological exposition of the very highest standard. Yet Gregory's exposition would never have reached that standard if he had not been pressurised by some very gifted opponents, who felt as strongly about their beliefs as he did. It would be exceptional today to find a public audience as alive to the nuances of theological debate and ready to argue such complex issues with confidence. It is therefore unfortunate that on occasions Gregory denigrates his opponents as somehow unworthy. This was certainly a common rhetorical device and was used in a much more extreme way by Athanasius (and, as will be seen, by Ambrose in Milan), but it lowered the tone of the debate. It was the problem that was intractable, not those trying to solve it, many of whom worked through to their own formulations with sincerity and intensive study. In fact, the Theological Orations provide one of the best arguments for the preservation of open debate in theology. And yet just as this great debate was going on, an imperial edict threatened to bring it all to an abrupt end. If one has to choose one swansong for the end of the Greek philosophical tradition, Gregory's Theological Orations are as good as any.

Before Theodosius arrived in Constantinople, Gregory suffered a major setback. Like many men and women of great intelligence and learning, he seems to have been naïve in his personal relationships. His adulation of Maximus, the visiting philosopher from Alexandria, bordered on the unbalanced. In a sermon delivered in the late summer, Gregory praised Maximus as a pillar of the Nicene faith, 'the best of the best; the noblest of the noble'. He appears to have been totally unaware that behind Maximus lay the ambition of Peter of Alexandria to control the bishopric of Constantinople. Peter seems to have assumed that

Gregory would be malleable, but Maximus reported back that Gregory's primary loyalty lay not with Alexandria, despite the protection the Egyptian sailors had given him, but with Meletius in the rival bishopric of Antioch. (It will be remembered that Athanasius had backed Paulinus in the dispute between Paulinus and Meletius, and Peter followed his lead.) Peter now devised a plot to install Maximus in place of Gregory. Maximus returned to Alexandria to receive further instructions while Gregory set out for a journey up the coast towards the Black Sea.

In Alexandria, Maximus received the full backing of Peter for a takeover of the Anastasia community so that he would be in charge there when Theodosius arrived and available to be elevated as the city's bishop if the emperor imposed his edict as law. He set off back to Constantinople with a group of Egyptian bishops whom Peter had delegated to consecrate him and a gang of 'sailors' who were to enforce the decision if there was any opposition. Maximus arrived to find Gregory still away. He appears to have won over two members of Gregory's clergy and to have tried to buy others. One evening Maximus and his followers marched into the Anastasia and began the service of consecration as priest to the Nicenes. When word got around as to what was happening, clergy loyal to Gregory and members of his congregation rushed to the scene. Their numbers were soon swollen by a larger crowd – which even included pagans, such was the fury that outsiders should try and intrude in the city's affairs. The Egyptians were soon driven out of the Anastasia, and after taking refuge in a safe house, they left the city in ignominy. Yet Maximus still had the temerity to petition Theodosius directly for the appointment! After all, he argued, Theodosius had specifically mentioned Peter of Alexandria, 'a man of apostolic sanctity', as an arbiter of the Nicene faith in his edict of 380, and he, Maximus, would be Peter's choice for bishop when the city was restored to the Nicenes. He even had a copy of Gregory's sermon praising him as an orthodox Nicene to use in his cause. But Theodosius refused to give any support to Maximus, who had to return unsuccessful to Alexandria. There is evidence that Peter and his successor Timothy continued to plot on his behalf well into the next year, claiming, in fact, that he had been duly consecrated before his ejection.

This was a major embarrassment for Gregory. His inability even to spot that there might be trouble did him little credit, and the whole affair, including his fawning approval of Maximus, had shown up his

VII

CONSTANTINOPLE, 381:
THE IMPOSITION OF ORTHODOXY

THEODOSIUS entered Constantinople on 24 November 380. The *adventus*, or entry, of an emperor to his capital was normally a festive event. The population would come out to greet him at the gates, singing and dancing as they did so. There would be panegyrics, welcoming orations full of praise, and a formal greeting by the city prefect. If the same itinerary was followed as was later for the emperor Justinian, Theodosius may have stopped first at the Church of the Holy Apostles, the finest church in the city before the building of the great basilica of Santa Sophia, to pay homage to the city's founder. Then he would have processed down the ceremonial way, the Mese, to the centre of the city, with rituals of welcome by other officials at each stage on the route, until he reached the Forum of Constantine and eventually the imperial palace. From here he would have moved through the palace and out on to the imperial box overlooking the crowds assembled in the hippodrome. If he was celebrating a military triumph, the day would continue with chariot races. There is no record of them. Theodosius may have had some small tactical successes, but no one could claim that the Goths were fully subdued It is unlikely that his reception by his subjects was as joyful or enthusiastic as he would have hoped.

It may have been this uncertainty and frustration that lay behind Theodosius' decision to enforce the Nicene Creed as soon as possible. He immediately summoned Bishop Demophilus to his palace and requested that he support the doctrine that God the Father, Jesus the Son, and the Holy Spirit were of equal majesty, a formula that equated with Nicene beliefs. Theodosius must have hoped he would capitulate, but Demophilus stuck to his principles and refused. As a result, he and many of his clergy were banned from the city. For years to come they are recorded as worshipping in the open air outside the walls. Theodosius was now forced to turn to Gregory, whom he asked to become the new bishop of the city. Gregory was delighted with the favour of the emperor but he knew only too well how unpopular the imposition was, and he was full of apprehension when Theodosius told him he would be formally installed in the Church of the Holy Apostles almost immediately, on Friday 27 November.

It proved to be a tense day. Soldiers lined the route from the hippodrome to the church and crowds massed behind them. No one would dare shout abuse directly at the emperor, but there were certainly calls for Theodosius to respect their faith. It was as if, Gregory later recounted, the city had been taken by conquest and this was a parade of the victors. The only hopeful sign on a day during which dark clouds hovered over Constantinople was a ray of sunshine breaking through just as Gregory entered the Holy Apostles. He and his entourage gratefully took it as a sign that God was on their side. He was eventually installed as bishop, though he accepted that it was only the direct protection of the emperor that allowed him to take on his new duties. There had even been disturbances within the church itself. From now on he used the Holy Apostles as his cathedral and it was here that the emperor and his court attended his services.

On 10 January 381, the emperor issued a letter (*epistula*) to Eutropius, the praetorian prefect of Illyricum, the most unsettled area of his half of the empire, asking him to impose the Nicene faith across his provinces. (It is possible that a similar law was issued at this time to the prefect of the east, but the evidence is not clear on this. There were reported expulsions of Homoian clergy throughout the east at this time, but they might have been local initiatives as Nicene supporters pressed home their advantage.) The prefects, one responsible for Illyricum and the other for the rest of the east, answered to the emperor for the efficient collection of taxes and the keeping of good order. If there was any dispute, between rival Christian factions in the diocese, for instance, the prefect would have to restore order. The prefects also monitored the appointment of bishops and ensured that tax exemptions were correctly applied. The law of January 381 was, in effect, asking Eutropius to recognise only those of the Nicene faith as bishops. It was a sweeping document, imposing a uniformity of belief such as no one had known before: 'The observation of the Nicene faith, handed down from our ancestors and affirmed by the testimony and declaration of the divine religion, destined to be continued forever, will be maintained. The contamination of the Photinian error, the poison of the Arian sacrilege, the crime of the Eunomian heresy, and the unspeakable, from the monstrous names of their authors, prodigies of the sects will be banished from hearing.' The Photinians, named after Photinus, Bishop of Sirmium from 344 to 351, were successors of Sabellius who believed that Jesus was only a temporary manifestation of God, rather than a distinct personality within the Godhead. The term 'Arian' seems to have been used loosely of subordinationists such as the Homoians. 'The purpose of the list [of heresies] in a secular law seems clear', writes the scholar R. Malcolm Errington: 'to give a secular judge, who inevitably was not competent to decide on the finer points of theology – he may well not even have been a Christian – clear instructions about the critical features of the Nicene creed to which he needed to pay particular attention in judging cases brought before his court.'[1]

There had to be a definition of the Nicene faith that the prefect could follow. The acceptance of an all-powerful God and Christ as the Son of God, 'under one name', was required, although there was no specific mention of the *homoousion*. Christ was to be recognised as 'God from God' and 'light from light'. When it came to the Holy Spirit, it was clear that Theodosius had realised that its status was uncertain and hotly disputed among the theologians of the Greek east. The original Nicene Creed had expected no more than simple belief in the Holy Spirit, while Gregory, in contrast, had argued only a few months earlier that the Spirit should be seen as fully divine and consubstantial with the Father and Son. Theodosius wavered – the prefect was to insist on no more than that 'the Holy Spirit should not be violated by being denied'.

Eutropius was instructed to deal harshly with the 'insane and demented heretics'. Not only did they have to surrender their present churches to the Nicenes, but they were not allowed even to build their own places of worship within a city, let alone claim any tax exemptions. Any disturbance or display of sedition was to be treated by expelling them beyond the walls of the city. A few months later, a further law forbade 'heretics' even to build churches outside a city wall. The law closed with its declared aim: that 'catholic churches in the whole world might be restored to all orthodox bishops who hold the Nicene faith'. This suppression of Christian worship was an outright rejection of everything that Constantine had promised in 313. Even though this specific letter is addressed only to the prefect of Illyricum, the mention of 'the whole world' suggests Theodosius' wider ambition.

Theodosius had already decided, probably as far back as November 380, after Demophilus had turned down his invitation to convert, that he would have to use a church council to give greater legitimacy to his Nicene policy. Invitations to meet in Constantinople had been sent out to selected bishops, the most prominent of whom was Meletius of Antioch. Although there was some talk of simultaneous councils being held in west and east, this assembly involved participants only from the east. Theodosius had as yet no jurisdiction in the west, but as the western bishops tended to support Paulinus against Meletius, they would not have attended such an assembly in any case.

The council was essentially a reconvening of Meletius' Nicene group from 379 (whose purpose then had been to settle the affairs of Antioch). This meant that there were no bishops from Egypt, Nicene or otherwise, nor from Illyricum. There were, of course, no subordinationists or other 'heretics'. The Church historian Socrates, writing in the following century, simply noted that those assembled were 'prelates of his [Theodosius'] own faith'. There was, however, a grouping of some thirty-six 'Macedonian' bishops whose endorsement of the Nicene Creed in its original form was considered orthodox enough to qualify them for membership. The Macedonians were especially influential in western Asia where the Nicene cause was weak, so it was hoped that their disagreements with their fellow Nicenes over the status of the Holy Spirit might be resolved. No one could call this a full council of the Church, nor did it see itself as such. In one message to the emperor, the participants referred to themselves as 'the holy synod of bishops from various provinces meeting in Constantinople'. (A synod refers to a local rather than an ecumenical council.)

Although he was now ageing, Meletius commanded immense respect. 'A most pious man, with a simple guileless manner: filled with God; a man of serene countenance and modesty' was Gregory's view,[2] and it was understandable that Theodosius would call on him to preside over the Council of Constantinople of 381, as it is known.[3] Theodosius' *epistula* enforcing the Nicene faith, and its hope that the whole world would now adopt Nicene orthodoxy, was noted and endorsed to the enthusiasm of the bishops, who realised how much patronage they, as Nicene supporters, would enjoy as they took over the churches of those who were now decreed to be heretics. Meletius acquiesced in the passing of a resolution from Theodosius that Gregory should be confirmed as Bishop of Constantinople, while the cause of Maximus was now formally rejected. A public rejection was needed because Ambrose, the Bishop of Milan, had given Maximus his support through writing directly to Theodosius, and the matter had to be settled once and for all. As it was this group of bishops that, in Antioch in 379, had proposed Gregory to go to Constantinople in the first place, there was unlikely to be any opposition to the resolution. The bishops clearly shared Theodosius' resentment at the attempts of Ambrose (whose story will be told in detail later) to interfere in the ecclesiastical affairs of the eastern empire.

But then disaster struck: Meletius died. The council was left without a leader and Antioch without a bishop. The agreement had been that Paulinus would succeed Meletius in the important see of Antioch, but the bishops assembled in Constantinople had always been uneasy about this plan and it soon became clear that Paulinus had little popularity. He was an ascetic man who had simply failed to create a network of local supporters. He did, however, have some backing from the western bishops, but this did not help him, as the easterners were determined to stand up to any intrusion, real or apparent, from the western Church into their affairs. It was now proposed that the matter be solved by electing a younger clergyman from Antioch, one Flavianus, to the vacant bishopric.

In his position as Bishop of Constantinople, Gregory now took over the chairmanship of the council. He suddenly found himself cast in a role for which he was totally unsuited, and it was his intransigence that proved his immediate undoing. Instead of letting the situation over Antioch resolve itself, he entered the fray with his own proposal that Paulinus should be supported as Bishop of Antioch. No doubt he felt he ought to honour Meletius' agreement, but he may also have been under pressure from Theodosius to support a pro-western policy to keep harmony within the empire. He found little enthusiasm for his proposal but refused to compromise. The leader of Flavianus' supporters, Diodore, the bishop of the apostle Paul's home town, Tarsus, approached Gregory with his candidate, but Gregory simply refused to listen. When Gregory made a speech to the assembled bishops in support of Paulinus' candidature, he made the fatal mistake of saying that he would resign his bishopric if his own proposal was not followed. The result was chaos. In his autobiographical poem, *De Sua Vita*, written when he had returned to Cappadocia, a bitter Gregory denounced the bishops: 'They screeched on every side, a flock of jackdaws all intent on one thing, a mob of wild young men, a new kind of gang, a whirlwind causing the dust to swirl as the winds went out of control, men with whom not even a ruler with the authority of fear or age would think it proper to reason, buzzing around as if they were in complete disorder, like a swarm of wasps suddenly flying in your face.'[4] Yet he had only himself to blame for the mayhem.

There followed a walkout. Virtually nothing is known of the theological debates of the council of 381, but Gregory was certainly hoping to get some acceptance of his belief that the Spirit was consubstantial with the Father. Whether he dealt with the matter clumsily or whether there was simply no chance of consensus, the 'Macedonians', bishops who refused to accept the full divinity of the Holy Spirit, left the council. (Some accounts suggest that the Macedonians may have left even before formal proceedings had begun.) Typically, Gregory berated the bishops for preferring to have a majority rather than simply accepting 'the Divine Word' of the Trinity on his authority. 'I stood and watched as the sweet and pristine spring of our ancient faith, which had joined that sacred and adorable nature of the Trinity in one, as formerly professed at Nicaea, was now wretchedly polluted by the flooding in of the brine of men of dubious faith.' He hinted vaguely that 'Authority', which can only mean the emperor, was putting pressure on the waverers so that they could combine against him.[5] Even taking this pressure into account, Gregory simply could not see that this was an issue on which it was perfectly reasonable for educated men to hold a variety of views. He now announced that he was ill and withdrew from the council chamber.

By now Theodosius was in despair. The emperor had the coercive power to pass what laws he liked, but imposing any kind of order on the Church was a completely different matter. Even a small council of bishops supposedly already adherent to the Nicene faith had dissolved into chaos, while the bishop of 'the second Rome' had shown himself to be a hopelessly inadequate leader. Theodosius decided to act firmly by summoning the bishops of Egypt and Illyricum, whom he hoped would give more ballast to the proceedings. They arrived in Constantinople by the middle of June to find Gregory still absent.

The Alexandrians saw their chance. Peter had recently died and his successor, his brother Timothy, was determined to exercise Alexandria's control over Constantinople and get rid of Gregory. They still had Maximus in the wings waiting to take over, and they now resurrected a canon from the Council of Nicaea that had laid down that no bishop could be translated from one see to another. As Gregory was still technically Bishop of Sasima, the see he had never occupied, it could be argued that his consecration as Bishop of Constantinople was invalid. This was the final straw for Gregory and he capitulated, returning to the council for the last time to make a resignation speech. The only thing that mattered, he told the bishops, was the Trinity, and with his usual lack of tact, he doubted whether anyone there other than himself had the skill or courage to expound it successfully. When he finished speaking there was silence, but he recounted later how many bishops then came up to him to express their sympathy – although no one begged him to stay.

Later the emperor himself received Gregory with considerable courtesy, applauding at the end of his speech, but again his resignation was accepted without debate; Theodosius knew he could not risk losing the support of the majority of the Nicene bishops by backing Gregory. There was some wider sympathy for Gregory in the city itself, where the intrusions of foreign bishops were always resented, but after a final oration on the Trinity in the Church of the Holy Apostles, which the emperor himself attended, Gregory left the city in June for his native Cappadocia. He later wrote that he had 'never seen a good outcome to any synod, or a synod which produced deliverance from evils rather than the addition to them . . . rivalries and manoeuvres always prevail over reason'.[6] Gregory died in 391.

The combination of a Nicene emperor who had already put in place a Nicene Church and a council that in genesis was Nicene in temperament should have led to a Nicene appointee as Gregory's successor to this prestigious see. In the event, this could not be risked. As yet Constantinople's population had shown no enthusiasm for the Nicene cause, and it made more political sense to appoint a man who was well known within the city and who had not compromised himself through support for any one faction. So it was that one Nectarius, an elderly city senator who had been a popular prefect in the city as a result of his patronage of the games, but who was still not a baptised Christian, was selected. One historian, Sozomen, perhaps the better source, claims he was chosen by the emperor himself; another, Socrates, says it was by the acclaim of the population.[7] Technically, his appointment before baptism was contrary to a rule passed at Nicaea, but this had not prevented a similar elevation for Ambrose in Milan a few years earlier. Nectarius appeared to know no theology, and he had to be initiated into the required faith before being baptised and consecrated. It was clear that he was being used to defuse potential unrest among the mass of the city's population in response to the imposition of the Nicene faith, but doubtless the bishops also saw him as an effective way of binding together the secular and ecclesiastical elites of the eastern empire, and he was given their unanimous approval.

There is another indication of the assembly's relative impotence within the city. Its proceedings went on into July and it must at some point have agreed on a revised Nicene Creed, perhaps even before the resignation of Gregory. Yet there is no record that the creed was ever promulgated, and presumably this is because it would have been deeply unpopular among the Homoians, who still appear to have made up the majority of the local population. In fact there is no mention of it anywhere until it was read out at the Council of Chalcedon in 451, seventy years later where it was accredited to the council of 381. The creed was based on that of Nicaea, with some differences (see Appendix). The final version showed something of the struggle that had gone on over the divinity of the Holy Spirit: '[We believe] in the Holy Spirit, the Lord and Life-Giver, who proceeds from the Father, who is worshipped and glorified together with the Father and the Son, who spoke through the prophets.' Here the Holy Spirit has been elevated to a higher status than in Nicaea, but there is no mention of it being God and none of consubstantiality. Gregory's formula had been rejected.

The sources of the changes in the creed apparently agreed at Constantinople from that of Nicaea are obscure. Some have argued that they originated with Epiphanius, the Bishop of Salamis, in Cyprus, who seems to have had a similar creed in his writings of the 370s, but there is no record of Epiphanius attending Constantinople, and many scholars believe that his text may have been rewritten later to fit the new orthodoxy. However, the clauses on the Spirit do bear some resemblance to ideas on its status put forward in the 370s by Basil of Caesarea. As with most statements hammered out in large assemblies, the final text was probably a compromise of the views of different contributors and traditions. Whatever its source, the Nicene Creed as developed at Constantinople, the form in which it is now used, does not contain any statement endorsing a Trinity of three consubstantial persons. There was certainly no consensus on the nature of the Holy Spirit.

With Nectarius now in charge,[8] the assembly was able to quash Alexandria's pretensions to control Constantinople and a number of canons were passed ensuring that this could not reoccur. One forbade a bishop to interfere outside his own see and, specifically, the bishops of Alexandria were restricted to administering the affairs of Egypt. From now on the authority of a bishop would run alongside the authority of the secular officials, the *vicarii*. With the bishops emerging as such powerful figures this made good administrative sense. However, Theodosius must also have been responding to the intrusive way in which bishops from both east and west meddled in each other's affairs and have hoped that the reform would help bring the squabbles to an end. Most significant of all, the council decreed that 'the bishop of Constantinople should have the next prerogative of honour after the bishop of Rome, because the city was the New Rome'. This was an astonishing development, not least in that it placed a city's political importance above that of its Christian heritage. It was a further reflection of Theodosius' determination that the Church should be bound within the secular political establishment. It was also a shrewd political move. With Nectarius in such a strong position, and new bishops in Antioch (Flavianus was not yet consecrated) and Alexandria (Timothy, the brother of the discredited Peter), it was the right moment to effect the change. In the long term, of course, the ancient bishoprics of Rome and Alexandria were deeply offended and the canon had the effect of intensifying their hostility against any future bishops of Constantinople, at least two of whom were to fall victim to their plotting (John Chrysostom was ejected in 404, and Nestorius deposed in 435). In short, under Nectarius, the council had been used to mount a coup that had reinforced the emperor's role as head of a politicised Church and arbiter of religious affairs in general.

The assembled bishops also took the chance to name as many heresies as possible, presumably to ensure that the churches and the patronage they attracted would be restricted to the Nicene faith alone. Eunomians, 'Arians', Macedonians and the Sabellians/Photinians were all excluded, as well as a sect known as the Apollinarians, named after

Apollinaris, Bishop of Laodicea, who claimed that Jesus did not have a human mind or soul. This perhaps went further than Theodosius himself wanted, as in a new law of 383 against heresy he did not include either Macedonians or Apollinarians, and there is nothing in the creed of 381 specifically excluding them.

With the conclusion of the assembly in 381, Theodosius issued further instructions to his civil servants. One surviving example is an *epistula* addressed to the proconsul of Asia, Auxonius – a proconsul was an official subordinate to the prefect. Asia was an important area to control because the three provinces for which the proconsul was responsible had not provided a single bishop for the Council of Constantinople. (This had been where the departed Macedonian bishops held sway.) The letter's definition of orthodoxy contains no reference to the creed just passed in the council. The Father, Son and Holy Spirit are simply declared to be one in majesty, power, glory, splendour and divinity, and it is stressed that there are three *personae* (the Latin term for the Greek *hypostaseis*) within the Godhead. Interestingly, here again there is no mention of the three being 'of one substance', presumably a recognition that even many Nicenes still did not accept this status for the Holy Spirit. Whatever the council had decided, Theodosius continued to use language that was reminiscent of the western approaches to the Trinity, which confirms that he viewed the council's proceedings as subsidiary to his own lawmaking. The imposition of the Trinity was an imperial matter, and the Church had little option but to acquiesce in Theodosius' law. Here, it helped, of course, that the vast resources and estates of each diocese were distributed to those bishops who moved within the boundaries of the imposed theological formula.

But there remained the problem of how a law such as this was to be administered. Theodosius must have been aware that the imposition of a specific text would arouse dissension from one faction or another and so lead to further theological wrangling that would upset his whole settlement. He thus hit on a different strategy, which was a good indication of his developing political skills. Instead of having to adhere to a creed, applicants for bishoprics simply had to be acceptable to a bishop named for the purpose by the emperor. The historian Sozomen says that the emperor had become personally acquainted with all his nominees before they left Constantinople. Nectarius was listed first, as befitted the new status of Constantinople, followed by Timothy as the arbiter of orthodoxy in Egypt. No name was given for Antioch as the dispute over Paulinus rumbled on.[9] In general the listing of the accepted bishops must have made the administration of the law much easier, in that any proconsul or prefect not sure whether an appointment was theologically acceptable could have it confirmed by the bishop named for that area and without further argument over the wording of correct belief. It even appears that an ambitious cleric could obtain a certificate of orthodoxy to show the secular officials. In the case of Ausonius' provinces in Asia, for example, there was no accredited Nicene bishop and he would have had to appoint outsiders to replace those bishops who were now declared heretical.

The imposition of such a wide-ranging and restrictive law was bound to be unpopular. All the contemporary historians of the period, even those supportive of Nicaea, speak of 'great disturbances as the Arians were ejected from the churches'.[10] Theodoret quotes a letter sent to Rome by the eastern bishops in which the Arians are described as 'wolves harrying the flocks up and down the glades, daring to hold rival assemblies, stirring sedition among the people and shrinking from nothing which can do damage to the churches'.[11] Things got so bad that Theodosius was forced to backtrack. In 383 he called a further council in Constantinople, and this time he invited the leaders of all the 'heretical' sects, including Demophilus and Eunomius. His hope, says Sozomen, was that 'they might either bring others to their own state of conviction or be convinced themselves; for he imagined that all would be brought to oneness of opinion if a free discussion was entered into concerning ambiguous points of doctrine'.[12] This was a remarkable volte-face. It suggested that Theodosius now realised the importance of getting a compromise even if this meant overthrowing the creed of 381 and allowing the Church as a whole to create a consensus.

Only a few months earlier, Theodosius had made his treaty with the Goths allowing them to stay as allies within the empire, but the emperor was certainly naïve if he expected that he could get any similar agreement on theological issues. He first suggested that earlier authorities should be consulted to see if they could offer some common basis for peace. This got nowhere: everyone was happy to accept the authority of these writers but then disagreed over what they had actually taught. Theodosius now asked for each sect to produce a creed of their own beliefs, and texts were handed in by Nectarius, Demophilus, Eunomius, and Eleusius, Bishop of Cyzicus, who represented the Macedonians.

The emperor then announced that he would only accept Nectarius' creed, which, according to Sozomen, in contrast to the creed of Constantinople, did apparently recognise 'the consubstantiality of the Trinity', and destroyed the rest. He may well have realised that the 'heretics', with their very different views, could not unite against him. 'The members of the other sects', Sozomen reported, 'were indignant with the priests for having entered into unwise disputations in front of the emperor.' Their arguments had exposed their lack of unity and allowed the emperor to move in to condemn them. Theodosius now passed new laws against heresies, although he appears to have been restrained in his enforcement of them. According to Sozomen: 'Some of the heterodox were expelled from the cities and deprived of the privileges enjoyed by other subjects of the empire. Great as were the punishments adjudged by the law against heretics, they were not always carried into execution, for the emperor had no desire to persecute his subjects; he only desired to enforce uniformity of view about God through the medium of intimidation.'[13] That the new settlement was seen as an expression of the emperor's imperial power was revealed as late as 388, when news reached Constantinople that the emperor might have been defeated and killed in a campaign against the usurper Maximus. There was a riot by the city's 'Arians' during which the house of the Nicene Nectarius was sacked. This suggests continuing resentment against Theodosius' settlement – which could only be expressed if he was believed to be dead – and perhaps explains why the creed agreed at the 381 council was never publicly announced in the city.

The initiatives taken by Theodosius in 381, even if uneven in their immediate application, irrevocably changed the spiritual lives of its Christian population. Richard Hanson, author of one of the most comprehensive studies of the Nicene debate, *The Search for the Christian Doctrine of God*, notes that the result of the Council of Constantinople was 'to reduce the meanings of the word "God" from a very large selection of alternatives to one only' with the result that 'when Western man today says "God" he means the one, sole exclusive [Trinitarian] God and nothing else'.[14] If Hanson is right, then there can have been few more important moments in the history of European thought. The freedom to speculate on what might or might not exist beyond this material world had been an intrinsic part of philosophical debate for centuries, and God, 'the gods', Aristotle's 'the Unmoved Mover' and Plato's 'the Good' had been among the many alternative ways of describing this ultimate reality. These alternatives were now being erased or subsumed into a composite 'Christian' God embedded in the Nicaea formula. Even today, studies of the philosophy of religion all too often start with definitions of 'God' as if there were no other way of conceiving the supernatural. This is surely the result of the narrowing of perspectives after 381.

It is not difficult to understand why Theodosius himself supported Nicaea. The formula of God the Father, Jesus the Son, and the Holy Spirit being of equal majesty appears to have represented the majority belief in Spain at this period and it was accepted by the conservative emperor. His court had been filled with officials from Spain and Gaul who would have held similar views and who had already shown that they were prepared to enforce them with violence. His beliefs would have been reinforced by Bishop Acholius of Thessalonika and possibly strengthened by Nicene bishops who had come to his court after the death of Valens. As a Latin-speaking Roman suddenly thrust into the Greek world, there is no reason why Theodosius should have known of the continuing debate within the eastern Church.

But there are two other reasons why he may have been drawn to the Nicene cause. The first is that the elevation of Jesus into full divinity fitted better with the current authoritarian zeitgeist. There were immense difficulties in finding a place within the ideology of the empire for a Jesus who was executed as a rebel against Rome. Second, the Goths and other tribes that Theodosius was fighting had been converted to Christianity at a time when the Homoian faith of Constantius had been in the ascendant, and they were to cling to this faith for decades to come. By creating a religious barrier between Homoian Goth and Nicene Roman, Theodosius could define a fault line along which he could rally his own troops against 'the barbarians'. In the west, in these same years, Ambrose of Milan was stressing the relationship between support for the Nicene faith and the success of the empire in war.

It is important to remember that Theodosius had no theological background of his own and that he put in place as dogma a formula containing intractable philosophical problems of which he would have been unaware. In effect, the emperor's laws had silenced the debate when it was still unresolved. If discussion had been allowed to continue within the Church, a broader consensus might have been established over time, one that could have preserved freedom of debate as well as a reasoned basis for any agreed formula (if, indeed, one was possible).

So what impelled Theodosius to suppress all alternative Christians beliefs so vigorously? It was here that he made an abrupt break with the policy of toleration upheld as recently as the 370s by Valentinian. It is likely that he was simply frustrated by the pressures he found himself under and genuinely believed that an authoritarian solution would bring unity to the embattled empire. At the same time control of dogma went hand in hand with greater control of the administrative structure of the Church. In this sense Theodosius could be seen as the heir of Diocletian and Constantine, bringing to fruition their attempts to create a more tightly structured empire that religious institutions were expected to serve. However, by defining and outlawing specific heresies, he had crossed a watershed. It soon became clear that once the principle of toleration was successfully challenged, as it had been by his new laws, the temptation to extend the campaign against dissidents would be irrestistible.

The first non-Christian sect to be attacked was the Manicheans, followers of the Persian prophet Mani, who believed in a universe in which good and evil struggled perpetually against each other. The sect had always been unpopular because of its Persian origins, and in 381 Theodosius ordered that no Manichean of either sex should be able to bequeath or inherit any property. This excluded Manicheans passing on family wealth from generation to generation, a basic right for Roman citizens. Then in 382, the emperor decreed the death penalty for membership of certain Manichean sects and put in place an informer system. It was to be the first step to the sect's elimination and to a wider campaign against non-Christian beliefs. While the emperor himself proved comparatively restrained in his own use of persecution, he had set up a framework that his more fanatical officials were able to exploit.

However, Theodosius' rule extended only to the east. The Latin-speaking west had not been represented at Constantinople, and here the Nicene settlement was to be imposed not by an emperor but by a bishop. We now turn to the career of the formidable Ambrose of Milan.

VIII

AMBROSE AND THE POLITICS
OF CONTROL

'YOU will not find that any one of the western nations have any great inclination for philosophy or geometry or studies of that sort, although the Roman empire has now been so long paramount there.'[1] This was the emperor Julian's own view of intellectual life in the western empire, where he had commanded the Roman armies on the Rhine. Even though this bleak assessment may have reflected the prejudices of a highly educated Greek, it is certainly true that the Latin world was not buzzing with theological speculation in the same way as the east. In his exhaustive commentary on the evolution of Nicene thought, the scholar Lewis Ayres has almost nothing to say on the western empire. 'Our knowledge of Latin Christology and Trinitarian theology [in the west] between 250 and 360 is extremely limited and certainly not that we can make certain judgements about its overall character.'[2] This suggests that the sweeping assertions of some commentators that the west was overwhelmingly Nicene need to be taken with caution. One particular problem was that the early Latin translations of the Greek scriptures were so clumsy that educated readers were put off by their crudeness. Gregory of Nazianzus himself complained of 'the narrowness of the [Latin] language and the paucity of their vocabulary', which in his view made 'the Italians' incapable of distinguishing between the terms used of the Trinity.[3]

It is hardly surprising that the Nicene Creed was largely unknown in the west as the Council of Nicaea had been made up of Greek-speaking bishops from the east. Western participation had been virtually nonexistent, and the Bishop of Rome was represented only by an

observer. The earliest recorded awareness of Nicene thought appears
to date from 359, when Constantius' determination to impose his subordinationist creed prompted a reaction by the western bishops meeting
at Rimini; they seemed to have been attracted to the Nicene Creed as
a bulwark against subordinationism.[4]

The most thoughtful of the western pro-Nicenes was Hilary, Bishop
of Poitiers in Gaul from 353. He had read widely in the works of
Tertullian and absorbed his ideas on the Trinity, but then had come
across the writings of Athanasius when these began to permeate the
west. As an outspoken champion of the controversial bishop, he was
exiled by the subordinationist emperor Constantius II to the east, to
Phrygia, where, unusually for a westerner in this period, he learned
Greek and became acquainted with Greek theology. By now he was a
fully converted Nicene supporter.[5] After Constantius had promulgated
his Homoian creed in Constantinople in 360, Hilary travelled to the
capital in the hope of persuading the emperor to allow him to debate
the Nicene alternative in public. He was unsuccessful, but the emperor
allowed him to return to Gaul, and the years before his death in 367
were devoted to networking among the western bishops. Most of his
work *On the Trinity* was written during his exile and draws on ideas
he must have encountered there and added to his reading of Tertullian.
Hilary was not an original philosopher, but he seems to have been
struggling valiantly to create a Latin terminology for the understanding
of the Nicene doctrine of God. But when he tried to tackle the problem
of how Jesus could suffer as a human being while not losing his full
divinity, he got himself into a terrible tangle, largely through his belief
that Jesus could not feel pain even in his human form. 'Though the
blow struck or the wound fell upon him or the knots tightened or the
ropes raised him, they brought to him the force of suffering but not
the pain of suffering.'[6] But if Jesus did not suffer at all, what was the
nature of the sacrifice on which the salvation of mankind depended?

Western support of Nicaea centred on the idea that there was a single
unified Godhead within which God the Father, Jesus the Son, and the
Holy Spirit related to each other as equals. Some fragments of theological texts that have survived describe God as a light from which Jesus
emanated as rays, or a 'flowing' of the Son from the Father. When
Theodosius in his edict of 380 decreed the single deity of the Father,
the Son and the Holy Ghost under the concept of equal majesty, this would
appear to be a fair summing up of what he may have been brought up

to believe in the Spain of the 360s and 370s. It is interesting that the Holy Spirit was given a much higher status in these western formulations than it received in the Nicene Creed of 325, but the boundaries between the three members of the Trinity were not clearly defined.

The western Church too was vulnerable to factions inspired by personal rivalry or theological differences. The status and patronage available to bishops was immense and the underlying tensions were exposed as soon as a bishopric fell vacant. In Rome in 366, over a hundred were killed in the street fighting that broke out on the death of Bishop Liberius before his successor, Damasus, was elected. Damasus' use of thugs to secure his victory was repugnant to most of his fellow bishops, and his moral authority was weakened for the rest of his reign. In 374, similar tensions between Homoians and Nicenes gripped the city of Milan after the death of the Homoian bishop Auxentius. This time the state intervened in the person of the praetorian prefect, Petronius Probus, who appears to have engineered the appointment of one of his protégés, the provincial governor Ambrose. In his report to Valentinian I, Probus claimed that Ambrose had entered the cathedral to restore order after the congregation there had been disturbed by Nicene intruders. He had then been acclaimed by the people as the new bishop even though he was not yet a baptised Christian. Valentinian accepted this version of events and Ambrose was duly baptised and enthroned within a week. Many in the Church were less impressed. The scholar Jerome was disgusted that 'a catechumen today becomes a bishop tomorrow; yesterday at the amphitheatre, today in the church; in the evening at the circus, in the morning at the altar; a little time ago a patron of actors, now dedicator of virgins'.[7]

Ambrose had been born in about 339. His father had been a prefect in Gaul, but after his death, while Ambrose was still a boy, the family had moved to Rome.[8] Although Ambrose had never been baptised there, his family had had strong links with the Nicene clergy of the city, and so it was as a committed, if still theologically uneducated, Nicene that Ambrose took office in Milan. He was soon mastering theology. His earliest works show a preoccupation with virginity, which he idealised as a higher state of being. However, as so often with those who rejoice in the rejection of sexuality, his emotional clumsiness did much to offend. Many families of the city were upset by his crude attempts to persuade their daughters to take vows of perpetual virginity, which undermined traditional Roman family values. One widow in particular was repelled by the way he insulted her when she considered remarrying. When in 378, just at the time of the disaster at Adrianople, a number of wealthy women died, their families were shocked when Ambrose suggested that they were better off dead than alive when there was the risk of being violated by invaders. This desire for control of others, whether these were virgins, widows, heretics, buildings or emperors, was to become the defining theme of Ambrose's reign as bishop. Even demons cowered before him. The son of the praetorian prefect Petronius Probus was troubled by an evil spirit, which confessed that Ambrose was the only man in the world he was afraid of.

In 379, Ambrose met the young emperor Gratian for the first time, in Milan. Gratian had now been emperor for four years, and his initial policy had been one of religious toleration. Before he had appointed Theodosius to fill the vacuum caused by Valens' death at Adrianople, he had specifically allowed the Nicenes whom Valens had removed to return to their sees while preserving any established Homoians in theirs. In August 379, however, he had issued jointly with Theodosius an edict forbidding 'heresy', although this was not followed by any expulsions of Homoians. Ambrose was determined to persuade the young emperor to support the Nicenes more aggressively, and when asked, he agreed to provide the impressionable Gratian with an outline of the Nicene faith. He worked at it busily over the winter of 379–380.

De Fide, 'On the Faith', the first two books of which were presented to Gratian in March 380, has been derided for its intellectual shallowness and its attempts to manipulate the emperor. Ambrose intimated that he had been asked to provide Gratian with details of the faith that would bring him victory, and throughout the work he linked imperial success to Nicene orthodoxy, specifically warning the emperor that if he campaigned in Illyricum, he risked being won over by 'Arians' and would suffer defeat in consequence. In one of his most extraordinary assertions Ambrose claimed that it was no longer the military eagles that led the legions but 'your name, Lord Jesus and Your Worship'.[9] That Jesus, who had died at the cruel hands of Roman soldiers, could be transformed into a leader of the legions illustrates how far Christianity had been integrated into imperial politics. Ambrose also adopted Athanasius' crude device of grouping all the subordinationists together and demonising them, and so contributed to the growing tradition of Christian invective that corroded serious theological thought. His exegesis of the scriptures was also rudimentary, 'little more than fantastic nonsense woven into a purely delusive harmony', as one assessment puts it.[10] In his scholarly work Ambrose drew on the texts of others – the fourth volume of *De Fide* relies heavily on Athanasius, for instance – and his fellow Christians were not taken in by his plagiarism. Jerome rebuked him for 'decking himself like an ugly crow with someone else's plumes' and, in a phrase typical of the writer's invective, ridiculed a work by Ambrose on the Holy Spirit as *totum flaccidum*.[11]

But Ambrose excelled in his brilliantly managed public performances. He was totally unscrupulous in seeking to publicly humiliate his enemies. The first of these events was the 'council' he dominated at Aquileia in 381. In the power vacuum created by Valens' death, Gratian had, through his edict of toleration, bid for religious leadership of the whole empire, and in the summer of 380 he called a general council of bishops from both east and west that would meet at Aquileia the following year. The city, an ancient Roman colony founded in 181 BC, was located at the head of the Adriatic where trade routes from northern Europe reached the sea. It had grown rich on both trade and its own industrial production and had a population of some 100,000. Under Constantine's patronage, a grand double church had been built – one building was reserved for catechumens and the other for those admitted to full church membership – and these were decorated with stunning floor mosaics that were only rediscovered under medieval silt in the early twentieth century.

To Gratian's embarrassment, however, he was then upstaged by Theodosius, who announced that his own council of the east would meet in Constantinople the same year. For some time, Gratian appears to have hoped that the bishops meeting at Constantinople would travel on to Aquileia, but this was never likely. It was now that Ambrose showed his genius for improvisation. He suggested to Gratian that the real challenge facing the western Church was the dispute between the Nicenes and the subordinationists centring on the continuing 'Arian' presence in Illyricum, and that the issues could be resolved at a smaller council. Ambrose's target in Illyricum was Palladius, the Bishop of Rataria. Palladius had been a bishop no fewer than thirty-five years, since 346, and was a convinced subordinationist. Ambrose had already mentioned him by name as a heretic in *De Fide*, and when Gratian had sent on a copy of the book to Palladius for comment, the latter had replied to Ambrose with disdain for this 'useless and superfluous

recitation of clever trickery'. Like most subordinationists, Palladius had
confidence in the superiority of his interpretation of the scriptures, and
he exhorted Ambrose to 'search the divine scriptures, which you have
neglected, so that under their divine guidance you may avoid the hell
towards which you are heading on your own'.[12] There was no love
lost here on either side.

When Palladius was summoned by the prefect of Italy to the council
at Aquileia in September 381, he assumed that there would be an
opportunity to see off Ambrose; there was no indication that free debate
would not be allowed. Yet when Palladius arrived at Aquileia, accompanied by another Homoian bishop, Secundianus of Singidunum, he
found to his horror that a small building close to the churches had
been set up like a law court, presided over by the Bishop of Aquileia,
Valerian, with Ambrose sitting beside him as if he were a prosecutor.
Instead of the great council of the west in front of which Palladius had
hoped to display his authority and learning, there were only some ten
bishops from Italy, all hand-picked supporters of Ambrose, and a few
other bishops from Gaul and North Africa. Palladius realised that he
had been set up.

Ambrose began the meeting by presenting Palladius with a letter
written by Arius, to Alexander in 320 and asked him whether he agreed
with it. This was a devious tactic. Many subordinationists had never
read Arius who represented only one current within the wider sea of
subordinationism. Palladius replied that he had come to debate the
nature of the true faith in general, not to discuss a text which he had
never seen before and that had no relevance. What he, Palladius, wished
to do was to initiate a discussion that could then define the agenda
for a full council. The surviving records show that the two bishops
now began tussling with each other for dominance. Ambrose tried to
get Palladius to sign a document condemning Arius; Palladius realised
that this would be tantamount to accepting the legitimacy of Ambrose's
stage-managed assembly and thus refused. For some time he managed
to escape getting drawn into Ambrose's net, keeping his silence when
repeatedly questioned on Arius, while insisting that Ambrose had no
right to act as an inquisitor. Ambrose was reduced to the feeble response
that Palladius' silence implied his acceptance of Arius' views.

Palladius then appears to have taken the initiative by moving the
argument on to firmer ground: the interpretation of scripture. He must
have realised that Ambrose's lack of theological training would have

left him vulnerable to what was subordinationism's strongest card. In the event, Ambrose wisely deferred to the superior knowledge of one of his supporting bishops, Eusebius of Bologna. Palladius cleverly kept the discussion focused on the scriptures without letting it drift to wider issues, but then made a fatal mistake: he misquoted the gospel of John and conflated two verses containing Jesus' assertion that 'the Father is greater than I'. Ambrose now announced that Palladius was falsifying scripture and Ambrose's supporters roared that he be anathematised. When Palladius tried to leave the room, he was restrained by force. Ambrose, claiming that he was holding the meeting on the direct authority of Gratian, pronounced that Palladius was a heretic. Palladius' companion, Secundianus, suffered a similar interrogation before he too was condemned.

The proceedings of this assembly show Ambrose's opportunism and the ruthlessness through which he exerted his authority. When he wrote to the emperor, ostensibly on behalf of the 'council of Aquileia', he claimed that he had established that Palladius and Secundianus were 'Arians' and that they must be deposed. He presented the small assembly of his bishops as if it represented 'the western Church' acting in defence of universal Christianity. The letter was even addressed to Theodosius as well as to Gratian on the grounds that the western bishops had a legitimate interest in the vacancy at Antioch, where the rights of Paulinus should be upheld against those of Flavian. (It is interesting that Ambrose made no mention of the Council of Constantinople, which had been held earlier in the year. One must assume that he didn't want it to be considered more important than his own – though he certainly knew of it through Acholius of Thessalonika, who attended the later sessions.) Theodosius' reply was dismissive. The eastern and western Churches, divided by geography and language, and increasingly by separate administrations, were by now drifting apart. When Bishop Damasus tried to regain the initiative for the west by calling a council to be held in Rome in 382 to which all eastern bishops were invited, only three easterners, among them Paulinus, discarded at Antioch, attended.

There is no evidence that Gratian acquiesced in Ambrose's demand to depose the two 'Arian' bishops. But Ambrose persisted. He was both helped and hindered by the weakness of the young emperor, who seems to have been particularly susceptible to the machinations of others when he established his court permanently in Milan in March 381. Milan's central location made it a good base from which to defend the northern borders of the western empire, and the young Valentinian II and his mother Justina were already settled there. Ambrose benefited from the possibility of direct access to the court, but it was clear that a number of important Christian figures arrived from Rome to take advantage of the shift of power to Milan. One of their successes had been to secure the removal of the Altar of Victory from the Senate in Rome, which had always been associated with the success of the Senate's deliberations. This was part of a campaign to withdraw state funds for ancient rites and went along with a refusal by Gratian to take on the traditional imperial title of *pontifex maximus*, chief of the priesthood.

The court's move to Milan was unpopular with those communities that had prospered from the imperial presence in Trier and Sirmium. There was additional resentment when Gratian recruited mercenaries from among the Alans, one of the Germanic tribes. He showed a somewhat un-Roman enthusiasm for their skill as archers, and his public appearance in an Alan costume might have been the moment when his credibility was irrevocably lost. Stories of the lack of control in his court and the proliferation of corruption abounded. Theodosius paid him less and less respect and in January 383 accorded his own eldest son Arcadius the status of an Augustus without even referring the matter to Gratian. From then on things went downhill for Gratian. In the summer of 383 the commander of the British legions, Magnus Maximus, revolted and crossed over the Channel to Gaul, and when Gratian marched north to confront him he found his army melting away. Left isolated in a province that offered him no support, he was killed by an officer who had defected to Maximus.

Gratian's death left the twelve-year-old Valentinian II as sole legitimate emperor in the west, but there was little the boy could do against Maximus, who now held power in Gaul and who proclaimed himself to be a Nicene, possibly in the hope of attracting Theodosius' support for his usurpation. Maximus offered to take Valentinian under his wing, but the young emperor was sufficiently well established in Italy, with a court of Italian aristocrats whose status depended on his continued rule, to be able to refuse. Although the details of any agreement are lost, both rulers appear to have recognised each other's position and the right to control their own territories without the interference of the other. Theodosius too accepted that he could do little to confront Maximus. They had, in fact, once served together in the elder Theodosius' army in Britain.

Valentinian received strong support from his mother Justina, the widow of Valentinian I, who appears to have had much of her late husband's tenacity. Both she and her son were Homoians, and they had built up a body of supportive clergy in Milan headed by an 'alternative' bishop, who had taken the name of Ambrose's Homoian predecessor, Auxentius. Their retinue also included Gothic troops who, like all the Germanic tribes, were subordinationists. The scene was set for a power struggle between the Nicene Ambrose and the Homoian court.

Once again Ambrose was to show his opportunism and genius for manipulation of a public event in his favour. The first conflict arose over the Altar of Victory in the Senate in Rome. A group of pagan senators, led by the city's prefect, Symmachus, took advantage of the change of emperor to formally request Valentinian for a restitution of all pagan privileges to Rome, including the return of the altar to the Senate. Symmachus was a consummate tactician, and rather than attempting to confront Christianity on behalf of the ancient pagan beliefs of the capital, he portrayed the issue as one of tolerance. Echoing the arguments of Porphyry and Themistius, he pleaded for the recognition of diversity of worship: 'The divine Mind has distributed different guardians and different cults to different cities. As souls are given separately to infants as they are born, so to peoples the genius of their destiny ... If a long period gives authority to religious customs, we ought to keep faith with so many centuries, and to follow our ancestors, as they happily followed theirs ... Allow us, we beseech you, as old men, to leave to posterity what we received as boys ... We ask, then, for the peace for the gods of our fathers and our country. It is just that all worship should be considered as one. We look to the same stars, the sky is common, the same world surrounds us. What difference does it make by what paths each seeks the truth? We cannot attain to so great a secret by one road.'[13] He reminded the emperor that when the altar had first been removed from the Senate, a famine had struck the city; the pagan gods were as adept at showing their displeasure by punishing wrongdoers as was the Christian god! Symmachus' eloquent plea convinced some of the Christians at Valentinian's court, but Ambrose was having none of it. In two letters to the emperor, the first a statement of general principle and the second a detailed reply to Symmachus' text, he presented his advice. If Valentinian accepted the request he would be supporting paganism itself, and he could not possibly make such a move without informing Theodosius (who, as

Ambrose knew, would surely back the bishop in the matter). As for Symmachus' plea for tolerance, 'Salvation is not sure unless everyone [*sic*] worships in truth the true God, that is the God of Christians, under Whose sway are all things: for He alone is the true God, Who is to be worshipped from the bottom of the heart; for the "gods of the heathen", as Scripture says, "are devils".'[14] When Valentinian acquiesced in his bishop's demand, the underlying issue of religious toleration, clearly presented by Symmachus, was firmly rejected. The debate – and Ambrose's victory – marked another turning point.

As Ambrose's confidence grew, there developed an extraordinary power struggle between the Nicene bishop and the Homoian court. It started in 385 when the court demanded access to one of the basilicas of the city for their own Homoian services. The church requested, referred to as the Basilica Portiana, was probably today's San Lorenzo, which may originally have been an imperial mausoleum and thus the emperor's preserve in any case. When Ambrose was summoned to the imperial palace to be told of the demand, a large demonstration followed him, and some of his supporters shouted that they would prefer to be martyred for their true faith than betray the Nicene Creed. The court had little option but to ask Ambrose to calm the crowd, which he did with the promise that nobody would invade any of the city's basilicas. He had outwitted the emperor and the demand for the basilica was dropped.

In a more determined move by Valentinian and Justina to assert their Homoian faith, they issued a law on 23 January 386 confirming that those who supported the creed laid down by Constantius II at Rimini and Seleucia, and subsequently at Constantinople in 360 – in other words the Homoian faith – should be guaranteed the freedom of assembly. The wording of the law made it clear that this was an affirmation of existing rights, not the creation of new privileges. Any 'tumult' against this law would be treated as treason. It was decided that the emperor himself would hold a major service at Easter in early April, and nine days before the feast a court official approached Ambrose with a formal request to use the Basilica Nova, the city's cathedral. If there were any disturbances, Ambrose himself would be held accountable. Ambrose had to be careful, and he responded by claiming that Church tradition did not allow a priest to hand over a church. The court countered by reiterating its earlier demand for the Basilica Portiana, and occupied the building, which was soon decorated with the imperial insignia.

Ambrose could not be seen to be instigating any opposition, and so it was that a 'spontaneous crowd' swarmed off to the Basilica Portiana. Troops were dispatched by the court to guard the entrances, with orders that they should let people in but not out again in the hope that they would eventually capitulate if left without food. Preaching in the cathedral, Ambrose skilfully portrayed himself and his own faith as under siege, and roused congregations not to open demonstration but to quiet resistance within both basilicas. He proclaimed that if he was attacked in any way, he would be a martyr. However, he remained exceptionally vulnerable, even more so when news came through that those protesting inside the Basilica Portiana had taken down the imperial hangings and had damaged them in the process. This could be construed as a direct insult to the emperor and liable to be punished severely.

In the event, it was the court that gave way. Many of the soldiers sent to the Basilica Portiana were Nicenes and susceptible to Ambrose's insistence that they would be betraying their faith before God. Some even deserted their posts. The court simply could not risk a refusal to obey orders or a massacre of Ambrose's supporters if they did stand firm. In addition, an ominous letter arrived for Valentinian from Maximus intimating that the young emperor would only survive in power if he supported the Nicene faith, which Maximus had already adopted. Valentinian gave in. The troops were withdrawn by the court and an uneasy calm descended on Milan. Ambrose was still subject to any direct enforcement of the law of 23 January, but his manipulation of the situation had been masterful.

Ambrose consolidated his success through a major building programme. When by June 386 another basilica, now known as Sant'Ambrogio, was nearing completion, Ambrose let it be known that he would be buried under its central altar. There was simply no precedent for such pretensions. Traditionally a church was dedicated to an earlier martyr, not the city's presiding bishop. Milan seems to have suffered little in the persecutions of the previous century, and when an earlier church had been dedicated, relics had been imported from elsewhere.

Many believed that this should happen again, but the bishop countered with the extraordinary claim that he had a presentiment where relics of the city's own martyrs could be found. He then led a crowd to a local memorial previously erected to two martyrs, Nabor and

Felix, whose fate had been recorded, and ordered the digging to start. Soon two sets of bones emerged. Ambrose later reported that there was fresh blood on them, which he interpreted as a sign that God had preserved the bodies as evidence that they were martyrs. He had also brought along two women possessed by demons, and with the bones before them, the demons cried out from inside them, proclaiming in their agonies that these were martyrs by the name of Gervasius and Protasius. Crowds accompanied the bloodied remains into the city and further miracles were announced, including the curing of a blind butcher who had rubbed his eyes with a handkerchief that had touched the bier on which the bodies had been carried. There were voices from the court mocking these opportune finds and the dubious evidence used to justify their legitimacy, but Ambrose had the remains buried in his new basilica within a day. The whole episode was presented as another victory for the Nicene faith.

By 387, Valentinian and Justina had been outmanoeuvred and their position was crumbling. There is evidence in the last months of 386 that leading officials were beginning to resign and leave Milan. Their weakness on a broader front was shown when they were forced to call on the help of Theodosius, who had to send them one of his generals to bolster their position. Valentinian's position was not helped by a visit of Ambrose to Maximus in Trier later in 386 in which Ambrose appears to have launched into recriminations against Valentinian. Consequently, during the summer of 387, Maximus moved into Italy, claiming that he was bringing the Nicene faith with him. There seems to have been no resistance to the usurper, and Valentinian was forced to flee with his mother eastwards to Thessalonika. Here he had his first meeting with Theodosius, and the two emperors counterattacked until Maximus was hunted down and killed at Aquileia. It was now that Theodosius forced Valentinian to renounce his Homoian faith as a price for his support. The Nicene faith had become the official religious policy of the empire, upheld by Valentinian, the late Maximus and Theodosius alike. Theodosius was clearly in charge, and having taken up residence in Milan, he was in a position to consolidate his faith in the west. He could be sure of the support of Ambrose, but which of them would prove the dominant partner in the relationship was still to be decided.

IX

THE ASSAULT ON PAGANISM

WHEN Justina and Valentinian fled to Thessalonika, they brought Valentinian's young sister Galla with them. The pagan writer Zosimus later recorded that no sooner had Theodosius cast his lustful eye on the young girl than he determined to marry her. The truth is probably more prosaic: Theodosius had recently been widowed, and the dynastic advantages of linking himself by marriage to his co-emperor's family were obvious. It seems clear that Theodosius was developing acute political skills. His compromise treaty with the Goths and his readiness to consider a religious settlement based on a consensus of theological views – the 'council of the sects' in 383 – suggest flexibility. He seems to have known when compassion was justified, and while he had no inhibitions about ordering the execution of Maximus and that of his small son, Victor, who had remained in Gaul, he protected the rest of Maximus' family. Even though he was faced with the evidence that many leading men in Italy and Gaul had abandoned Valentinian in favour of Maximus, he did not launch a witchhunt against them. One can begin to see a man who was learning how to carry out the complex and often impossible task of ruling an empire under threat without intensifying discontent.

Now, in the autumn of 388, Theodosius was in Milan. He was to remain there for three years, leaving the eastern empire in the hands of his son Arcadius and a trusted set of praetorian prefects and proconsuls. Theodosius knew that so long as he did not directly challenge Valentinian's status, he was unlikely to be dislodged, and his long-term plans might well have been to emerge as emperor in the west. He would, however, have to make a relationship with Ambrose. The two men first met when Theodosius arrived for a service in the cathedral and, following eastern practice, expected to join the clergy for communion. Ambrose, who was insistent on keeping the Church distinct from the court, was forced to rebuff him. It was a deeply embarrassing moment and showed just how poorly defined the relationship between Church and state remained. And it was not long before Ambrose took the opportunity to point out to the emperor his 'Christian' duty.

In 388 Theodosius had been irritated by a request for advice from a local governor concerning the sacking of a Jewish synagogue at Callinicum on the Euphrates by a Christian mob led by their bishop. The emperor simply suggested that the bishop should be ordered to bear the cost of restoring the building. When Ambrose heard of the matter, he tried to present the emperor with a very different response to the incident. Reparation, he argued, would involve asking the bishop to betray his faith, and if the bishop refused there would be more trouble, which would bring the risk of a Christian emperor creating new martyrs. Ambrose further dramatised the affair by claiming that he would be happy to take responsibility for giving 'the orders that there would be no building in which Christ was denied'.[1] Theodosius quietly sent a command to the local governor cancelling his original instructions. While Valentinian I had been prepared to support Judaism – and Julian had even begun the rebuilding of the Temple in Jerusalem – now an emperor was condoning a Christian attack on a Jewish place of worship. It was a further assault on the concept of religious toleration. Ambrose followed his success with a tendentious letter requesting that the bishop's violence should be ignored and a sermon before the emperor in which he implored Theodosius to take on the protection of the Church against its enemies.

These were delicate matters. Theodosius had, of course, already shown in his law of January 381 that he was prepared to throw his weight behind one definition – and, as it had turned out, Ambrose's definition – of the Christian faith and impose it by law. Yet by now he must have realised that the ancient rituals and religious beliefs of the empire were still firmly embedded and could not be suppressed in the way that Ambrose demanded. This had been recognised by earlier Christian emperors. Constantius, for instance, had issued a request in 342 to an urban prefect specifically asking that temple buildings situated outside the city walls should remain intact on the grounds that the ancient ceremonies they hosted provided enjoyment for the people.

Fifteen years later, on a visit to Rome, Constantius inspected the ancient shrines of the city, 'asked about the origins of the temples and expressed his admiration of their founders'.[2] Theodosius himself had shown caution in attacking pagan shrines. In 382 he had received a request from Palladius, the military commander in Osrhoene on the Persian frontier, asking whether he should close the famous temple at Edessa, presumably as a result of demands by local Christian groups. Theodosius had replied pragmatically that because of its great artistic value, it should remain open. Yet his moderation was soon undermined by his more hotheaded Christian officials. The praetorian prefect of the east, a fellow Spaniard, Maternus Cynergius, was particularly ruthless, and appears to have destroyed Edessa and its treasures. His vandalism unleashed the aggression of others, notably bands of fanatical monks who delighted in the destruction of shrines.

To this day the word 'pagan' has the negative connotations that its early use by Christians gave it – the word originally described an un-tutored country dweller – but it is important to remember that these places of worship had been the focus of community life and ritual for centuries. To their guardians, Christians appeared as sacrilegious barbar-ians – 'men by all appearances, though they lived like pigs', as one shocked observer put it.[3] In 386 the orator Libanius bravely warned Theodosius of the devastating effect that tearing down ancient temples in the countryside would have on peasant life. He detailed how 'the black-robed tribe [the monks] . . . hasten to attack the temples with sticks and stones and bars of iron . . . utter desolation follows, with the stripping of roofs, demolition of walls, the tearing down of statues and the overthrow of altars . . . the priests [i.e. of the sanctuary concerned] must either keep quiet or die'. This is one of the last pleas for religious toleration to be recorded in the ancient world. The archae-ological evidence for this destruction, in both the eastern and western empire, is pervasive.[4]

Although Libanius' oration was addressed to the emperor, there is, in fact, no record that it ever reached him. But Theodosius was clearly concerned about the unsettling effect these rampaging Christians, whether officials or monks, were having on public order. In 386, he replied to a request from Egypt that it was better that the overseer of the temples of the province should be a non-Christian, since it would be wrong to entrust the buildings to those whose beliefs would not allow them to care for them. The emperor was acting to preserve temples just as his officials were destroying them. After the death of Cynegius in 388, Theodosius was able to confirm his distaste for this destruction by replacing him with a pagan aristocrat, Tatianus; his son, Proculus, also a pagan, was appointed the prefect of Constantinople. It seems that it was the lack of public order that concerned Theodosius rather than the upholding of his own orthodoxy. A law issued to Tatianus in June 388, and thus applicable to the whole of the eastern empire, forbids religious debate of any kind. 'Let no opportunity be offered to anyone to enter a public place either to debate about religion or to hold discussions or to bring about any kind of deliberations.' Another ruling issued by Theodosius in September 390 ordered monks to stay in deserts or 'great empty spaces' – in other words, to keep away from cities and large shrines.

However, the stifling of free debate went hand in hand with conciliation with the pagans, and now Theodosius turned to Rome. There was good reason for such a move. With Arcadius established as his successor in the east, it was crucial that Theodosius obtained for his younger son Honorius, born to his first wife Flaccilla in 384, an equal status in the west. For this he needed the support of the Senate and the aristocracy in Rome, many of whom were still pagans, so in July Theodosius, with Honorius in his retinue, set off south to the ancient, if now largely redundant, capital of the empire.

Theodosius was welcomed to the Senate with a panegyric from a Gallic orator, Pacatus, which was so rooted in traditional formulas as to give no hint that the emperor was a Christian. It was noted how Theodosius' birthplace in Spain was also that of the emperors Trajan and Hadrian, and how his military victories were reminiscent of those of Scipio Africanus, who had defeated the great Carthaginian general Hannibal. He was declared to have the virtues of revered emperors such as Augustus and Trajan – *clemens* (clemency), *civilitas* (courtesy) and *amicitia* (friendship), the last of which, Pacatus opined, was clothed in purple, wreathed in gold and installed upon the imperial throne. There was even a comparison of the emperor to Jupiter and Hercules. Appropriate mention was made of Honorius and none of Valentinian, who had been sent to Trier to preside over Gaul. The senators must have been thankful that their support for Maximus was overlooked and they dutifully decreed the making of statues of Theodosius and his co-emperors, each with the inscription 'exterminator of usurpers and founder of public safety'. Theodosius responded as the senators must have hoped. Pacatus was rewarded with the proconsulship of the province of Africa and the aristocratic Symmachus with a consulship (although Theodosius refused to restore the Altar of Victory to the senate house). Symmachus must have been particularly relieved, as he had actually visited Maximus in Milan to offer him his allegiance. The most successful of these pagan aristocrats was Nichomachus Flavianus, who was awarded a prefecture with responsibility for Italy, Illyricum and Africa.[5]

By 390, Theodosius' position was relatively secure. There was no powerful interest group able to challenge him, he had avoided any major military disasters, and his compromises seem to have led to domestic peace, even if there was some concern over the troublesome activities of Christian mobs. His change of orders in the Callinicum affair, though deeply ominous in that it appeared to legitimise unprovoked Christian attacks on Jews, was achieved quietly and without any apparent loss of face. In other threats to his authority, notably the defacement of his statue in tax riots in Antioch in 387, Theodosius' response had been comparatively restrained: only those proved to have been guilty were punished and there was no retribution against the citizenry as a whole. But now a major incident was to threaten all he had achieved.

Thessalonika was an important city, the capital of the province of Macedonia, and a thriving port. It had one of the larger hippodromes of the empire, holding perhaps 100,000 people, and as such was prey to the tensions unleashed by the chariot races and their stars, the successful charioteers. The garrison of the city was made up of Goths under a commander by the name of Butheric. It was Butheric who imprisoned one of the most popular charioteers on what seems to have been a charge involving homosexual rape. When he failed to appear in his chariot at the next games, the crowds erupted. Resentment against the Goths added to their anger, and Butheric and several of his officers were murdered and their bodies dragged through the streets.

Theodosius was furious when the news reached him in Milan, but this time, in contrast to the tax riots in Antioch, orders for retribution were given without delay. It remains unclear whether these were given directly by the emperor or elaborated by his officials, such as Flavius Rufinus, his *magister officiorum*, a ruthless figure in his own right, as the command travelled eastwards to Thessalonika. What followed was a rush of bloodletting in which some 7,000 may have died. By the time

Theodosius had realised the enormity of what he had initiated and issued counter-orders, it was too late. The recognition of his own responsibility is suggested by an order issued soon afterwards that all executions in the empire were to be delayed for thirty days so that each could be reviewed. The shedding of more blood could not be risked.

The massacre was a major public embarrassment for the emperor, as much for the deaths caused as for the image it presented of a ruler unable to control his emotions. For Ambrose, here was a chance to establish a psychological hold over Theodosius. In a private letter, he assumed the guilt of the emperor, whose actions he attributed to his unruly temper, and requested that Theodosius show penitence. Ambrose intimated that he would not give the emperor communion until he did so. The events that followed are difficult to interpret. Theodosius did indeed come to the cathedral and profess penitence, but the *humilitas* he showed in doing so could well have been a carefully calculated pose by which he knew he could resolve the situation. *Humilitas* was one of the range of virtues an emperor could use in the stage-management of himself before his subjects. Certainly Theodosius had become aware that the Church was another medium through which he could present himself to the public. His initiative seems to have succeeded, in that accounts of the massacre and the penitence of the emperor were reported in contemporary documents as if the emperor's guilt had been successfully removed. He could now participate again fully in Church activities.[6]

Theodosius' reconciliation with Ambrose had taken place at Christmas 390. Just a few weeks later, in February 391, he issued the first of a series of laws against paganism. This was a major change in his religious policy. Sacrificing had been banned by earlier emperors, but there is no evidence of any order restricting pagan worship being issued during the reigns of Valentinian I and Valens. Even if pagans could not actually sacrifice animals on an altar, it is clear that the old festivals were still being celebrated around the temples, with animals being killed and then feasted on outside their sanctuaries. The new law repeated that 'no-one is to stain themselves with sacrifices', a prohibition that had been in force since Constantine, but it now stipulated that '. . . no-one is to enter shrines, no-one is to undertake the ritual purification of temples or worship images crafted by human hand'. It is clear from the listing of the recipients that, despite the repetition of 'no-one', its main audience was intended to be local officials. It is even more surprising that this decree was issued at Milan, as it would have to be Nichomachus Flavianus, the pagan prefect Theodosius had appointed shortly before, who would administer it. It was followed in June, when Theodosius was on his way back to Constantinople, by a law aiming at Christians who reverted to paganism: 'If any splendour of rank has been conferred upon or is inborn in those persons who have departed from the faith and are blinded in mind, who have deserted the cult and worship of the sacrosanct religion [i.e Christianity] and given themselves over to sacrifices, they shall forfeit such rank so that, removed from their position and status, they shall be branded with perpetual infamy and shall not be numbered even among the lowest dregs of the ignoble crowd.' Status was important in the late Roman Empire and Theodosius must have known how devastating this law would be.[7]

Another law issued in June was directed at Alexandria and shows just how difficult it was for the emperor to control Christian aggression. The law has not survived, but in so far as it can be reconstructed, Theodosius appears to have authorised the closing down of some pagan rituals still being held in a building taken over by Christians. However, his measured pronouncement was subverted by local fanatics who exploited his intervention so as to justify an attack on one of the great temples of Alexandria, the Serapeion, regarded as the most impressive complex of religious buildings outside Rome. As Christian mobs, encouraged by their bishop, Theophilus, moved in on the temple, pagans fled into the sanctuary after taking Christian hostages. The killing of these hostages was followed by an assault on the temple led by the bishop, the city prefect, Evagrius, and the local garrison. There was a moment's hesitation when the enormity of breaking the boundaries of the sanctuary and defacing an effigy of the god Serapis held the crowds back, but when Theophilus struck the statue, the attack began. The destruction of the temple was a psychological turning point. When, soon after, the Nile flooded the valley with its fertile silt as usual, the Christians felt they had proved that the pagan gods were not responsible for bringing the waters. Moreover, after the violence had died down, it was claimed that the destruction was what the emperor had ordered. The direct involvement of Evagrius made this difficult to contradict, and Theodosius only managed to reassert control by removing Evagrius from his position in April 392. A much safer man, an earlier prefect, Hypatius, replaced him until a permanent successor could be found.

When news reached Theodosius that rioters were being dealt with leniently by the local courts, he ordered Hypatius to enforce appropriately severe penalties.

Yet at the same time a new wave of anti-pagan activity began. In April 392, the law restricting monks to the deserts was repealed, allowing them to join the renewed destruction of pagan shrines. Then, in November 392, a law was issued that in comprehensiveness had had no equal since the pharaoh Akhenaten's attempt to eliminate the ancient gods of Egypt in the fourteenth century BC. Not only was any activity associated with pagan rites suppressed, but any symbol of paganism, even in domestic shrines, was banned. The pagan gods were reclassified as evil spirits. Local officials were given widespread powers to enter homes to search out offending material. It is hard to gauge the effectiveness of this policy. Traditional beliefs and customs are not easily eliminated, and there is a mass of evidence to show that many rituals continued or simply reappeared in a Christian guise. The law of November forbade, for instance, the lighting of lamps before shrines, but these soon reappeared in front of Christian altars and martyrs' tombs. (Jerome excused the practice by claiming that a detestable pagan practice was acceptable when done for Christian purpose.) There is no doubt, however, that the laws against paganism meant a shift of resources and spiritual energy towards Christianity. The temples of the Roman forum were being restored into the 380s, but shortly thereafter Jerome was able to write that 'the gilded Capitol [the Capitoline Hill, site of the great temple to Jupiter] falls into disrepair, dust and cobwebs cover all Rome's temples. The city shakes on its foundations, and a stream of people hurries, past half-fallen shrines, to the tombs of the martyrs.'[8] The Olympic Games, held every four years in honour of Zeus, and by now well over a thousand years old, were celebrated for the last time in 393.

Ambrose has often been held to blame for Theodosius' sudden change of policy after 389. The brief period between the emperor's penitence and the first law of February 391 is cited as evidence that Theodosius had discovered sin (as defined by Ambrose) and was busy improving his relationship with God. There may be something in this, in that the laws were a departure from the more measured and tolerant approach Theodosius had adopted to the range of spiritual allegiances to be found in the empire, and suggest a deeper, more personal impulse that overrode his maturing political sensitivities. However, much as Ambrose liked to emphasise his power over the emperor, there is little evidence of a close relationship. There is no known example of them spending time alone together, for instance, as one would expect of a personal confessor. Moreover, the more sweeping and extreme of the laws were promulgated after Theodosius had left Ambrose's sphere of influence.

A more plausible explanation relates to the promotion of the *magister officiorum*, Flavius Rufinus, who returned to Constantinople with Theodosius in 391. Rufinus had established himself as a powerful figure in Italy and, as already suggested, may have elaborated Theodosius' commands to the garrison at Thessalonika. He had a reputation for religious fanaticism. Back in Constantinople, he had been awarded the prestigious post of consul, and it appears that he had been the moving force behind the relaxation of the restrictions on the roving monks. The laws of April 392 seem to reflect a power struggle within the court – those ordering severe treatment of Christian rioters in Alexandria coming from the pagan Tatianus, those releasing the monks from the Christian Rufinus. Then, in what seems to have been a coup, Rufinus replaced Tatianus as praetorian prefect in August 392, and followed up his success with a series of laws aimed at the Lycian aristocracy from which Tatianus and his family came. In 394, he ordered the execution of Proculus, which took place in front of his displaced father. The wide-sweeping law of November 392 seems, therefore, to reflect the victory of Rufinus. Rufinus remained in place for the rest of Theodosius' reign, but when after the emperor's death he plotted a coup which would have led to him becoming co-emperor alongside the young Arcadius, he was assassinated by his rivals in November 395.

When Theodosius moved back to Constantinople in 391, he had left Italy comparatively undefended. He had probably wished to avoid appointing a strong man there who might have threatened his plans to keep the west for his son Honorius. Valentinian, who remained in Gaul, under the protection of a leading general, Arbogast, must have grasped that he was gradually being isolated by Theodosius. His confidence undermined by his exclusion, he asked Ambrose in the spring of 392 to come to Gaul to baptise him. Yet before the bishop arrived, Valentinian was found dead at his court in Vienne, probably at his own hand. Suicide resulted in exclusion from a Christian burial, so when Ambrose brought the corpse back to Milan and buried it with imperial honours, the impression given to the wider world was of an unsolved murder, which gossip attributed to Arbogast. Arbogast was determined to protect himself by appointing a new Augustus, one Eugenius, who already had links with the eastern court of Theodosius and who might therefore not be seen as a threat to the emperor. Theodosius was deliberately slow to recognise him: if Eugenius was accepted as Augustus in the west, it would destroy Theodosius' dynastic ambitions for Honorius. Yet delay brought its own problems. Eugenius was mild-mannered but effective. He and Arbogast launched a successful campaign across the Rhine, and the new Augustus proved an impressive networker in Italy. Though nominally a Christian, Eugenius was receptive to the pagan senators of Rome, even sending them some of his prisoners from the Rhine campaign for slaughter in the Colosseum. When he arrived in Milan in 393 he was welcomed by the prefect, Nichomachus Flavianus. Ambrose conveniently arranged a provincial tour so that he would not have to be in the city to declare his own allegiance, while Eugenius wrote to Theodosius professing friendship. His gestures were finally rejected when in January 394 Theodosius declared that Honorius had been elevated to the highest imperial status, that of Augustus. The Theodosian dynasty was now in place.

Meanwhile, in Italy, Nichomachus Flavianus was ready to exploit the opportunity Eugenius' support had given him. All the resentment against Theodosius' anti-pagan laws was expunged in a major revival of the ancient pagan cults of Rome. The Altar of Victory was triumphantly returned to the senate house. Temples were restored and a mass of ancient rituals were celebrated once more. Nichomachus himself presided as a priest in a variety of cults, including those of Mithras, Sol Invictus and the Egyptian deities Isis and Serapis. Symmachus' son married Nichomachus' daughter in a gesture of aristocratic solidarity.

This reaction in Italy spelled a major crisis for Theodosius. He risked losing the west and being humiliated by the public rejection of his stance against paganism. By the spring of 394, both sides were preparing for war. The events that followed were later presented by Christian historians as a confrontation between Christianity and paganism, but in essence this was a traditional power struggle of a type common in imperial history. Theodosius drew heavily for his troops on Goths and other Germanic groups, including the Goths he had settled as allies in Thrace in 382, and in the summer of 394 he crossed through Illyricum towards Aquileia. It was a troubled time for the emperor, as his wife Galla had just died in childbirth, together with the child. In the short term there was no hope of a new male heir, and the urgency of consolidating the succession for his two surviving sons must have been acute. Meanwhile, Arbogast began gathering his forces in Milan and Nichomachus Flavianus mobilised the resources of Italy in support. As Nichomachus' prefecture extended to Africa, he was also able to arrange the transport of corn from there. Eugenius had become a figurehead in these machinations. He had probably always been malleable to the plans of Arbogast, who remained a pagan, and he was now forced to fight for his position.

The two sides met at the river Frigidus near Aquileia in early September 394. Arbogast was an experienced general and he chose a well-defended position on high ground. Theodosius' first assault was a disaster. Thousands of Goths died and morale collapsed as word went round that Theodosius was sacrificing his mercenaries to keep his own Roman forces intact. (Later Christian writers claimed that the Goths had died because they were still Arians, as yet unconverted to Nicene Christianity.) According to the historian Theodoret, who was instrumental in presenting the battle as a religious confrontation, Theodosius spent the following night in prayer. He was rewarded at daybreak with a vision of John the Evangelist and the apostle Philip, which gave him the courage to counterattack. Then, suddenly, there was a blast of the notorious *bora*, a wind that sweeps down from the Alps and cuts to the bone, which covered the battlefield in dust, preventing Arbogast's men from firing their missiles and javelins. It was now the turn of Arbogast's troops to suffer a collapse in morale, and Theodosius was able to rally his forces for a final assault on his position. Eugenius, who had stayed on high ground with his troops, was captured and executed; Arbogast fled but committed suicide, as did Nichomachus Flavianus. Theodosius was compassionate to the other survivors, not least because the emperor urgently needed good men. The historian Rufinus, writing shortly after the battle, linked the fortuitous arrival of the *bora* to the miraculous intervention of God, and by the time of Theodoret, two generations later, Eugenius had been placed fighting alongside statues of Jupiter and Hercules in a last stand for paganism. 'Such was Theodosius in peace and war,' concludes Theodoret, 'ever asking and never refused the help of God.'[9]

The accounts of the Battle of the River Frigidus by Christian historians such as Rufinus and Theodoret provide an excellent example of how historical events were now presented. Traditional Greek and Roman historians such as Thucydides and Tacitus had allowed no place for divine intervention. Events were explored through the natural and human forces that shaped them, with a strong emphasis on the activity of individuals. This made their narrative intrinsically interesting and immediate, not least as it showed how human societies worked. The historian Ammianus Marcellinus, who was probably writing his history at the very time of the battle, was heir to this tradition. There is a strong emphasis on narrative, which is full of detail of the personalities of his time and the way in which they shaped the events around them. Ammianus mentioned religion only in passing, and as such appealed to the eighteenth-century historian Edward Gibbon, who praised him in his *Decline and Fall of the Roman Empire*: 'It is not without the most sincere regret that I must now take leave of an accurate and faithful guide, who has composed the history of his own times without indulging the prejudices and passions which usually affect the mind of a contemporary.'[10]

By contrast, in the new 'Christian' history the hand of God is seen as essential to explaining the unfolding of events. The Battle of the River Frigidus is not won through the superior tactics of Theodosius but through the intervention of God via the medium of the *bora*. This confirms an approach to history that links belief in God with success in war. This had already been evident in Eusebius of Caesarea's account of the Battle of the Milvian Bridge, and in his *De Fide*, Ambrose attributed the victories of an emperor to Nicene orthodoxy, with God sending defeat to those who clung to Arianism. Ambrose's assertion in *De Fide* that Christ leads the legions shows how powerful the new ideology had become. Some sixty years later, in 452, Attila the Hun's retreat from Italy is attributed by Christian historians to a meeting with Pope Leo in which the pope persuaded him to withdraw. One version has Peter and Paul appearing with swords and threatening Attila with death if he does not do so. (The truth is perhaps more prosaic: Attila was running short of food, his army was weakened by disease and he was aware that he was vulnerable to a counterattack at his rear.) In *The Ecclesiastical History of the English People* by the Venerable Bede (AD 731), the first history of England, the Christian king Aethelfrith leads his army against the city of Chester and slaughters some 1,200 pagan priests who assembled, without weapons, to pray against him. 'Thus', wrote Bede, 'the prophecy of the holy bishop Augustine [the first missionary to England, not the theologian from North Africa] was fulfilled, namely that those heretics would suffer the vengeance of temporal death because they had despised the offer of everlasting salvation.'[11] This partisan history in which God intervenes at the right moment to ensure the triumph, violent or otherwise, of Christianity entirely lacks the psychological depth and intrinsic quality of the great historians of the classical world. It reveals the dramatic changes to intellectual life brought about during these years.

Theodosius died at Milan on 17 January 395, shortly after his victory at the river Frigidus. His body was laid in state in the cathedral and Ambrose gave the funeral oration in the presence of the ten-year-old Honorius, which claimed Theodosius and his dynasty for the service of God. While traditionally the funeral rites of an emperor would celebrate his military successes by reference to the great victories of the Roman past, Ambrose evoked instead Old Testament precedents such as the victory of Elisha over the Syrians in the Book of Kings. The emperor's campaign against paganism was highlighted. Theodosius had 'imitated Jacob in uprooting the faithlessness of the usurpers, he put the images of the pagans out of sight, for his faith put all the cults of the idols out of sight, and consigned to oblivion all their religious celebrations'. He had defeated Maximus and Eugenius, who had gone straight to hell, while he, Theodosius, 'now enjoys perpetual light and lasting tranquillity . . . he has merited the companionship of the saints'. Among these 'saints' were Gratian, Constantine and his mother Helena (part of the oration dwells on the story of her finding of the True Cross, the earliest account of this legend, and the placing of one of its nails in the imperial diadem). Valentinian II gets no mention. A prominent place was also given to the ceremony of penitence in the cathedral that Theodosius underwent after the massacre at Thessalonika. 'He wept publicly for his sin', Ambrose told his audience. 'What private citizens are afraid to do, the emperor was not ashamed to do . . . nor did a day pass thereafter on which he did not bemoan that fault of his.'[12] To Ambrose, the emperor had recognised the supremacy of the Church over temporal power.

In fact, the story was a very different one. It was the power of the emperor that had defined the Church. It was Theodosius who had provided the legal framework within which Christianity had been given dominance over paganism and the Nicene Creed precedence within Christianity. This was recognised by his Christian admirers from Ambrose onwards when they portrayed Theodosius as the quintessentially orthodox emperor who had seen off both Christian heretics and pagans. But Ambrose's rewriting of history in favour of the Church obscures the political reality. It was the emperor, not the bishops, who was seen by many as representing God on earth. The military historian Vegetius, whose account of military practice, the *Epitoma rei militaris*, was probably addressed to Theodosius when he was in Italy between 388 and 391, records a recruit's oath: 'By God and Christ and the Holy Spirit and by the emperor's majesty, which, by God's will, ought to be beloved and venerated by the human race ... For when the emperor receives the name of Augustus, faithful devotion must be given to him, as if to a deity present in the flesh [*sic*] ... For the civilian or soldier serves God when he loves faithfully him who reigns with God's authority.'[13]

In contrast to the picture presented by Ambrose, Theodosius had not been rigid in the way he imposed his faith. When he became aware of the resilience of the 'Arians', he proposed a compromise solution that, if successful, would have created a broader and more tolerant Church. He did try to rein in his more fanatical officials. But he had also initiated a policy, radically different from any that had gone before it, that allowed power to shift towards the 'Catholic' Church at the expense of other traditional beliefs – 'Arian' Christian, Jewish and pagan. In the assessment of the historian R. Malcolm Errington, Theodosius 'created a general climate of opinion within which highly-placed Christian extremists, whether bishops or court officials, could act virtually uncontrolled'.[14] Throughout the empire, debate that had been lively until 380 now withered and within Christian communities respect for authority was now placed above intellectual freedom. The consequences for the future of European thought would be immense.

X

EPIPHANIUS' WITCHHUNT

DURING the mid-370s, Epiphanius, the Nicene Bishop of Salamis in Cyprus, compiled his *Panarion*, 'a medicine chest' of remedies against heresies. 'Able but anti-intellectualist, of wide but ill-digested learning and intransigent zeal for "correct" doctrine, inordinately lacking in judgement, tact and charity, but also inordinately venerated for his force of personality, impressive bearing and rigorous asceticism', Epiphanius was a scourge of heretics.[1] He had the ability to humiliate the diffident and to draw strength from the prejudices and fears of the credulous. Epiphanius assumed that there had once been a pure faith but that it had been sullied, first of all, of course, by the sin of Adam in the Garden of Eden, but later by Hellenism and Judaism. These had their own heretical offspring; in the case of Hellenism, the followers of Plato, the Stoics, Pythagoras and Epicurus. Epiphanius then recorded no fewer than sixty Christian heresies, many associated with the debates over the Trinity, that emerged after the Incarnation. The *Panarion* is, in fact, one of the best sources for the diversity of early Christian belief. It also documents the growing obsession with heresy. Originally, the Greek word *heiresis* had meant a choice, in particular the choice of the school of philosophy an individual may have elected to follow. Now, in Christian terminology, it had come to mean a wilful rejection of orthodoxy, and any heretic was subject to the threat of eternal hell fire.

The Church had always prided itself on its apostolic tradition, the doctrine that faith had been handed on in pure form from the teachings of Christ through the apostles and on through a succession of bishops. With the declaration of the Nicene Trinity as orthodoxy, it had now to be assumed that this was the doctrine the Church must always have taught. Gregory the Great, pope from 590 to 604, claimed that even the patriarchs who lived before Moses 'knew that one Almighty God is the Holy Trinity', although he had to admit that there was little evidence that they preached about it. So where did this leave those earlier theologians who had openly preached subordinationism?

The greatest missionary of the fourth century was undoubtedly Ulfilas, who converted the Goths to Christianity in the 340s. He also translated the Bible into Gothic, inventing an alphabet for the purpose. At the time, subordinationism, as later reflected in the Homoian creed of 360, was the dominant belief in the empire, and it was passed on by Ulfilas, himself a convinced subordinationist, to the Goths, remaining a symbol of their identity after it was rejected by the rest of the empire in 381. Thus Ulfilas could never be accorded sainthood because his beliefs had now become heretical. Sainthood was now the reward for correct belief as such, not saintliness in the conventional sense of the word.

A more serious case was that of the third-century theologian Origen (*c.*184–254). Born in Alexandria of Christian parents, Origen committed himself to a life of pastoral care and study after the traumatic experience of seeing his father martyred. Although he himself believed in the ideal of celibacy, he accepted sex as a gift of God – not as an instrument of demonic possession, as some of his contemporaries did – so long as it was confined to the needs of procreation. He also believed that couples should be able to remarry after divorce on the grounds that confining their sexuality to a new marriage was a lesser evil than the alternatives. For Origen, the power of God was tempered by his readiness to forgive, and he startled his followers by arguing that Satan was not evil by nature but only because he willed himself to be evil; this will could be overcome by the forgiveness of God. While Origen believed in hell, it was only as a temporary corrective measure before the sinner was reunited with God. It made no sense, he said, to talk of a powerful and forgiving God who could be so easily thwarted by humans that he had to respond with their permanent rejection.[2]

Origen towered above his contemporaries for the range and originality of his thinking and his optimistic outlook on life. To many he was an intellectual hero: Gregory of Nazianzus believed that he was the greatest mind in Christian history.[3] Eusebius of Caesarea, the biographer of Constantine, gave him a central place in his history of the

Church, and Jerome described him in his work *Famous Men* as 'an immortal genius'.[4] His output was prodigious and his extensive library remained in Caesarea (in Palestine), where he lived for the last twelve years of his life, for his admirers such as Gregory of Nazianzus to exploit.

Origen was the first major exegetist, or interpreter, of the Bible. In one of the finest intellectual achievements of the third century, he began by putting together the different Greek versions of the Old Testament so that discrepancies could be ironed out. (He always believed that the Hebrew text was superior to the Septuagint, its Greek translation; he was one of the very few Christians with the learning to read it.) In his comments on the biblical texts, Origen championed the use of allegory; he accepted that a literal reading of the text must have some value, but greater study and prayer would always lead to a deeper moral and spiritual meaning. The story of Adam and Eve, for instance, could be interpreted symbolically as the story of the fall of mankind from grace. When they left the Garden of Eden in 'coats of skin', this should be seen as an allegory for their taking on material bodies. This creative interpretation could override textual problems, as can be seen in Origen's treatment of Jesus' cleansing of the Temple. The synoptic gospels all place this episode just before the Passion; John, in contrast, includes it early in his account of Jesus' ministry. Origen accepts that John is historically inaccurate but justified in his revised chronology because he is aiming to show that the Church needed purification: it is 'a spiritual truth in historical falsehood'.[5] With regard to the lack of references in the gospels to Jesus' divinity, Origen argued that a literal reading certainly presented Jesus as human but that his divinity within would be revealed by prayerful study of the texts, which in itself would be aided by the divine Word. He scorned those who argued for a more literal interpretation of the Bible by suggesting, for instance, that one should believe that God had physical attributes, such as eyes and hands, as the Old Testament accounts attested. For Origen, God was on a plane far above the human world. He also argued that one should not take the resurrection of the body at the Last Judgement at face value. It is a sign of his intellectual range that he drew on the works of the finest medical mind of the second century AD, the pagan Galen, to argue that the human body is always in flux and after death takes on a new ethereal form; it is in that form that it will rise at the Last Judgement.[6] This sophisticated theology won Origen many admirers

among the more intellectual Christian thinkers. He made it possible
for there to be genuine arguments over the meaning of texts and so
helped preserve the possibilities of freedom of debate within theology.
But he also had his critics. More conservative minds were unsettled
by his creative scholarship and ability to think originally about theological issues. 'The stupidity of some Christians is heavier than the
sand of the sea' was Origen's riposte.[7]

For Origen, God was pure spirit, beyond time and space, and the
very source of goodness. He had created a large number of souls who
were endowed with reason and free will. Some of these, however, had
drifted away from him. Those who remained close to the Creator might
be ensouled as angels or stars; those who drifted further might appear
in human bodies. Origen did not despise the material world: God had
created it to provide a home for fallen souls before they were reunited
with him. Unlike Augustine, who was to teach that man was so heavily
weighted with sin that he could never regain the grace of God through
his own efforts, Origen believed that the soul had powers of reason
and free will that it could harness to move towards God. In this he
was drawing on Plato's concept of an ascent through reasoned thought
to a fuller understanding of the Forms and 'the Good'.

Origen believed that Jesus had existed from the beginning of time
but that the Son was distinct from the Father and was used by him to
mediate between the Father and the inferior material world. Thus Jesus
was subordinate to the Father, who placed him within a human body
for his mission. The Holy Ghost too was subordinate and placed by
Origen at the head of the created order.

Over a century later, after the parameters of theological debate had
been narrowed by Theodosius' decree, many Christian thinkers were
still prepared to accept Origen's greatness and the depth of his theological insights while ignoring his subordinationism. But in his hunt
for heresies, Epiphanius could not let the legacy of Origen lie intact.
In his *Panarion* he attacked Origen over his subordinationism, his belief
in the pre-existence of souls and his denial of the resurrection of the
body. To Epiphanius, Origen was the arch-heretic who had inspired
Arius.

Epiphanius had been born in Palestine, and in 393, now an old man,
he returned home to extirpate the Origenist heretics he believed flourished there. His chief target was the worldly and confident Bishop of
Jerusalem, John, who was reputed to have subordinationist sympathies,

but he started his campaign by sending a band of monks to confront two of the most important intellectual figures of the region. The scholar Jerome lived in a monastery in Bethlehem, where he practised a rigid asceticism and worked on his Latin translation of the Bible; Rufinus, less ascetic and more measured in his scholarship, was settled in a monastery on the Mount of Olives. The two men had been friends since childhood and both were known for their support of Origen. Jerome's use of Origen's commentaries on the Bible was such that scholars have been able to reconstruct lost works of Origen from Jerome's plagiarism.[8] Rufinus was more of an independent scholar, and had studied the master for six years under Didymus the Blind, the famous scholar of Alexandria, who also admired Origen.

When Epiphanius' monks arrived, Rufinus barred the gates of the monastery to them and told them that they would be driven off with cudgels if they persisted in trying to enter. The welcome the rebuffed monks received from Jerome was very different. An isolated and often embittered man, Jerome had come to Bethlehem to work on his translation of the scriptures after his obsession with sexual asceticism had aroused such distaste that he had been forced to leave Rome. (He had been secretary there to Pope Damasus in the 380s.) He was known for his vituperative responses to anyone who challenged his ideas. The more notorious examples of his invective that have survived include an assault on one Jovinian, who had been unwise enough to argue that the married state was preferable to the celibate, and on a certain Vigilantius, who had deplored the credulity with which relics were venerated.

It therefore comes as a surprise that when Epiphanius' monks were ushered in, Jerome agreed at once that he would abjure Origen's works. It was a climbdown that is hard to explain. Jerome had travelled with Epiphanius to Rome on one occasion, and there may have been a friendship he did not wish to jeopardise; or he may have distinguished between Origen's exegesis, which he himself had plagiarised, and Origen's dogma, which he was ready to reject. Yet one feels that the answer lies somewhere in Jerome's desperate insecurity and emotional isolation. He simply could not risk being labelled unorthodox and so was all too ready to submit to his visitors' bullying

In September 393, Epiphanius himself arrived in Jerusalem for the so-called Dedication Festival, which drew in monks and bishops from all over the Christian world. When John allowed him to preach, the old man launched into an abusive attack on Origen which was clearly aimed at the Bishop of Jerusalem. Jerome was also there, and his account describes John and his clergy grinning like dogs, scratching their heads, nodding to each other and referring to Epiphanius as a silly old man.[9] Eventually John sent his archdeacon to shut him up. Epiphanius had gone far beyond the bounds of good behaviour in using a host cathedral to denounce its bishop. John retaliated a few days later by preaching a sermon in which he undermined his visitor by setting out his own Christian faith in such an orthodox fashion that Epiphanius had to accept that there was nothing heretical in it. This seems to have deflated Epiphanius, and he sought sanctuary with Jerome before retiring to a monastery at Besanduc, near his birthplace, that he had founded many years before. His attack on John had failed, but he had managed to push Jerome and the Bishop of Jerusalem into opposing camps.

One result was that Jerome's monastery at Bethlehem refused to have anything to do with the local clergy who remained loyal to John. At Besanduc, Epiphanius received a visit from Jerome's brother Paulinus; astonishingly, he seized the man and consecrated him as a priest to serve Jerome's monastery in Bethlehem. This was an outrageous intrusion on John's prerogatives and John retaliated by excommunicating the members of Jerome's community, forbidding any contact between them and the diocese's clergy. Epiphanius returned to Cyprus, from where he wrote a furious letter to John saying he should have been only too glad to have had extra clergy found for him and demanding that he repudiate the heretical views of Origen, which he listed in detail. John, realising by now that he was dealing with someone who was seriously deranged, wisely refused to reply. Not to be deterred, Epiphanius sent copies of his letter to all the Palestinian monasteries, urging them to sever their ties with John. Epiphanius had now succeeded in creating a state of civil war in John's diocese.

If Epiphanius lacked any sense of judgement, Jerome proved as bad. His monastery too had received a copy of Epiphanius' letter to John, which was written in Greek. One of Jerome's guests, Eusebius, from Cremona in Italy, could not speak the language and Jerome offered to provide him with a Latin translation, in which he embellished the letter to make it sound even more offensive than it was. Jerome's abusive comments littered the margins. In a farcical turn of events, the translated letter then somehow disappeared from Eusebius' desk and found its way back to John and Rufinus, who spotted the embellishments to the translation. Anxious to protect his own reputation in the west, where he feared he would now be regarded as a heretic, John let his supporters in Rome know what Jerome had done. Jerome replied with the weak argument that translators should always seek out the sense of a work rather than just make a literal translation, and this was no more than he had done.

It was to his credit that John realised that a compromise had to be found. He suggested that Theophilus, Bishop of Alexandria, should mediate. The first attempt was disastrous, because Theophilus sent as his representative one Isidore, a priest who had already written to John and Rufinus supporting their stand against Jerome. A leaked copy of the letter had reached Jerome, and he refused to accept its author as a conciliator. Theophilus persisted. A letter John sent him showed that the bishop was eager to defuse the issue, and a carefully worded letter sent by Theophilus to Jerome avoided placing any blame on him. Just as Christ had been humble and the scriptures had preached brotherly love, so too Jerome should seek peace with his bishop. Jerome's reply is another illustration of his intense social isolation. Grateful for the attention, he submitted to Theophilus' request. 'Let him [John] be as he used to be when he loved me of his own choice . . . If he shows himself like that, gladly I hold out my hands and stretch my arms to him. He will have in me a friend and a kinsman, and will find that in Christ I am as submissive to him as to all my Christian brothers.'[10] It is one of the few moments when one feels compassion for the cantankerous old scholar. Some of the details of the reconciliation that followed are obscure, but it did take place. Paulinus was welcomed as a member of John's clergy and the excommunication was lifted from Jerome's monastery. Jerome and Epiphanius no longer attacked John for Origenist heresy.

This conflict had only occurred because an orthodoxy had been proclaimed to which earlier thinkers, long since dead, were now expected to conform. An opening had been provided for unscrupulous men such as Epiphanius to exploit to the confusion and upset of all. With the rejection of Origen, one was also, of course, rejecting the tradition of free and creative scholarship of which he was such an excellent example. If Epiphanius had not intervened, scholars would have been able to continue to study Origen's works, drawing out their treasures and ignoring what they felt unable to support, just as any scholar does of his forebears. Although Origen continued to find his supporters, he was finally condemned as a heretic at the Council of Constantinople in 553.[11]

If Origen had been restored to the status he deserved, then so might have been his belief that a forgiving Father would hardly condemn human beings to eternal hell fire. Greek and Roman religion placed relatively little emphasis on the afterlife; it was concerned with life in the here and now. This did not preclude speculation on whether the soul survived as an independent entity, as Plato had argued, or a discussion on the nature of the underworld (Hades), but Christians gave far greater prominence to life after death.[12] Their powerful emphasis on reward or punishment was a significant development. There were of course references in the gospels to suffering in the hereafter for those who rejected God, but early Christians had rarely mentioned hell. Instead they concentrated on the rewards of their faith in Christ. According to *The Shepherd* of the Roman Hermas, written in about AD 140, all Christians would go straight to heaven. Others, such as Tertullian, writing some fifty years later, distinguished between martyrs, who would be rewarded in heaven, and the rest, who would remain in a waiting place underground until the Last Judgement. There are only very few references in other texts to a hell where burning takes place, and at the time Origen was writing, ideas of the afterlife were still centred on rewards for Christians rather than punishment.[13]

An important development is recorded in *On Mortality*, written by Cyprian, Bishop of Carthage, in 252. Plague had broken out in Carthage and Cyprian makes the astonishing assertion that it should be welcomed because Jews and pagans would now be thrown into hell more quickly while Christians would likewise be speeded to heaven. This can be seen as a seminal moment when, in contrast to earlier Greek tradition, disease was no longer regarded as something to be approached through observation and analysis in the hope of a cure, but rather something to be placed in the wider context of divine reward or punishment for one's beliefs.[14] *On Mortality* also makes clear that hell is now seen to be a place where non-Christians will go as a matter of course.

In the fourth century, the age of mass conversion and major controversy, the belief emerges that even Christians can be sent to hell. In the bitter debates over the Trinity, each side regularly condemned the other to everlasting punishment – as Palladius did for Ambrose in the passage already quoted (p. 110). But the most ominous shift in emphasis took place during the long life of Augustine (354–430). At the start of his theological development, when he still believed in free will and reason, Augustine argued that it was only through a conscious rejection of God that anyone could be condemned to hell. But later, when his concept of original sin gripped his ever more pessimistic imagination, he taught that no one could escape the wrath of God unless God chose to save them; if God's grace was not forthcoming, they would surely burn eternally. In the last chapters of his *City of God* (completed before his death in 430), Augustine seems to revel in the punitive and unforgiving nature of his Creator: 'The whole of mankind is a "condemned lump"; for he who committed the first sin [Adam] was punished, and along with him all the stock which had its roots in him. The result is that there is no escape for anyone from this justly deserved punishment, except by merciful and undeserved [*sic*] grace; and mankind is divided between those in whom the power of merciful grace is demonstrated, and those in whom is shown the might of just retribution.' He goes on to suggest that 'there are many more condemned by [divine] vengeance than are released by mercy'. In other words, the majority of humankind is destined to burn in hell.[15] Augustine could provide little evidence in favour of this bleak vision, but it was accepted by the Church almost without debate and became embedded in orthodox Catholic belief for centuries to come.

The condemnation of Origen was thus a profound loss to Christianity. Not only did Augustine's extreme theology make nonsense of the concept of a loving and forgiving God, but the threat of hell was now used to manipulate obedience. In the tortuous theological discussions of the fourth and fifth centuries, when the boundaries of orthodoxy were constantly shifting, each side was ready to exploit their opponents' fears. Theodosius was shrewd enough to include the threat of divine punishment for those who defied his decrees. But no free debate can take place if the participants risk being condemned to eternal suffering for suggesting ideas that Church or state might then denounce as heretical.[16]

XI

ENFORCING THE LAW

WITH heresy now defined, the active suppression of heretics gathered pace. One can trace the process by telling the story of the last years of Eunomius, known for his thoughtful advocacy of the 'unlikeness' of Father and Son. In 380, Eunomius had been able to preach freely at Chalcedon, where he had attracted a large following. He was still free to participate in the council that Theodosius called to Constantinople in 383 after strong opposition to Nicaea had forced the emperor to rethink his policy. By chance, Eunomius' submission has survived. In it, he spelled out in detail his view that the Son must be a later creation and distinct from God the Father. He concluded with the hope that his detractors would be condemned by the emperor. He must have been aware that his pleas were unlikely to be listened to, but whatever the pressures placed on him, Eunomius was not prepared to compromise on his intellectual integrity.[1]

With the reassertion of Nicene orthodoxy in 383, Theodosius moved more resolutely against the Eunomians. On 25 July 383, Eunomius was placed first in a decree that forbade Eunomians, and other named congregations, from assembling or building places of worship; six months later, another decree called for the confiscation of any existing property and the expulsion of all Eunomian clergy. One of his admirers, the historian Philostorgius, recorded that Eunomius was now forced to teach in secret: his church had become an underground organisation. Remarkably, Eunomius still had his contacts within the court of Theodosius himself, and while Theodosius was dealing with Valentinian and Maximus, he seems to have turned a blind eye to their presence. But when news reached him in Milan that there were Eunomians among the eunuchs of the imperial bedchamber, the emperor reacted with a further law in May 389 that treated these men as traitors. In the summer, Eunomius himself was arrested and exiled to Caesarea, the capital of Cappadocia, where he was allowed to live on an estate outside the town. After Theodosius' death, there were further laws against the Eunomians, and their documents could be searched for and burned. Eunomius was moved to a monastery, where he died in 396.

The use of the law to provide a respectable cover for the isolation of dissidents is familiar to us today, but it breached some very ancient conventions of the Greek and Roman worlds and marked a new departure in Roman law. As Caroline Humfress has demonstrated, in traditional Roman law there was no category of 'wrong belief'.[2] There were, however, laws against astrologers and diviners, and those accused of *maleficium*, sorcery: emperors were deeply suspicious of those who might foment unrest through foretelling the future. The Manicheans, for instance, had always been regarded with suspicion because reading the stars was an important part of their ritual. If heretics could be accused of *maleficium*, then they could be dealt with within existing law.

A key case in the development of a new approach was that of the Spanish Christian Priscillian. Priscillian set himself up as a prophetic leader who enjoined strict asceticism on his followers and who held independent and original ideas on the origin of the soul. Like so many charismatic figures, he soon built up an enthusiastic following, especially among upper-class women. He even gathered enough support to be ordained as Bishop of Avila in 380, despite having been condemned by Church leaders. Although a journey to Rome to gain the backing of Bishop Damasus ended in failure, Priscillian's return to Spain via Milan gained him some influence at court among those who opposed the growing power of Ambrose, who had sided with the Spanish bishops in rejecting Priscillian. In Spain he also had the support of the emperor's deputy, the *vicarius*. Priscillian might have been an outcast from the Church, but with the state on his side his position appeared impregnable.

Then everything changed. When Priscillian was condemned once more by a council of bishops meeting in Bordeaux, he appealed directly to Maximus, who had seized power in Gaul and set up court at Trier, in the hope that the new 'emperor' would offer him support. But the bishops launched their own prosecution of Priscillian before Maximus, which was taken up by one of Maximus' court prosecutors with the charge of offences associated with sorcery. The *maleficium* consisted of showing an interest in magical studies, holding nocturnal meetings with women and praying naked, but these flimsy charges could hardly conceal the fact that Priscillian was being targeted because he threatened the Church's authority. Maximus, uncertain of his own status, and wanting to attract the goodwill of Theodosius, chose to support the bishops, and Priscillian was found guilty and executed. This was the first time since Constantine's grant of toleration that a secular court had condemned a Christian to death primarily for his religious beliefs. It was only the beginning. 'By the end of the fourth century,' writes Caroline Humfress, 'the charge of *maleficium* had become a convenient category under which crimes relating to heresy could be subsumed.'[3]

But there still remained the problem of knowing what was and what was not heretical. In 395 the proconsul of Asia, Aurelianus, was presiding over the trial of a bishop, Heuresius, who was accused of being a follower of Lucifer, Bishop of Caglieri, who had been excommunicated. Completely out of his depth, Aurelianus wrote to the emperor Arcadius, Theodosius' son, who had succeeded him, asking for an imperial rescript on the definition of heresy. The response was uncompromising: 'Those persons who may be discovered to deviate, even in a minor point of doctrine, from the tenets and path of the Catholic religion are included within the designation of heretics and must be subject to the sanctions which have been issued against them.'[4]

In the years that followed, the definition of heresy and the treatment of heretics absorbed most of the energy of the government. The very complexity of Christian debates meant, however, that it was impossible to create a secure boundary between heresy and orthodoxy and at local level personal rivalries could easily be transformed into accusations of heresy. One such case involved the Bishop of Synnada in Phrygia, Theodosius, who travelled to Constantinople to ask for imperial help against heretics in his diocese. While he was away, these 'heretics' declared that they had converted to 'orthodoxy' and seized his churches. The advantages of holding on to the assets of a Church, its land and its buildings, made charges of 'heresy' or proclamations of 'orthodoxy' for material advantage highly attractive.

In 428, Theodosius II, the grandson of Theodosius I, was forced to put in place a more rigorous definition of heresy. As the preamble to his law suggests, it was the struggle over Church assets that was the problem. 'The madness of heretics must be so suppressed that they shall know beyond doubt, before all else, that the churches which they have taken from the orthodox, wherever they are held, shall immediately be surrendered to the Catholic church, since it cannot be tolerated that those who ought not to have churches of their own should continue to detain those possessed or founded by the orthodox and invaded by such rash lawlessness.'[5] There followed a list of heresies. First came the Arians, Macedonians and Apollinarians, then Novatianists and Sabbatians, followed by another grouping of sixteen heresies, and finally the Manicheans were listed as 'at the lowest depth of wickedness'. The silencing of theological debate followed. When, in 457, the emperor Leo I (457–474) asked the Bishop of Melitene, in Armenia, whether he wanted a council to discuss theological issues, the bishop shrewdly replied: 'We uphold the Nicene creed but avoid difficult questions beyond human grasp. Clever theologians soon become heretics.'[6] A hundred years earlier such a reply would have been an insult to the tradition of free thought, which was intrinsic to Greek culture. The very concept that there were ideas 'beyond human grasp' that should be avoided for that reason would have been incomprehensible to anyone with an educated mind.

One irrevocable loss during these years were works of theology. A law of 409 targeted at the books of heretics required their *codices* to be burned. (A *codex* was a bound book, which had by now largely replaced scrolls of papyrus.) 'If perchance any person should be convicted of having hidden any of these books under any pretext or fraud whatever and of having failed to deliver them [for burning], he shall know that he himself shall suffer capital punishment, as a retainer of noxious books and writings and as guilty of the crime of *maleficium*.'[7] This shows how elastic the 'crime' of *maleficium* had become: it could now be extended to cover even the possession of heretical books. How these books were selected and tested for orthodoxy is unknown; it is likely that the libraries of heretics were simply confiscated or destroyed.

Other laws of the first half of the fifth century document the continuing assault on paganism. Pagans were easy to isolate, and their sheer variety of deities, spiritual beliefs and philosophies made them vulnerable to the forces of organised monotheism. However, as Theodosius I had realised, there were dangers here. Although in principle the emperors supported the closing down of pagan temples, they were worried that this could lead to disorder. So when Porphyry, the Bishop of Gaza in

Syria, arrived in Constantinople in 400 to petition the emperor Arcadius for armed support in his campaign against local pagans and temples, the emperor urged caution. He told the bishop that he preferred a more gradual elimination of temple activity. However, according to the account given by Porphyry's biographer, Mark the Deacon, published after the bishop's death in 420, Porphyry won over the empress Eudoxia, and when she gave birth to a son, the future emperor Theodosius II, this was seen as a sign that God himself supported the campaign. The baby even apparently nodded his assent to the plan and Arcadius capitulated to the bishop's demands. Soldiers were provided for Porphyry, and when he returned to Gaza, the pagan temples were duly burned to the ground and their contents ransacked. To add to the humilation of the pagans, stones from the most sacred part of the sanctuary of the Temple of Marnas, which is reported to have burned for days, were repositioned as paving stones, so that they would be walked on by human and animal alike.[8]

By 423, however, there are signs that supporting or turning a blind eye to locally inspired attacks on paganism was becoming counterproductive. It was clear that Christianity was being used by opportunists as a front for the destruction of their rivals and that looting was taking place under the pretence that it was God's work. Theodosius II issued a law in an attempt to restrain the disorder. 'We especially commend those persons who are truly Christians, or who are said to be [sic], that they shall not abuse the authority of religion and dare to lay violent hands on Jews and pagans who are living quietly and attempting nothing disorderly or contrary to law. For if such Christians should be violent against persons living in security or should plunder their goods, they shall be compelled to restore not only that property which they took away, but after suit they shall also be compelled to restore triple or quadruple that amount which they robbed.'[9] It may be that this law was issued as a result of specific outrages, for by 435 the state had renewed its campaign against the resilient pagans. It was ordered that 'All persons of criminal [sic] pagan mind we interdict from accursed immolations of sacrificial victims and from damnable sacrifices . . . and we order that all their shrines, temples, sanctuaries, if any even now remain intact, should be destroyed by the magistrates' command and that these should be purified by the placing of the venerable Christian religion's sign [the Cross].'[10] But even this did not have its effect, and in a letter to the praetorian prefect of the east issued in January 438,

Theodosius opined: 'We must exercise watchfulness over the pagans and their heathen enormities, since with their natural insanity and stubborn insolence they depart from the path of the true religion. A thousand terrors of the laws that have been promulgated, the penalty of exile that has been threatened, do not restrain them, whereby, if they cannot be reformed, at least they might learn to abstain from their mass of crimes and from the corruption of their sacrifices. But straightway they sin with such audacious madness and Our patience is so assailed by the attempts of these impious persons that even if We desired to forget them, We could not disregard them.'[11] Although paganism had virtually disappeared from cities by now, it remained strong in outlying areas, and petitions to the emperors from bishops and new attempts by the authorities to quell traditional beliefs continued.

Similar examples are recorded of the marginalisation of Jews. The diatribes launched by John Chrysostom, Bishop of Constantinople between 398 and his deposition in 403, against the resurgence of Judaism in his diocese are a vivid reminder of how entrenched Christian attitudes had become. Just as Ambrose had forced Theodosius I into condoning the destruction of the synagogue at Callinicum, so 'holy men' would challenge the emperor if he was seen to be lenient. The Syriac *Life of Symeon Stylites*, for instance, includes a threat of divine retribution to the emperor for his apparent favouring of the Jews. 'Now that you have become a friend and companion and protector to unbelieving Jews, behold suddenly the righteous judgement of God will overtake you and all who are of the same mind of you in this matter. You will lift up your hands to heaven and say in your affliction, "Truly this anger has come on me because I broke faith with the Lord God."' Whether as a result of this threat or others, or even his personal inclination, Theodosius responded in 438: 'We finally sanction by this law destined to live until all ages that no Jew, no Samaritan . . . shall enter upon any honors or dignities; to none of them shall the administration of a civil duty be available, nor shall they perform even the duties of a defender of a city . . . with an equally reasonable consideration also, We prohibit any synagogue to arise as a new building.'[12] Although Jews were still free to exercise their religion in their existing synagogues, they were losing their opportunity to participate in government, and the long process by which they were segregated from 'Christian' society had begun.

The power of the state over aberrant Christian, Jewish and pagan activity was strengthened by the integration of the bishops within the judicial system. As early as 318, Constantine had allowed cases to be transferred from municipal to Church courts. By 333, any one party to a case could ask for the transfer, and it was stipulated that the testimony of bishops should be privileged over that of any other witness. This meant in effect that a Christian could arrange for his affairs to be settled by a man of his own faith, an undoubted advantage if his adversary was a pagan. There is a case from Syria in the 380s where, as reported by Libanius, a band of monks had dispossessed some peasants of their land on the pretence that it was sacred to a particular saint. When the peasants protested, they were dragged by the monks before the Church court, where the bishop ruled against them. By this period, sitting in court was a regular part of most bishops' lives. A bishop's court had the same rights as secular courts to order the torture of witnesses of low status, the imprisonment of the accused and the administration of corporal punishment, although there seem to have been some restraints on the practice. One fifth-century Syriac rule for clerics reads: 'Do not scourge anyone, but if there is a reason because of which you are compelled to scourge, either scourge to frighten, or send the guilty ones to the judges of the world [e.g. the secular courts].'[13]

The evidence for the work of episcopal courts is surprisingly fragmentary. Bishops had held jurisdiction over their own communities well before Constantine's law gave them access to other cases, and there had already been an established tradition of Christian law. A document known as the *Apostolic Constitutions* of 380 gives guidelines under which bishops should operate. Their role for violators of Christian conduct, the *Constitutions* notes, was to be like a good physician who removes afflicted parts of a body to restore the whole to good health. This, of course, gave them the freedom to deal with heretics, who could be defined as 'diseased flesh'.[14] The bishops appear to have adopted those laws of the state that specifically concerned religious issues. These included the laws of apostasy, for instance, which condemned Christians who turned to pagan rites, to altars or temples, to sacrifices or idolatry, to Jewish rites or 'the infamy of the Manicheans'. The bishop's court now became the forum where such cases were settled, and even seem to have developed their own case law. Basil of Caesarea and Gregory of Nyssa are known to have broadened the definition of apostasy given by imperial law to include the practice of magic. In short, the ecclesiastical and secular courts were working in conjunction with each other in the upholding of Christian orthodoxy, a process that was to continue and reach its climax in the eastern empire in the reign of Justinian in the sixth century. In the west, it is evident that Augustine conducted the major campaign he waged against the Donatists largely through his court.

While free discussion of the issue was now limited, the premature 'settlement' of the Trinity by Theodosius in 381 had left important questions unresolved. The one that was to consume the eastern Church for many years to come was how to relate the fully divine Jesus, one in substance with the Father, to Jesus as a human being as he appeared in the gospels. What was the nature of Jesus' divinity while he was on earth? Was it somehow suspended at the moment of his birth and taken up again at the Resurrection, or did it persist throughout his earthly ministry? Could he, for instance, have a divine soul, of a different quality from that of an ordinary human being, in a human body? When Mary gave birth, what did she give birth to – a man or a god? In his everyday life, did Jesus pass backwards and forwards from divinity to humanity, acting as divine when he carried out miracles and as human when he ate and drank with his disciples? Were his teachings to be allocated to either his divine or his human capacity according to their content? Did his divinity affect the degree to which he could endure the suffering he apparently underwent for the saving of mankind?[15]

When the problem had been discussed in the early Church, two opposing parties emerged. The Adoptionists, on the one hand, believed that Jesus was fully human but had been 'adopted' by God, at either his birth, his baptism or his resurrection. But the 'divinity' conferred on him by his adoption in no way compromised his humanity and he suffered for mankind on the Cross without any lessening of the agony that other humans would feel. At the other extreme were the Docetists, who argued that while Jesus went through the motions of being human, he was actually divine all the time. Clement of Alexandria, for instance, claimed that while Jesus appeared to eat and drink, he did not actually digest the food or have any need to excrete waste! It somehow just disappeared. The problem this approach left was whether he could actually suffer on the Cross if his body was not subject to human feelings and pain. Without any pain, the Crucifixion was hardly an impressive act of salvation.

There was a great deal of open ground, one might say, in the bitter debate that followed, a hotly contested 'no man's land' between these extremes. After 381, the debate was made more, rather than less, difficult by the need to reconcile a definition of Jesus' humanity with Nicene orthodoxy. Arius had avoided the problem simply by saying that Jesus was a lesser divinity and that his divinity was never so great as to deprive him of the pain of suffering. Now this option was no longer open to orthodox Christians, and the debate reached a new level of intractability as a result. The wrangling that followed was intensified by the rivalry between the bishops of 'upstart' Constantinople and of Alexandria, which still festered at the loss of its ancient status in 381.

A new Bishop of Constantinople, Nestorius, took office in 428. He claimed to be a scourge of heretics, and in his inaugural sermon before Theodosius II he asked for imperial support in his crusade, in return for which he promised victory in war: 'Give me, king, the earth purged of heretics, and I will give you heaven in return. Aid me in destroying heretics, and I will assist you in vanquishing the Persians.'[16] Such, however, was the confusion over what was or was not orthodoxy and the personal and political antagonisms of the period that very soon it was Nestorius who was declared the heretic! He had, perhaps unwisely, entered the debate over the humanity of Jesus by suggesting that the redemption of mankind might be threatened if the human side of Jesus was submerged and that Mary could hardly be called the mother of God, not least because this risked making her into a goddess herself. Cyril, Bishop of Alexandria from 412 to 444, saw his chance to challenge the diocese of Constantinople through its bishop. Cyril wished to emphasise the divinity of Christ, notably by according Mary the title *theotokos*, 'bearer of God'. The Alexandrian preference was for a Jesus 'of one nature', with a divine soul and a human body, in other words, the divinity of Jesus having a much higher status than the humanity. Cyril launched bitter accusations of heresy against Nestorius, unscrupulously misrepresenting his views in the process.

Theodosius responded to this dispute in 431 by summoning a council to Ephesus but he neglected to provide sufficient imperial supervision. Cyril and his supporting bishops arrived early and bullied their way to success not least through bribery of Theodosius' court; this was so extensive that Cyril's own clergy in Alexandria complained their diocese had been reduced to poverty. The emperor deposed Nestorius, but when faced with immense outrage from Nestorius' supporters, he backtracked and forced Cyril to accept a statement that Christ was both perfect god and perfect man and as the latter, 'one in substance' with humanity. The title *theotokos* was allowed to stay, with the result that this statement, accepted by Cyril in 433, was somewhere between Cyril's original position and that of Nestorius.

Even so, Nestorius remained condemned. His was a new 'heresy' – the difficulty lay in pinning down what it was. To give some legal status to the condemnation, Theodosius defined it through classifying it. Nestorius was declared a follower of the first-century 'magician' Simon Magus, regarded by some as 'the father of all heresy'. In 435, a law decreed: 'Since Nestorius, the leader of a monstrous teaching, has been condemned, it remains to apply to those who share his opinions and participate in his impiety a condemnatory name, so that they may not, by abusing the appellation of Christians, be adorned by the name of those from whose doctrines they have impiously separated themselves. Therefore we decree that those everywhere who share in the unlawful doctrines of Nestorius are to be called "Simonians" ... We also decree that no one should dare to possess or read or copy the impious books of the said lawless and blasphemous Nestorius concerning the pure religion of the orthodox, and against the doctrines of the sacred synod of the bishops of Ephesus. These books it is required to seek out with every eagerness and burn publicly ...'[17]

The law was extended against named followers of Nestorius, and probably also in 435, it decreed 'that Irenaeus [Bishop of Tyre] who not only followed the accursed sect of Nestorius, but promoted it, and took steps along with him to subvert many provinces, to the extent that he himself was at the head of this heresy, having been stripped of all his ranks and also of his own property ... should endure exile in Petra, so that he may be tormented by lifelong poverty and the solitude of the region'.[18]

Nestorius' triumphant adversary, Cyril, was unscrupulous in many ways, but he was an able theologian. Rather than supporting his beliefs with texts from scripture, however, he relied on selected Church fathers, notably Athanasius, to whom he credits the title *theotokos*. [19] As we have noted, the Nicenes had found it difficult to refute the many sayings of Jesus that suggested he was subordinate to God the Father; now, a hundred years later, theologians were substituting later authorities for the gospels. In 448, a small synod of bishops met at Constantinople to deal with Eutyches, a monk who was accused of heresy as one who claimed that Christ had only one nature. When Eutyches said that he accepted the teachings of the Holy Fathers at Nicaea but preferred to rely on scripture for his beliefs as it was more trustworthy than the Church fathers, his statement was met with 'disturbance'. Everyone knew by now just how intractable an issue would become if the scriptures had to be consulted for elucidation. This shift to reliance on later sources, and authorities, marked an important development in the history of theology that was to reach its culmination in the declaration of the Council of Trent (1545–63) that scripture itself is not to be interpreted 'in any other way than in accordance with the unanimous agreement of the Fathers'.

When Cyril died in 444, his successor as Bishop of Alexandria, Dioscorus, attacked the concessions he believed Cyril had made to the Nestorians in accepting that Jesus had two natures. Dioscorus wished to emphasise the divinity of Christ in line with the declaration of Mary as *theotokos*, and claimed to support the 'one nature' of Jesus formula that Cyril had held before his concessions of 433. Tension rose when it was discovered that Nestorians, including Irenaeus, were regaining their influence in the area around Antioch, where Nestorius had been exiled. After successful complaints to the emperor, a new law was issued in 448 that reveals how Theodosius saw his role as the representative of God on earth: 'We think it appropriate to our kingship to remind our subjects about piety. For we think that thus it is the more possible to gain the goodwill of our Lord and Saviour Jesus Christ when it is the case both that we are zealous so far as is in our power to please him and we stimulate those subject to us to that end.' In practice this meant that 'Since it has come to our pious ears that certain men have written and published teachings which are dubious and not precisely in accord with the orthodox faith as set out by the holy synod of holy fathers who assembled at Nicaea and at Ephesus and by Cyril [of Alexandria] we order that any such writings, coming into existence, whether formerly or now, should be burned and committed to complete annihilation, so as not even to come to public reading, with any who can bear to own or read such compositions in books being liable to the extreme penalty.'[20] Such a sweeping law could be interpreted to include virtually any writing defined by the state or a local bishop as unorthodox. It is impossible to know how many works actually were burned, but the historian Averil Cameron notes that, in the east, 'Books ceased to be readily available and learning became an increasingly ecclesiastical preserve; even those who were not ecclesiastics were likely to get their education from the scriptures or from [orthodox] Christian texts.'[21] It marks a major blow to the literary culture that had been so deep-rooted among Christians and pagans alike.

In 449, Dioscorus masterminded his own council in Ephesus to which the Bishop of Rome, Leo, contributed a compromise formula. But his episcopal statement, pleading for a two-nature formula under which Jesus would be seen as divine when he was performing miracles and human when he showed any form of weakness, came close to Nestorius' original proposal and Dioscorus would not even allow it to be read. The council then degenerated into violence and intimidation. The Bishop of Constantinople, Flavian, was beaten up and died soon afterwards; Leo, furious at his rejection, denounced the fractious assembly as 'a robber council'.[22]

Theodosius II died in 450, after the longest reign of any emperor, some forty-two years. Pulcheria now took as her consort one Marcian, a soldier, who was elevated to emperor. He was keen to win the political support of the alienated Leo, not least because he needed to shore up the west from collapse at the hands of the Germanic invaders. So Marcian summoned yet another council, which eventually met in 451 at Chalcedon. The *acta* of the council are remarkable for being headed not by the names of church leaders but by that of the emperor and a list of his senior officials. Marcian began by asking the bishops to provide their own statement, but when it arrived, his legal advisers condemned it as muddled and not much different from what had been agreed at the 'robber council'. The imperial officials now drew up their own document, which, in order to reconcile Leo to the process, incorporated his *tome* as well as some of Cyril's assertions.

The 'Chalcedonian formula' that the officials produced acknowledged that Jesus was both truly God and truly man, of the same substance with the Father in the Godhead but also in one substance with 'us' in manhood, except as regarded sin. Mary was confirmed as *theotokos*, the bearer of God. Yet within the single *hypostasis* – person – of Jesus, there were two natures, human and divine, which existed as distinct, 'without change, without division, without separation'. This explained nothing. As Christopher Stead puts it: 'The Chalcedonian definition was a fairly limited achievement; it was a statement of the conditions that had to be met, within a given horizon of thought, for a satisfactory doctrine of Christ; it did not amount to a positive solution.'[23] It remained unclear whether the two natures had existed before the Incarnation – if so, would not this make it less likely that Father and Son could be called 'of one substance'? – or whether the human nature of Jesus was grafted on, as it were, at the moment of his birth, which would make Mary's title of *theotokos* less easy to justify. It was hard to imagine how one being could combine human and divine natures without the divinity, especially as defined by Nicaea, not dominating the human. Again how could Jesus' humanity be of 'one substance' with the rest of humanity if he was also distinct from the rest of humanity in being unable to sin? The bishops, either as a result of imperial pressure or because they felt the text adequate, accepted it, even though the 'two natures' formula smacked of Nestorianism. To underline the point that Christian belief was now firmly integrated into the state, Marcian insisted that his army officers swear allegiance to the new creed.

In the west, the Chalcedonian settlement was seen as a triumph for Leo. It was, in fact, the very first time a Bishop of Rome had successfully intervened in the making of Church doctrine. Leo was a determined and forceful man and he cleverly linked the formula to his own papal authority. The debate had never been as heated in the west, and the declaration of a Christ of two natures was soon accepted. But no proper theological explanation was produced, and when in 513 a Greek bishop asked a later Bishop of Rome, Symmachus, for an authoritative untangling of the problem, the philosopher Boethius reported that the request caused great consternation. It was regarded as a settled matter, upheld by the papacy as part of Christian doctrine and thus not open to further discussion.[24]

In the east, however, the council proved to be, in the words of Patrick Gray, 'a monumental disaster'.[25] The Alexandrian clergy could not believe that the council had accepted a formula that was so close to Nestorius' belief, and in Egypt and Syria hardline factions emerged that firmly rejected Chalcedon. Again monks caused disruption and in 452 Marcian had to respond: 'Your outrageous behaviour, in violation of the rules laid down for monks, has brought on a regular war levied against the common good order, has collected crowds of gangsters and other such habitual criminals; has stirred up arms for slaughter and devastation and every ill among those resident in the countryside.'[26] Moreover, Marcian insisted that the monks were not capable of discussing theological issues. But those who believed in a single nature of Christ, the Monophysites as they later came to be known, claimed that they stood for the true Church and insisted that they would eventually triumph over the Nestorians as the Nicenes had done a century before over the machinations of the Arians. In the next sixty years, emperor after emperor tried to find a formula that would reconcile them to the Chalcedonians, but without success. With time, their intransigence became more and more deep-rooted, and even the masses became conversant with every word of the debate. In the 490s there were riots in Constantinople when a new liturgy contained a phrase that appeared to tend towards Monophysitism.

In 527, the greatest emperor of late antiquity, Justinian, came to the throne of the eastern empire. He was backed by his determined wife Theodora, whom he had raised from a dubious past as a circus artiste. Justinian had his bad moments, especially during the Nika riots of 532, when only the resolution of Theodora, who sent in the troops to massacre the insurgents, saved his throne, but he showed immense resilience in his plan for the regeneration of the empire. The western empire had fallen with the abdication of the last emperor, Romulus Augustulus, in 476, but Justinian reconquered northern Africa and, after a protracted and destructive campaign, much of Italy. He now had extra grain supplies from Africa in addition to those arriving in Constantinople from Egypt. Unlike the fledgling successor states of the west, the Byzantine Empire was able to sustain its trade routes, and some areas, such as the hinterland of Antioch and Gaza, are known to have become prosperous on the export of oil and wine. City life continued, though at a reduced level, whereas it disappeared almost completely in the west. In short, Justinian was able to maintain a secure border, guarded by fortresses on the eastern frontier, and still have the resources to create one of the finest buildings of late antiquity, the church of Santa Sophia, at a time when church building in the west had virtually ceased.

Justinian also tried to find a solution to the theological controversy that was splitting his empire. He was not a theologian but, like his predecessors, he believed in religious unity under the auspices of an emperor appointed by God. His famous law codes (promulgated between 529 and 534), which brought together a thousand years of Roman law into a coherent body of interlocking texts, were issued in the joint names of Lord Jesus Christ and the emperor himself. In one of his laws of the 530s, he ordered all to come forward for Christian baptism. 'Should they disobey, let them know that they will be excluded from the state and will no longer have any rights of possession, neither goods or property; stripped of everything, they will be reduced to penury, without prejudice to the appropriate punishments that will be imposed on them.'[27] The death penalty was decreed for all who followed pagan cults. In 526, the last Egyptian temple had been closed down, and in 529, the philosophers in Plato's Academy, which had survived for 900 years, were dispersed.[28] 'The sixth century is a period in which the philosophical glory that was Greece is wearing thin,' writes one scholar. 'Philosophers, and especially pagan ones, are rare birds indeed, flocking together for shelter and survival in various parts of the empire.'[29] A great intellectual tradition had withered.

This determined attempt to create a unified Christian state was marred by the continuing debate over the Chalcedon formula. When he came to power, Justinian originally accepted Chalcedon. He knew its Nestorian features would earn him the support of the people of his capital, Constantinople, Nestorius' own see, and that it would also keep open a channel to the Church in Rome. He was unwilling to jettison Chalcedon in search of a new settlement, but he thought it might be possible to find a way of getting the intransigent Christians in Egypt and Syria back into the Chalcedonian fold. His first manoeuvres to draw them in failed as miserably as those of his immediate predecessors, and by the 540s he had hit on another approach: if he could condemn Nestorianism outright, notably the Three Chapters, the works of three key Nestorian theologians, then the anti-Chalcedonians might soften. It was a tricky strategy because these theologians, Theodore of Mopsuestia, the historian Theodoret, an opponent of Cyril, and Ibas, Bishop of Edessa, had been considered orthodox in their day. Justinian desperately needed the support of the Bishop of Rome, Vigilius, and the western bishops if he was to make any progress. Vigilius was summoned to Constantinople, where Justinian bullied him into supporting the condemnation of the Three Chapters. But the emperor's action had the opposite effect. By now the Chalcedonian formula had achieved a sacred status in the west, and there was no support there for changing it, especially as this meant condemning works by those who had been assumed to be orthodox Christians. The western bishops were furious that Vigilius had betrayed them, and the North African bishops even united to excommunicate him. When Justinian called a council to Constantinople in 553, it proved a disaster. Pope Vigilius, caught between the emperor and the western bishops, found an excuse for not attending. His absence was concealed in the final edition of the Acts of the Council so that his opposition to Justinian was not made public, but the Three Chapters were condemned at the council. The hapless Vigilius later announced that he *did* support the condemnation, but he had misjudged the anger of his fellow western bishops at his betrayal. After he died, on his way back to Rome, his body was refused burial in St Peter's. In response to the council's decision, the anti-Chalcedonians now set up their own Churches, resulting in the Coptic Church in Egypt and the Jacobite Church in Syria. They preached that Jesus had only one nature, even though this contained both divine and human elements, in contrast to the 'two nature' formula of Chalcedon.[30]

Although the Council of Constantinople of 553 had failed in its aim of bringing peace between the factions, among its acts was a statement of how Christian orthodoxy was to be judged. The council pledged its allegiance to 'the things we have received from Holy Scripture and from the teachings of the Holy Fathers and from the definitions of one and of the same faith by four sacred councils'. In addition, all these so-called councils – the Council of Nicaea of 325, the Council of Constantinople of 381, the Council of Ephesus in 431 and the Council of Chalcedon of 451 – which had been subject to imperial pressures and in many cases had been unrepresentative of the Church as a whole, were now given special status as ecumenical, i.e. of the whole Church, councils. By 600, in Rome, Pope Gregory the Great was equating these four councils with the four gospels as the cornerstones of Christian orthodoxy.

But with the possible exception of Ephesus in 431, when the machinations and bribery of Cyril shaped the proceedings and led the way to his desired outcome, it was the emperors who had actually defined Christian doctrine. This definition was then incorporated into the legal system so that orthodoxy was upheld by both secular and Church law, and heretics were condemned by the state. It is important to reiterate just how radical a development this was and the degree to which it diminished intellectual life. There were still those who stood apart from the Church – the Monophysites in the east, the Donatists and the Arian Goths in the west – but these could be treated as outside the law, as were pagans and Jews. The legal codes of Justinian reiterated the suppression of the rights of Jews in civic, economic and religious spheres, and they were subject to continued abuse in theological tracts as well as assaults on their synagogues.[31]

With orthodoxy enforced, the Greek mind turned inwards. The most influential religious thinker of the age was Dionysius; his works were claimed to be those of Dionysius the Areopagite, who was described in the Acts of the Apostles as a follower of Paul. This gave him un-rivalled status, even though the evidence now suggests that his works date not from the first century but from as late as AD 500. Dionysius was a mystic, and he described how the human soul could ascend towards deification to become lost in the mystery of God. As he put it in his *Mystical Theology*:

'My argument now rises from what is below up to the transcendent and the more it climbs, the more language falters, and when it has passed up and beyond the ascent, it will turn silent completely [*sic*], since it will finally be at one with him who is indescribable.'[32] Otherworldliness and a reluctance to have any reasoned debate on the nature of the Godhead now pervaded the Byzantine world. 'Even know-ledge and discourse themselves are limited to the dim perceptions allowed in the human world, through the signs and messengers that God chooses to vouchsafe.'[33]

Justinian stands in a direct line from Theodosius' laws of 381 and brings them to their logical conclusion, the creation of an empire based on a single monolithic faith. Even those laws of Theodosius that had been applied to a single prefecture were now extended in the Code to the whole of the rest of the empire. But, as this chapter has shown, heresy and orthodoxy were defined largely as the result of power strug-gles within the Church, with the opposing factions competing for impe-rial support. The state, in its turn, often had to intrude simply to restore order. Once the state had decided to intervene in support of orthodoxy and in opposition to heresy, the outcome was an authoritarianism based on irrational principles, which presided over the demise of ancient traditions of reasoned debate.[34]

XII

AUGUSTINE SETS THE SEAL

ON the death of Theodosius in 395, the empire was divided between his two sons, Honorius and Arcadius. As we have seen in Chapter Eleven, in the eastern empire the precedent set by Theodosius, under which Christian doctrine was enforced by the state with the support of the Church, culminated in the theocratic state of Justinian. In the west, in contrast, political authority was crumbling fast and no emperor was in a position to impose orthodoxy as Justinian had done in the east. The intellectual climate was also very different. The Romans had never been great philosophers. Even Cicero, one of their most original minds, had largely absorbed his ideas from Greek sources. In the Christian era, the gap between the east and west grew ever wider, largely because the number of Romans who could read Greek fell dramatically. It is often forgotten just how isolated the western Church was from its much more sophisticated sister in the east. In vain did Augustine write to Jerome for more translations of Greek theological works; many of the greatest never reached the west. Even the gospels were known only through inadequate translations and no Latin speaker seemed to have been able to read the letters of the apostle Paul in the original Greek until the late fifteenth century.[1] No Bishop of Rome and virtually no westerners had attended any of the major Church councils, and the Latin translations of their proceedings that reached Rome were incomplete; Augustine was unaware of the Council of Constantinople of 381, which had taken place only a few years before his conversion.

The combined efforts of Theodosius, his successors and Ambrose had been to ensure that Nicene orthodoxy was imposed in the west.

All this might have been lost in the ensuing breakdown of order if a rationale for an authoritarian Church wedded to the doctrine of the Nicene Trinity had not been articulated by Augustine. Augustine provided the theological façade that allowed the Church to consolidate the status and authority it would never have achieved without Theodosius' initiatives.

Augustine cannot be understood outside his own exploitation of the theology of Paul. In the Greek world, in the first century AD, Paul's letters and theology had laid the foundations for a Christianity that took root outside Judaism. Later he became less influential. In the second century he had been championed by Marcion (see p.43), but Marcion had been declared a heretic. The Church father Tertullian went so far as to call Paul 'the apostle of the heretics'.[2] Paul suffered further by becoming associated with Gnosticism, a movement rejected by the mainstream Church in the third century, and with the despised Manicheans, who placed him second to Mani as a religious leader. As a result, many theologians wrote their works without any reference to Paul, and those that have survived often concern his personality rather than his letters. He is, for instance, presented as the companion to one Thecla, whom he converted, but to whom some accounts give greater prominence than they do to Paul. At the beginning of the fourth century, when Constantine built the first great churches of Rome, that erected in honour of St Peter was one of the largest, while the supposed place of Paul's martyrdom on the road to Ostia was marked by no more than a small shrine.

It is only in the final decades of the fourth century that Paul became of interest in the west. In the 380s, a massive basilica was built around his shrine, financed by many Christian grandees, including Theodosius himself. In the first depiction of Christ in Majesty, in the church of San Pudenziana in Rome (390), Peter is accorded the place of honour at Christ's right hand, but Paul comes next, immediately on Christ's left. This is a dramatic and unexpected elevation.

The roots of this change can be traced to the 360s, when one Marius Victorinus produced the first Latin commentary on Paul. Little is known of Victorinus, who appears to have been African by birth and a teacher of rhetoric in Rome. Jerome writes that 'in extreme old age, yielding himself to faith in Christ, he wrote some very obscure books against Arius in a dialectical style,which can only be understood by the learned, as well as commentaries on the apostle Paul'.[3] However difficult

Victorinus is to read – and one modern commentator confesses to finding him 'totally incomprehensible'⁴ – he reflects a new interest in Paul. Five more Latin authors, including Jerome and Augustine, would produce Pauline commentaries by 410. Paul's most popular text was the Letter to the Romans, which comes to predominate over his other writings to such an extent that it has been called 'one of the most influential documents of western history'.⁵ Some fifty commentaries on Romans had been written in the Latin-speaking west by 1300, although many of these were derived from earlier ones. In contrast, there is little interest in Romans in the east, where theologians were drawn to the more mystical impulses of Pauline theology, his Christology, and his teachings on the sacraments and the Holy Spirit.⁶

For the historian of ideas, the question is why, after centuries of neglect, Paul suddenly became so prominent. A clue might be found in a poem written in 416 by a Christian in Gaul who was watching the empire collapse around him.

> This man groans for his lost silver and gold,
> Another is racked by the thought of his stolen goods,
> And of his jewellery now divided amongst Gothic brides,
> This man mourns for his stolen flock, burnt houses, and drunk wine
> And for his wretched children and ill-omened servants.
> But the wise man, the servant of Christ loses none of these things,
> Which he despises; he has already placed his treasure in heaven.⁷

To those who had been used to the security of living in the comparative peace and stability of the Roman empire, the disruptions of the fourth and early fifth centuries must have been devastating. One only has to read the accounts of the shock effect of the sack of Rome in 410 to sense the disorientation the news, often spread by refugees, brought with it. It is always hard to evoke the mentality of an age, but one can sense the helplessness of those who lived through these years and, as a response, the readiness to see salvation in another world.

With this in mind, the sudden popularity of Paul's Letter to the Romans makes sense. The letter was written probably in AD 57 with the aim of securing the assistance of the Roman Christian community in a mission to Spain that Paul hoped to undertake, yet its importance is as one of the fullest and most penetrating expositions of Paul's theology. His own vision of God that he set out in his letter is not a comforting one: God bristles with anger at those who have offended him. The entire human race is sunk in depravity, 'under the power of sin'. Throughout the letter, 'sin' is presented as a malign power that holds humanity in its grasp. 'God has imprisoned all human beings in their own disobedience' (Romans 11:32). Paul has a particular obsession with sexual misconduct, 'the filthy enjoyments and practices with which they [non-Christians] dishonour their own bodies' and the 'degrading passions' that cause both sexes to commit homosexual acts. (Romans 1:24–32). Not only is the human race mired in sin, any search for salvation through living according to the Jewish law, or, indeed, any system of law, is deeply flawed. Having dismissed humanity's own efforts to set itself right with God, Paul tells his readers that they can only be made righteous through the grace of God as a result of the crucifixion of his son, Jesus Christ. 'Sin will have no dominion over you, since you are not under Law, but under grace' (Romans 6:14). The crucifixion has, in fact, transcended the Jewish Law: the traditional observance of it has been replaced by need of faith in Christ: 'We shall be saved by him from the wrath of God.'

The two crucial premises that underlie the theology of 'justification through faith' that Paul develops in Romans are, therefore, the wrath of God and the inadequacy of human efforts to regain his pleasure as a result of the pervasive power of sin. Hence the need for Christ's sacrifice on the Cross. Paul's theology has become so deeply embedded in the Christian tradition that other ways of conceiving the human condition have been obliterated. Is he right in saying that anger is such a dominant feature of God and that human beings are helpless? What evidence can he provide for his assertion that sin settles like a stifling blanket over all human endeavour? Origen, after all, put forward an alternative position in which God is essentially forgiving and souls are endowed with the free will and reason to make their own way towards him. As so often in the Christian theological tradition, different conceptions of God are in conflict here (even if these conflicts are usually obscured in introductions to theology), and it is hard to find a means to resolve the differences between them.

We do not know what influences impelled Paul to create such a pessimistic picture of God and humanity. Although no direct connection has been made between Paul and the Essenes, the Qumran community whose activities are recorded in the Dead Sea Scrolls, there are numerous similarities in their ways of thinking. The Essenes were deeply ascetic and found sexuality, in particular, repugnant. They saw the world as one divided into light and darkness and were required 'to love all the children of light and abhor all the children of darkness, each one according to the guilt, which delivers him up to God's retribution'. This comes close to the punitive god of Paul, who divides the world into saved and unsaved.[8] Paul's own personality also seems relevant. In Romans itself he tells how 'I have been sold as a slave to sin. I fail to carry out the things I want to do, and I find myself doing the very things I hate ... I know of nothing good living in me' (Romans 7:14–20). This is a man who feels unable to fight 'the sin' within himself. Perhaps it is not surprising that he envisages the whole of humanity in a similar state. But it is also important to note that Paul was writing at a time when the second coming of Christ was widely predicted, and his letters, which reflect the urgency to commit oneself to Christ before it is too late, were never intended to become the theological treatises into which they were turned by later commentators.

The writings of a man who believed that all are helpless before the wrath of God were now discovered in an age that could well believe itself to be suffering this wrath. A work that had been neglected in the west for 300 years suddenly found a new audience. This might have proved a temporary phenomenon, with interest in Paul waning as life became more settled in later centuries, if Paul had not been taken up by Augustine and turned into a cornerstone of western theology so that, as one scholar, Paula Fredriksen, has written, 'much of Western Christian thought can be seen as one long response to Augustine's Paul'.[9]

Born at Thagaste in northern Africa in 354, Augustine had studied at the university at Carthage. For some time in his twenties, when he was teaching in Carthage, he was attached to the Manicheans, and it must have been then that he first came across Paul. Like Paul, the Manicheans were preoccupied with good and evil, light and darkness, and had a morbid fear of the physical world. When he moved to Italy in 383, first to Rome, and then to Milan, where he became the city orator, Augustine rejected the Manicheans and progressed through an extensive study of Plato and his followers, towards Christianity. It was, however, a tortuous process for him to reach a resolution of his inner uncertainties, a process brilliantly described some years later in his *Confessions*, in which he tells the reader how his conversion was eventually effected by reading a verse of Paul from the Letter to the

Romans (13:13–14): 'Not in revelling and drunkenness, not in lust and wantonness, not in quarrels and rivalries. Rather arm yourself with the Lord Jesus Christ: spend no more thought on nature and nature's appetites.' Augustine now adopted Paul as a Christian rather than a Manichean mentor.

After he had moved back to North Africa in 388, Augustine first became a priest and then, in 395, bishop of the coastal city of Hippo. It was in the 390s that he developed what can only be described as an obsession with Paul, although, unable to read Greek, he was dependent on Latin translations of the linguistically complex originals. Between 391 and 395, he wrote two commentaries on Romans, three substantial treatises on questions arising from Chapters Seven to Nine, and a response to queries on the letter from an old friend from Milan, Simplicianus. It was in this last letter that he set out his belief that, in line with Paul's thinking, all human beings are doomed to be mired in sin and it is only through the grace of God, which no one merits, that one can be saved. Why God picks out anyone from the humanity that has fallen away from him as a result of the sin of Adam is, to Augustine, *occultissima*, 'totally unclear'. (It is similarly unclear what Augustine means when he describes God as 'loving', although he once made an analogy with a schoolmaster who beats his pupils because he 'loves' them.) It is in his letter to Simplicianus that he uses the term *peccatum originale*, 'original sin', for the first time, and in future years he developed this to argue that even at birth no one is free of the sin of Adam, which has been passed through the act of sexual intercourse from generation to generation. By now the belief in hell had become firmly embedded in Christian thought, and it was to hell that all, even unbaptised infants, would go for eternity unless God reached down to save them. It was the integration of Augustine's pessimism with the emerging doctrine of eternal hell fire that made the implications of his theology so unsettling. It is hardly surprising that he faced opposition, even outrage, from his contemporaries, but in the important debate with Pelagius, who did believe in the free will of the individual to do good, he prevailed, and the concept of 'original sin' became part of Christian doctrine.[10]

Yet even if there is little one can do to save oneself, the believer should still aim to lead a Christian life by following the teachings of the Church. By the 390s, Nicene orthodoxy was as much part of the Church in the west as it was in the east, even if it was difficult to enforce in an empire that was being invaded by Germanic tribes who were 'Arians'. In North Africa, the imperial Church instituted by Constantine (see p. 50 above) was in a minority as the Donatists still dominated the region. There remained sophisticated subordinationists among the Latin-speaking believers, and one of these, Maximinus, had a famous public debate with the elderly Augustine in 427 that many observers felt ended in Maximinus' favour. [11] Whatever the later dominance of Augustine's position within the medieval Church, in his own time he was an embattled figure, even in his own diocese.

Augustine had absorbed from his readings of Plato the idea of an unchanging truth that exists 'above' in an immaterial world but is intelligible to humans, and he adopted this concept in an early work after his conversion, *Contra Academicos*, 'Against the Sceptics' (386–387). But while for Plato this truth could only be found through a long process of reasoning – he did not expect his 'Guardians', an intellectual elite in themselves, to fully understand the immaterial world before the age of fifty – Augustine bypassed this long journey (and with it the process of reasoning itself) and argued that one could find truth by a leap of faith. One of his favourite texts was Isaiah 7:9: 'Unless you believe you will not understand.' In other words, if one absorbed a belief, for instance about the Trinity, then the act of believing wholeheartedly would lead to an understanding of the doctrine. This leap of faith was based on trust in God: 'For we do not yet see our good, and hence we have to seek it by believing and it is not in our power to live rightly, unless while we believe and pray we receive help from him [God], who has given us the faith to believe that we must be helped by him.' [12]

Augustine's use of the word 'faith', *pistis* in Greek, *fides* in Latin, shows up the difficulties of the term. To have faith in someone is to show trust in them. This is essentially an emotional or intuitive response that may not involve reason at all. Jesus' disciples doubtless had faith in him and Augustine asks his readers to have a similar trust in God. He is aware that one's faith, in individuals, for instance, can lead one astray, but once one has a trust in God, then that in itself validates the faith. This is understandable – we can recognise that in everyday human relationships trust in another person evokes trust in return and so cements the relationship, and this analogy could certainly be used of a relationship with God. Yet Augustine also goes on to talk of 'the content of faith'. By this he means the teachings of the Church as contained, for instance, in the creed. These must be believed because they are taught through the authority of the Church.

So where did the authority of the Church as the arbiter of doctrine come from? Augustine had to give pride of place to the scriptures, but as anyone who has tried to draw any kind of coherent theology from the mass of writings of the Old and New Testament knows, this could soon lead to problems. The Arian debates had shown that both sides were able to quote the scriptures ad infinitum without convincing their opponents. The interpretation of the scriptures had therefore to be placed in the hands of the Church, and this in effect meant that scripture came to be interpreted so as to support what had become established by the Church as orthodoxy. The core of orthodoxy was, of course, the Nicene Trinity. Yet if the thesis of this book is right, this doctrine had only become orthodox because it had been enforced by the state. The underlying problems in the making of Christian theology, and thus defining the specific doctrines that make up 'the content of faith', are clear. A doctrine might become established, perhaps through law, and then scripture had to be interpreted to support it, rather than the doctrine growing organically from scripture itself. There remained enormous problems in knowing what part, if any, reason played in the process. If one is presented with doctrines that can only be understood if they are believed through trust in God and the authority of the Church, then the contribution of reason, though not necessarily eradicated from the Christian tradition, certainly becomes diminished.

In a world where beliefs were still fluid, a large number of Augustine's theological works were defences of Christian orthodoxy. There are many examples where anxious correspondents, at sea in the shifting currents of theological thought, asked him to provide a response to a particular problem, and Augustine uses these treatises to hit out at his opponents. The titles of no fewer than twenty-six of his works contain the word *contra*, 'against'. It was inevitable that he would also have to produce a defence of the Nicene Trinity. He dreaded the task. He understood that a mere declaration that the Trinity was 'an article of faith' would not be sufficient, yet he was intelligent enough to see all the unresolved philosophical problems that lurked behind the Nicene definition. An early response, in the last book of his *Confessions,* ran as follows: 'Who understands the omnipotent Trinity? Yet who among us does not speak of it, if it indeed be the Trinity he speaks of? Rare is the soul that knows whereof it speaks, whatever it may say concerning the Trinity. They dispute, they quarrel but for want of peace no one sees that vision.'[13] In a famous medieval legend Augustine is portrayed wandering along the seashore, where he meets a young boy – usually depicted in art as an angel – filling a shell with sea water and pouring it into a hole in the sand. When Augustine asks him what the point of this activity is, the reply comes that he is showing that it is easier to empty the sea into a hole than explain a single iota of the mystery of the Trinity.

It was only in 400 that Augustine started his work on the problem, and it took him until 420 to complete. In 414, he had to respond to one Evodius of Uzalis, who asked how one was to know God and the Trinity. Augustine's weary reply was that he could hardly give priority to a work that only a few would understand at the expense of his other writings, sermons and discussions of the Psalms, which appealed to the many.[14] But so great was the interest in the work that about 415, a copy of the incomplete text was taken from his study and published, to the fury of its author. Five years later, the work was at last finished and Augustine agreed that it could now be read aloud to listeners and copies made of the long text.

Quite apart from the philosophical problems he encountered in explaining the Nicene Trinity, Augustine had no access to some of the best work on the subject, that of the Cappadocian Fathers; there is no record that Gregory of Nazianzus' *Theological Orations* had been translated into Latin by this time. Instead Augustine appears to have relied heavily on Latin authors such as Tertullian, who had coined the Latin word *trinitas*, Hilary of Poitiers, and the 'incomprehensible' Marius Victorinus. Some commentators have argued that his lack of knowledge of the more sophisticated Greek thinkers was fatal to the whole enterprise. In his *The Promise of Trinitarian Theology*, Colin Gunton asserts that although Augustine claimed to rely on scripture and tradition for his understanding of the Trinity, in fact 'he either did not understand the trinitarian theology of his predecessors, both East and West, or looked at their work with spectacles so strongly tinted with neo-platonic assumptions that they have distorted his work. The tragedy is that Augustine's work is so brilliant that it blinded generations of theologians to its damaging weaknesses.'[15]

Nevertheless, *De Trinitate* is a profound and complex work. In his biography of Augustine, Serge Lancel describes it as 'a mighty river which sweeps powerful ideas along on a course that is rich in meanders and swelled by unexpected tributaries'.[16] Whatever concerns one has about the underlying pessimism of Augustine and his readiness to accept the authority of the Church without question, there is no doubting the brilliance with which he penetrated every nook and cranny of the problem. As with much of his theology, he was able to develop orthodox thought in new and original ways.

Augustine took as his initial premise the belief that the mystery of the Trinity is a revelation of God and that it must be accepted in faith. His Trinity is one of Father, Son and Holy Spirit who are inseparable, equal, and operate as a divine unity. Despite the passages in scriptures where God, Jesus or the Holy Spirit appear to act on their own, Augustine believed that all three act together whenever the divine interacts with the material world. Even in the Old Testament Jesus was present as part of the Godhead. Having established the orthodox, Augustine set out to defend it. In Books I to IV of *De Trinitate*, he examined the scriptural basis for the Nicene Trinity. As earlier commentators were suffused with subordinationism, Augustine has to carry out a painstaking re-examination of every scriptural text to show that a Nicene gloss can be placed on it. Gregory of Nazianzus had undertaken much the same task in his *Theological Orations*, and like Gregory, Augustine had to indulge in a great deal of special pleading and even casuistry to reinterpret each text to suit his ends. A major problem he encountered was that many texts talked of Jesus having been sent by the Father. Most earlier commentators had suggested that one who is sent must be a lesser, subordinate being to one who does the sending, but Augustine asserts that there is no reason why the sender and the sent have to be unequal. His subordinationist critics responded by asking why there is no scriptural passage in which the Father is sent by the Son or the Holy Spirit (and whether such a sending would, in fact, be conceivable). It is clearly an issue that cannot be resolved. When confronted by texts such as John 14:28, 'The Father is greater than I', which can hardly be interpreted in any way other than as an expression of the subordinate nature of Jesus, Augustine simply claims that Jesus is here speaking in his human capacity. This is unlikely to have convinced the more sophisticated of his critics. The gospel writers could not have anticipated how their texts would become entangled in later theological debates, and would have been surprised to hear that the words of Jesus they quoted could be divided into 'divine' and 'human' pronouncements.

Having dealt with the scriptural background, in Books V to VII

Augustine explored the philosophical problems of the Nicene Trinity: how the language of substance, essence and personality can be interpreted. Here he has to express in Latin what had been examined more subtly in the works of the Greek fathers. Yet, like the theologians in the east, he had major problems associating the Holy Spirit with Father and Son. The only distinction between the three that Augustine allows is in terms of their relationship. The names 'Father' and 'Son', one 'unbegotten' and one 'begotten', define the relationship between these two members of the Trinity. The name 'Holy Spirit', on the other hand, does not contain any definition of a relationship, and Augustine, like Gregory of Nazianzus, employed the word 'procession' found in John 15:26, where the Spirit processes from the Father. But while Gregory and the eastern theologians assumed that this verse meant that the Holy Spirit processes *only* from the Father, Augustine argued that in order to keep the relationship of the threesome intact, the Holy Spirit must also process from the Son, in what became known as the 'double procession'. When the Greek Church heard of this formulation, they were outraged at the apparent distortion of John's text, and when the Catholic Church endorsed Augustine's view, the ensuing confrontation – known as the *filioque* controversy, from the Latin for 'and from the Son' – was one of the factors that led to a final schism between the Roman Catholic and Greek Orthodox Churches in 1054.

Perhaps the most interesting parts of *De Trinitate* can be found in books VIII to XV. Turning to a verse from Genesis (1:26) – 'Let us [God] make man in our image and in our likeness' – Augustine argues that if humans are made in the image of God, then there may be traces of the tripartite Godhead in the human mind. Somewhat arbitrarily, perhaps, he divides the mind into three parts: the mind itself, its knowledge of itself and its love of itself. All three are of the same substance and equal – just like the Trinity. Self-knowledge and self-love process from the mind, but here the analogy breaks down: one can hardly call 'the mind' the 'Father' of 'self-knowledge' and 'self-love'.[17] In Book X, Augustine discusses the human faculties memory, understanding and will, which enjoy the same relationship – although it is hard to see how the three of them work together as a single force. Nevertheless, this analogy is an imaginative idea that suggests an intimate link between God and humanity. As one commentator has put it: Augustine 'suggests that we will only find ourselves if we look for God, and that only in finding ourselves will we find God'.[18] This seems a good starting point for further reflection, and even if the analogy of the human mind echoing the Trinity is not always convincing, Augustine's insights are often seen as an important contribution to the philosophy of mind.

Ultimately, *De Trinitate* is overwhelming and was unsurpassed for centuries. Thomas Aquinas' *Treatise on the Trinity* is largely a sophisticated restatement of Augustine's ideas while in the Protestant tradition, Calvin adopts Augustine's interpretations of scripture.[19] Perhaps the vital point to make here is that the Trinity does not excite the imagination. Edmund Hill, a recent translator of the work, talks of how 'it has come about that the doctrine of the Trinity has been effectively detached from the wider movements of Christian spirituality and devotion in the west, and the mystery has come to be regarded as a curious kind of intellectual luxury of theological highbrows, a subject on which not many priests are eager to preach sermons, nor congregations to listen to them'.[20] This, according to Hill, is because later generations, especially those in the Middle Ages, missed the point that Augustine was providing a complete programme for the Christian spiritual life, although it is true that the doctrine of the Trinity has perplexed theologians and laymen alike through the centuries.[21] The contrast with the drama of the Nativity, the Crucifixion and the Resurrection of Christ to which ordinary believers could easily relate is obvious. *De Trinitate* shows that the whole discussion of the Trinity takes place at a forbiddingly erudite level, far above the comprehension of all but the most sophisticated minds. More than 1,600 years later, the German theologian Karl Rahner was to note that the everyday devotional beliefs of most Catholics would not change at all if there was no Trinity, so little does the doctrine engage their minds.[22] Its imposition as dogma, by an imperial decree, did nothing to root it in the everyday life of the Church.

Despite his impressive attempts to find a rational basis for belief in the Nicene Trinity, Augustine always maintained that the concept remained a mystery, essentially a revelation of God that one had to accept in faith. This is echoed in the *Catechism of the Roman Catholic Church* (1994), which refers to the Trinity as 'a mystery of faith, one of those mysteries that are hidden in God, which can never be known unless they are revealed by God . . . God's inmost Being as Holy Trinity is a mystery that is inaccessible to reason alone'.[23] This might be acceptable theologically, even if it raises conceptual problems, relating, for instance, to the nature of revelation and the authority of the Church, which have to be addressed. The problem was that Augustine then went on to cast doubt on the process of reason itself, especially as it related to the study of the natural world. It is one thing to accept, as all the great Greek thinkers did, that there are limits to reason; it is another to fail to recognise what a major contribution reason can make to human knowledge and understanding in, say, mathematics and science. Augustine had already used the concept of 'faith' to displace Platonic reasoning; he was now to confront the tradition of Aristotle, the use of reason to define cause and effect from empirical evidence collected by the senses.

Augustine was not sympathetic towards the study of the natural world. In his *Soliloquia*, an early work, he asks himself the rhetorical question of what he wishes to know. 'I desire to know God and the soul. Nothing besides? Nothing whatsoever.'[24] As so often with Augustine, his attitude darkens with time, not least in his approach to the natural world. One can see the development of his thought through a study of the way he uses the term *curiositas*, what Aristotle would have seen as the healthy 'desire to know', above all to explore and understand the world available to the senses. To Augustine, *curiositas* is always *un*healthy in so far as it diverts attention away from God. In the *Confessions*, he provides a critique of the term as essentially sinful. 'There is another form of temptation, even more fraught with danger. This is the disease [*sic*] of curiosity . . . It is this which drives us to try and discover the secrets of nature, these secrets which are beyond our understanding, which can avail us nothing, and which man should not wish to learn.'[25] He later talks pejoratively of curiosity as the 'lust of the eyes' and then, in his final works, as a sin associated with the fall of the soul into the iniquity of the world as a result of the disobedience of Adam. The weight of original sin is such, he argues, that it has left no more than a tiny spark of reason intact in the human mind. His views – and here he has much in common with the eastern theologians of the day – led, in the words of one scholar, to 'a pre-occupation with the minutiae of theological doctrine, as well as a distaste, sometimes bordering on the pathological, for the speculations and investigations of worldly natural science'.[26] There are still those who argue that Christian thought was in some way more sophisticated than that of the pagan world, even that medieval Christianity initiated modern science, but this argument is difficult to sustain when the most influential of the western theologians, Augustine, takes such a jaundiced view of the study of the natural world and the use of reason based on empirical observation that goes with it. It took Thomas Aquinas to restore faith in the power of the reasoning mind to Christian theology, while Augustine's works remained the first call of those who opposed his endeavour.

But there is something even more ominous about Augustine's legacy: he brings to an end the long tradition, described in Chapter Three, that one should not use force to convince. As we have seen, many earlier Christians, Lactantius being the most sophisticated among them, had endorsed the principle of toleration. Only a few years before Augustine, Gregory of Nazianzus had argued that to enforce belief against the will of the believer was similar to damming up a river: when the water eventually broke through the dam, its force would be all the greater. Only beliefs held willingly, he suggested, had any real value.[27] The precedent had now been set by Theodosius and Ambrose that Church and state could combine in the persecution of heretics and pagans, but it was Augustine, infuriated by the intransigence of the Donatist majority in his diocese, who provided its theological justification. Such is the threat of hell fire that the end justifies the means. 'What then does brotherly love do? Does it, because it fears the short-lived furnaces for the few, abandon all to the eternal fires of hell? And does it leave so many to perish everlastingly whom others [i.e. the Donatists] will not permit to live in accordance with the teaching of Christ?'.[28] Thus the idea of persecution became embedded in medieval Europe. Burning alive, the traditional Roman punishment for counterfeiting coins, was adopted for those who 'counterfeited' the teachings of Christ.[29]

In the east, emperors had taken the initiative in forcing the conversion of all, a process that culminated in the sweeping legislation of Justinian. Augustine was writing at a time of political and social disintegration after Rome had been sacked for the first time for centuries, in 410. It was understandable that he would be preoccupied with the return of order, and this was the theme of his last major work, *The City of God*, written in direct response to the sack of Rome. Its central thesis is that there are two cities, that of God in heaven, and that of Rome on earth. Rome does not deserve to survive because its pagan gods will never offer it full protection, and in any case, an earthly city can never provide the true happiness of God's kingdom. Governed by human beings, it will always be corrupted: there is no reason why rulers should be any better than the ruled – Augustine would have no truck with Themistius' portrayal of the ruler as 'divine law descended from on high'. The best that can be hoped for is that the state will support the Church on earth, yet as human beings are naturally sinful and hence disorderly, the main purpose of the state is to keep order. 'The peace of the whole universe is the tranquillity of order. Order is the arrangement of things equal and unequal in a pattern which assigns to each its allotted position.'[30] To Augustine this 'allotted position' included the maintenance of the institution of slavery, which he described as 'punishment for sin': 'It remains true that slavery as a punishment is also ordained by that law which enjoins the preservation of the order of nature and forbids its disturbance.'[31] Augustine's lasting contribution to political thought lies in his justification of authoritarian regimes that see virtue in order per se, rather than in any abstract ideal such as justice or the defence of human rights, or even in the teachings of Jesus themselves. At a stroke Augustine supplants centuries of Greek thought, expressed notably in Plato's *The Republic* and Aristotle's *Politics*, which viewed the government of the city primarily in terms of the well-being of its citizens. Moreover, when Church and state become mutually supportive in the upholding of order, then the punishment of heretics becomes a matter of state policy. This would be the norm in medieval Europe.

Augustine's negative view of mankind was still prevalent in Europe as late as the seventeenth century. 'As frail, fallen vessels in an age where the state's arm was still relatively short, seventeenth century Christians had to be imprisoned within the confines of a gendered, hierarchical and deferential society to ensure that the divine moral order was passably upheld ... An Augustinian view of human nature also sustained the penchant of seventeenth century theologians and lawyers for divine-right absolute monarchy.'[32]

Augustine's underlying premise – that there is a single truth that can only be grasped through faith; that human beings are helpless; that God is essentially punitive, ready to send even babies into eternal hell fire; and that one has a right, even a duty, to burn heretics – challenges the whole ethos of the Greek intellectual tradition, where competition between rival philosophies was intrinsic to progress. Those like Aristotle and his followers in astronomy, medicine and the natural sciences would have found it hard to comprehend Augustine's condemnation of their endeavours. Aristotle's assertion that 'while no one is able to attain the truth adequately ... everyone [*sic*] says something true about the nature of things, and, while individually they contribute little or nothing to the truth, by the union of all a considerable amount is amassed' would have been anathema to Augustine. The freedom to speculate freely as an individual had no place in his system: he was terrified by the idea that all might contribute to the finding of truth. Augustine bequeathed a tradition of fear to Christianity, fear that one's speculations might be heretical and fear that, even if they were not, one might still go to hell as punishment for the sin of Adam.

But why did Augustine's views become so central to western Christianity? There is no intrinsic reason why his thought should be so privileged, especially as, in hindsight, one can see so clearly how his own pessimism shaped his theology. One reason, already suggested, was that in an age of political, social and economic breakdown, pessimistic theologies fitted the zeitgeist more effectively. With the breakdown came the collapse in western Europe of the conditions in which intellectual life could take place. When conditions improved, several centuries later, the Church had integrated Augustine's work so successfully that he had become the gatekeeper of a closed world that remained fearful of any expression of dissent. None of this would have been possible if Theodosius had not set the precedent of establishing the 'truth' and condemning all those who opposed it as 'demented heretics'. Augustine, a natural conservative and supporter of what had been decreed to be orthodox, articulated the theological links between the emperor's decrees and medieval Christianity.

XIII

COLLAPSE IN THE CHRISTIAN WEST

ALTHOUGH the eastern empire was to suffer some devastating blows as the Arab expansion of the seventh and eighth centuries deprived it of much of its territory in Africa and the near east, it retained a stability at its core and even a flexibility in its response to the crisis that enabled it to survive for a further thousand years. The western empire, in contrast, suffered an almost complete breakdown of order as invasions ravaged its territories and successor states struggled to impose their own order. Much of what we would call civilisation – urban life, access to goods through trade, literacy and basic comfort – was diminished or even disappeared completely. The purpose of this chapter is to show how the conditions for intellectual and cultural life were absent for several centuries and only revived when trade breathed new life into the western economy and provided the wealth and the need for effective administration that could sustain a learned elite.[1] I believe that only against this background can the legacy of Theodosius' decree in the west be assessed.

Valentinian I had managed to preserve the northern frontiers of the western empire intact until his death in 375. The onset of the disintegration of the western empire could be dated from 383, when the usurper Maximus crossed from Britain, where he had been commander of the legions, and came to rule all Gaul, Spain and Britain, before his further expansion into Italy in 387 led to his defeat by Theodosius. The ease with which the authority of Gratian was overthrown in much of western Europe was an ominous sign, and even after Maximus' death Roman rule was never restored north of the Loire. The ancient imperial capital of Trier was abandoned in favour of a new centre of

command at Arles to the south. Soon villa life, towns and Roman
industries began to collapse. In north-western Europe, urban living
virtually disappeared after AD 400: a town like Lyons shrank from 160
hectares to a mere 20.

The events of the next seventy years show signs of increasing disintegration: large numbers of Germanic tribes crossed the Rhine in 406,
Rome itself was sacked by the Gothic Alaric in 410, and the remaining
legions, which were now supported by large numbers of mercenaries,
were unable to coordinate counterattacks. The Vandals swept first into
Spain in 409, and then in 429 into North Africa. They reached the
gates of Hippo in 430 when Augustine lay dying there. Gaiseric, the
Vandal leader, was able to attack Rome by sea in 455; in 458 he
captured Sicily, which had been a Roman province for 700 years. Both
North Africa and Sicily had been important sources of tax and grain
and were now lost. A few Roman generals had temporary successes
but usually only through the recourse of using one of the invading
peoples against the others. In the *Life of Severinus*, the last days of a
frontier guard on the northern borders are described as they lose contact
in the 450s with administrators to the south, fail to be paid and eventually disband themselves. Officially the end of the empire came in 476
when the last emperor, the boy Romulus Augustulus, was deposed. His
place was taken by a German, Odoacer, who in theory at least was
acting as the representative of the eastern empire, but Odoacer was
murdered in 493 by the Ostrogoth Theodoric, who imposed his own
rule on much of Italy.

Although Theodoric and his Ostrogothic successors worked hand in
hand with the remnants of the Roman elite, central rule had vanished.[2]
Justinian's invasion to restore Roman rule in the west, launched in
535, brought even more disruption, and about 560 Pope Pelagius I
refers to 'the devastation which more than twenty-five years of continuous warfare, still now by no means abating, inflicted on Italy'.[3] Plague
was a further drain on the population from the 540s, before in 568
another set of invaders, the Lombards, swept into northern Italy.

In recent years some historians have glossed over the effects of these
massive disruptions as if Germanic rulers smoothly replaced the Roman
administrations. It is true that there were treaties, such as the one
concluded with the Visigoths in Aquitaine in 419 that allowed the
invaders to settle, while some Roman aristocrats appear to have maintained their estates intact.[4] The Ostrogoths, a minority within a much

larger Italian population, used effective Roman administrators, of whom Cassiodorus and Boethius were the best known, and even restored some of the decaying buildings of Rome. Yet this all took place in a crumbling economy, and it is important to turn to the archaeological evidence to get a fuller picture of what was happening.

When the empire was at its height, the effective control of *mare nostrum* – 'our sea', the Mediterranean – allowed the Romans to exploit its trading potential to the full. The accumulation of years of experience in a stable landscape meant that even smallholders could afford mass-produced goods, many of which were of a high standard. Excavations show that peasant households enjoyed a variety of well-crafted pots of different shapes and sizes, for storage, cookery or display. Although there were major consumers – the legions and privileged cities such as Rome and, later, Constantinople, whose grain supplies were guaranteed by the emperors – the economy of the empire was characterised by a network of small-scale free enterprise as merchants, manufacturers and craftsmen collaborated to supply the consumer needs of a steady market. Studies of lead and copper pollution (from Roman industrial sites) trapped in the ice cores of the Arctic show that it rises from almost nothing in prehistoric times to a peak in the Roman period, then reverses to prehistoric levels and does not regain the scale of Roman activity until the sixteenth century. Similarly analysis of shipwrecks from the period AD 100 to 300 show impressive trading networks throughout the Mediterranean, again unequalled until the sixteenth century.

It is the disappearance of this industry and trade that provides the most evocative evidence of economic collapse. Britain is an extreme example, but during the fifth century virtually every building craft simply vanishes from archaeological sites. Brick-making ceases and is not seen again for 800 years; stone is no longer quarried or tiles manufactured. It is not until the Normans in the eleventh century that large stone buildings such as castles and cathedrals reappear. It is possible to argue that living standards fell even below those of the Iron Age peoples of the island before the Roman conquest, since these, at least, enjoyed trading contacts with the continent. As elsewhere in Europe, the monetary economy simply ceased to exist. At Hoxne in Suffolk, a hidden cache of treasures from the early 400s, at the end of the empire, was made up of 14,000 coins as well as silver and gold ware. Two hundred years later, the early seventh-century Anglo-Saxon ship burial of a pagan king at Sutton Hoo a few miles from Hoxne contained a total of only forty coins from Gaul, apparently retained as prestige items. The contrast between the monetary wealth of an Anglo-Saxon king and that of a rich Roman individual in the last years of the empire is extraordinary.

The evidence from Italy reflects the same collapse. Here a population estimated at seven million in the first century AD dropped to as low as four million in the seventh century. A hundred dioceses recorded in late antiquity vanish completely from the sources.[5] Small towns were particularly hard hit, and many of the surviving Italians relocated to fortified hillsides or found protection as serfs or soldiers of local lords. At a material level, tiles, which had been known for centuries and which had, during the years of stability, roofed quite humble dwellings, disappear, as they had in Britain. The aqueducts into Rome were cut in the late sixth century, and it is not until the sixteenth century that any were reconnected. The size of cattle slumps below pre-Roman levels.[6]

A vivid image of the desperation of the age survives from the letters and works of Gregory the Great, pope from 590 to 604. In his embattled Rome, the population had recovered to some 90,000 from a low of 30,000 in the mid-sixth century, although most of the newcomers were refugees from the Lombard invaders in the north. He paints a grim picture of the world as he sees it: 'Towns are depopulated, fortified places destroyed, churches burnt, monasteries and nunneries destroyed; fields are deserted by men, and the earth, forsaken by the ploughman, gapes desolate. No farmer dwells here now; wild beasts have taken the place of throngs of men. What goes on in other parts of the world, I do not know: but here, in the land in which we live, the world no longer announces its coming end, but shows it forth.' Rome itself is disintegrating: 'the senate is gone, the people perish, pain and fear grow daily for the few who are left: a deserted Rome is burning . . . we see buildings destroyed, ruins daily multiplied.' Gregory's world is pervaded by the sense of living 'in the last times'. [7] While he keeps close contact with southern Italy and Sicily, where there are Church estates and it is still possible to reach Carthage and the Dalmatian and the Gaulish Mediterranean coast by sea, the rest of Europe is by now largely out of reach. His mission for the conversion of England in 597 was in the circumstances a major undertaking.

It was not only the Germanic tribes, Anglo-Saxons, Franks,

Burgundians and assorted Goths, who were building new kingdoms out of the void; much of the former western empire, the entire coast of North Africa, southern Spain and Sicily, was lost in the seventh century to the Arabs, who swept up as far as Poitiers in France before they were defeated. With the relationship with the older and more sophisticated Greek church breaking down, and so much lost to Islam, Rome emerged as the single isolated religious centre of the barbarian west.[8]

The Church had an advantage over the fragile secular rulers as its hierarchy had survived the social breakdown; bishops had become increasingly sought after for their administrative skills. A position in the Church enabled aristocrats to maintain their status, as in the case of Sidonius Apollinaris, a former prefect of Rome before the fall of the western empire, who was consecrated Bishop of Clermont in 470 and who lived out his life on his estates in Gaul in uneasy proximity to the local Gothic rulers. Fundamental to the consolidation of Church power was the conversions of Arian or pagan kings who brought their subjects with them. The Frankish king Clovis converted from Arianism to Catholicism at the end of the fifth century. The Visigoth Reccared, another Arian, became Catholic in 589 (although the Visigothic kingdom would be overrun by the Arabs in 711). When the pagan Kentish king Aethelbert was converted by the monk Augustine, who had been sent to Britain by Gregory in 597/8, some 10,000 (probably an exaggerated number) of his subjects were also baptised. Although these mass conversions gave little scope for individual commitment, it meant that the Church hierarchy and the secular rulers supported each other and, however much pagan practice continued in the countryside, the influence of Church power grew enormously. Christianity continued to spread, so that by 750 it extended from Italy to Gaul and present-day Germany, northern Spain and Britain. A deeply symbolic moment came when Leo II consecrated Charlemagne as Holy Roman Emperor in Rome in 800 and set up an institution that lasted, despite its tensions between pope and emperor, for a thousand years.

Yet it would not be until the eleventh and twelfth centuries that papal jurisdiction was fully accepted within western Christendom. For the time being this proved, perhaps paradoxically, an immense advantage for the Church. The lack of papal authority meant that new dioceses could be established by bishops on their own initiative and local varieties of Christianity could take root and flourish in a way that would have been impossible in a hierarchy imposed from above.

The sixth-century Rule of St Benedict, for instance, decreed that each Benedictine house should be independent under its abbot, which enabled each community to respond to local needs. In Ireland, 'Christianity accommodated its modes of organization to the small scale kingdoms and the politics of cattle and kinship and had adapted biblical precepts in ways that made local sense'.[9]

One of the most important developments sustaining this diversity was the rise of shrines and the cults of saints, even if some of these saints had actually been pagan holy men who had subsequently acquired 'Christian' status. For centuries, saints gave religious institutions and the faithful a sense of identity, means of protection and economic vitality. In Tours, the soldier-saint Martin was used as a patron of his city, his vengeance promised to those who threatened it. (Many of the 'miracles' associated with him involve the destruction of pagan shrines.) The West Saxon kings used the martyr St Edmund as their own protector. Monasteries with important relics, such as Fleury on the Loire, which had seized the bones of St Benedict from Monte Cassino, freely used the sacred power of these bones in their litigation and disputes with encroaching landowners. In short, the spread of Christianity involved a process of collaboration between local rulers, the partisans of local holy men, and ancient spiritual forces.

This is a very different cultural world from that of the Romans. In the declining years of the empire, it was still possible for a man to enjoy a traditional education in the classics. Boethius' famous *Consolation of Philosophy* (c.524) is a work by a Christian rooted in the classical world and infused with the philosophy of Plato. Born c.480, Boethius translated Aristotle's books on logic in a form that enabled them to survive in the west while most of Aristotle's work vanished for 800 years. He was planning to compile a major work in which the philosophy of Plato and Aristotle was integrated when he was arrested, imprisoned and executed by Theodoric (524–526), whom he served as an administrator. Another of Theodoric's Roman civil servants, Cassiodorus (490–c.585), spent his last years gathering ancient manuscripts in his estate at Vivarium in southern Italy, where monks copied them for him. A century later, Isidore, the Bishop of Seville from 600 to 635, compiled a large etymology of Latin words: a reconstruction of his sources suggests he had a library of some 200 authors with perhaps 475 separate works. This can be compared with the third-century Roman library of the poet Serenus Sammonicus with its 62,000 papyrus rolls.

During this period many ancient manuscripts must have decayed and disappeared. We do not know what happened to the libraries of the scholars described in earlier chapters. Most of Origen's thousand works, part of what was the most celebrated Christian library in the ancient world, at Caesarea in Palestine, seem to have been discarded when he was declared heretical. It has been suggested that some of the finest libraries of ancient Rome, those of the imperial palaces on the Palatine Hill and those in Trajan's sumptuous forum, were destroyed during a siege of Rome in 546. There is some evidence that one or two private libraries were preserved in Rome and Ravenna. Overall, however, hundreds of thousands of works must have been discarded, allowed to rot, or consumed by fire.

The disappearance of books went hand in hand with a slump in literacy. It is true that the Church still expected its clergy to be able to read and write – and Pope Gregory in particular was determined to maintain standards among his clergy – but even so there was a dramatic decline in proficiency. In sixth-century Gaul, the aristocratic Gregory, Bishop of Tours from 573 until his death in 594, explained that he felt impelled to write his *Ecclesiastical History of the Franks* when those around him lamented: 'Woe to our day, since the pursuit of letters has perished from among us and no one can be found among the people who can set forth the deeds of the present on the written page.' By the standards of his day, Gregory was educated, but as one commentator has suggested, 'Judged by anything like a classical standard Gregory is guilty of almost every conceivable barbarity. He spells incorrectly, blunders in the use of inflection, confuses genders, and often uses the wrong case with the proposition.'[10] One study of eighth-century charters in Italy shows that even among the social elite who were required to witness them, only 14 per cent were able to sign their own name. Even in the eleventh century, very few lay people could write their name at the end of a charter, whose Latin they would not, in any case, have been able to understand.[11] The problem lay partly in the failure of the Church to spread literacy outside the confines of the clergy. Paradoxically it was the Irish, who had never been 'civilised' by the Romans, who maintained some level of scholarship, first by preserving the high status of the *filid*, the scholar-poets, and second by mastering Latin with far greater accuracy than those whose native language it was. The missions of saints Columba and Columbanus to mainland Britain, France and northern Italy were as much cultural as religious expeditions. Ireland also produced the most original thinker of these centuries, Eriugena, who knew enough Greek to be able to introduce the mystical works of Pseudo-Dionysius to the west and to write his Neoplatonist work *The Division of Nature* (*c.866*). (Like many other intellectual initiatives, it offended the Church and was declared heretical in the thirteenth century.)

Latin survived as the working language of the Church, but much more of the Roman cultural heritage might have been preserved if there had been an ethos that valued classical learning. Augustine had challenged that ethos in his *De Doctrina Christiana*, where he argued that secular learning should be despised unless it supported the understanding of the scriptures. His writings were an important influence on Gregory the Great, whose access to other works was limited, but in the words of Robert Markus, 'Augustine read Cicero, Virgil, Plotinus, Ambrose, Cyprian and other ancient writers, Christian and non-Christian. Gregory read Augustine.'[12]

In view of this, the claim that is often made that monasteries were powerhouses of culture seems a dubious one. The ethos within these communities was one of obedience to authority. In the case of the Benedictines, there was indeed a requirement that they listen to sacred readings, but the choice was limited, by Benedict's Rule, to the Old and New Testaments, the works of the 'Holy Catholic Fathers', those of John Cassian on monastic life, and the Lives of the Church fathers. This helps to explain why monastic libraries were very small. In Anglo-Saxon England, the library used by the Venerable Bede at the twin monastic foundations of Jarrow and Monkwearmouth is, at 200 works, truly exceptional. Much of it was brought from Rome in the late seventh century by two abbots, Benedict Biscop and his successor Ceolfrith. In his *The Anglo-Saxon Library*[13], Michael Lapidge concluded: 'The typical Anglo-Saxon monastic library probably owned fewer than fifty volumes, all of which could be housed in a simple book-chest.'[14] In addition to the scriptures, there were twenty essential titles, which included the works of Augustine, Jerome, Gregory the Great and Isidore. Eusebius' *History of the Church* and Cassian's *Institutes*, together with a few works of Christian-Latin poets, make up the total repertoire. Lapidge goes on to show how the claims by scholars that Anglo-Saxon monastic libraries were well stocked with classical literature are based on virtually no evidence other than a few fragments of manuscripts.[15] Continental libraries were somewhat larger.

An inventory of the library at Reichenau (on Lake Constance in Switzerland) in 821 shows a total of 415 *codices*. Only a small number of these were non-religious works, although these did include Virgil's *Georgics* and *The Aeneid* and Vitruvius' *De Architectura*.[16] Part of the problem was the cost of parchment, a large *codex* would have required the hides of a hundred cows, and there was thus an incentive to wash down less favoured (usually classical) texts for reuse. One important exception to this melancholy tale was the monastery at Fulda in central Germany. It was large, with some 600 monks, and very wealthy, and under its abbot, the scholarly Hrabanus Maurus (*c.* 780–856), it amassed a vast collection of both classical and Christian texts, probably some 2,000 in all. Several ancient works, including a large section of the *Annals* of Tacitus, have only survived because the monks of Fulda copied them out in the ninth century.

With so little at their disposal, it is no surprise that the scholarship of even the most intelligent men was limited. They were poorly supplied with evidence of the past, and moreover, that past was now presented in terms of the spread of Christianity. So when one comes across men of great intelligence such as the Venerable Bede in Jarrow, one has to admire them for their attempt to maintain learning in such dire circumstances. While the largest body of Bede's work consists of biblical exegesis, he tried to understand secular subjects as well. He examined the relationship between the moon and the tides and used astronomical formula in his calculation of the 'correct' date for Easter. His Latin is sophisticated for his period, although he admits that the only secular work he allows himself to use is a grammar purged of any reference to paganism. The restrictions imposed by his sources and his beliefs ensure that his famous *Ecclesiastical History of the English People* concentrates on only one major issue: the progress of Christianity in England. The narrative is shaped by Bede's conviction that his own people, the Northumbrians, had been called to bring salvation. Thus he plays up the role of the Germanic newcomers and is actively hostile to the Britons, who deserve, as we have seen, to be massacred if they do not accept the Christian faith. He has none of the acute moral sensitivities of the great classical writers such as Thucydides and Tacitus, with their detached assessments of how those in power exploit their position to destroy the weak. Neither of these historians could have written approvingly that, after Aethelfrith's massacres of pagan priests, 'the prophecy of the holy Bishop Augustine was fulfilled . . . namely that those heretics would also suffer the vengeance of temporal death because they had despised the offer of everlasting salvation'.[17] There are so few surviving sources from this period that it is difficult to assess Bede's accuracy as a historian, but a comparison with another surviving work, Stephen of Ripon's biography of the Northumbrian bishop Wilfrid, suggests, in the words of one scholar, that Bede is 'highly selective and discreet' in his own version of events.[18] There is certainly nothing of the breadth and tolerance for 'foreign' cultures shown by that great father of history, Herodotus, 1,100 years earlier. So much had intellectual horizons narrowed.

The rise in the use of relics for religious, economic and political purposes suggests that the mass of the population had become more credulous. But this would be an inappropriate conclusion. Those seeking healing in classical times would sleep at the Temple of Asclepius in the hope of a cure in much the same way as Christian pilgrims would flock to a church some centuries later. In fact many Christian shrines had formerly been pagan ones. Pope Gregory, a man who was always pragmatic and moderate, told his missionaries to England that they should not try to destroy ancient shrines but sprinkle them with holy water and then allow them to continue as centres for Christian worship. (Note the contrast with the destructive fanatics of the east.) What is different is that the educated elite now accepted miracles when in earlier times they would have ridiculed them. One can see the transition in Augustine. In his early works, after his conversion, he acknowledged the miracles of Jesus in the New Testament but wrote that they were no longer needed now that Christianity was established. By the closing chapters of *The City of God*, at the end of his life, however, he had become a fervent supporter of the miraculous.[19] Similarly there remains an element of restraint in the way that Pope Gregory reflected on the miraculous: he preferred to relate miracles directly to holy men rather than their bones, but he still saw the hand of God as present everywhere in the natural world. His contemporary, Gregory of Tours, was completely immersed in the miraculous effects of holy bones, especially those of St Martin of Tours. In his Gaul, or Francia as it became when the Franks established their rule, the literature was dominated by the hagiographical lives of saints and their deeds. St Martin of Tours was credited with many more miracles than Jesus – 207 according to Gregory's account.[20]

The cumulation of developments was to ensure that for centuries the possibility of critical theological (and other intellectual) discussion faded from Europe. What was needed was the revival of the social and economic conditions that could foster urban elites and thus the possibility of intellectual discourse.

It is in the eighth century that the very first signs of a revival of trade can be found. A gradual accretion of prosperity in northern Italy (primarily in Venice and in the Po valley, where a new class of Lombard landowners arose) and Francia was given a boost by two factors. The first was the conquest of northern Italy by Charlemagne in the late eighth century, which brought the two economies, one either side of the Alps, together, to the mutual benefit of each. Second there was the beginnings of trade with the Islamic states of the eastern Mediterranean. These could provide silks, incense, drugs and spices that originated even further east. Some raw materials, including slaves, could be traded in return. The revival of trade had little to do with the Church (which on occasions tried to ban the flourishing commerce with Islam). As the Venetians, the most successful of the traders, consolidated their settlements on the islands of the lagoon, they placed their first cathedral, San Pietro in Castello, in the eastern extremities of the city, far from the political and economic core. Many of the rejuvenated cities of northern Italy found themselves in dispute with the landowners and the Church, although accommodations were often made.[21]

The first 'renaissance' of European culture took place in the reign of Charlemagne, who ruled as King of the Franks from 768 and Holy Roman Emperor after his coronation by the pope in 800 until his death in 814. Charlemagne looked back to the past glories of the Roman emperors and his programme was one of *renovatio*, 'renewal', of an effective and centralised imperial rule to which both Church and state would be subjected. He never had the power to recreate the autocracy of an efficient Roman emperor, nor would his clergy have allowed it. They valued their comparative independence too highly. At the Synod of Frankfurt of 794, over which Charlemagne presided, his Church leaders criticised the attempts of the eastern emperors to rule the Church in the tradition of Constantine and Theodosius. They were no readier to accept the hegemony of the pope. This meant that Charlemagne's court at Aix-la-Chapelle could provide a focus for cultural activity without competition from a powerful Church hierarchy. His initiatives, such as the increased use of written law codes and administrative documents, stimulated education. It was during these years that Hrabanus

Maurus compiled his collection of classical and Christian manuscripts at Fulda. Yet this revival of learning depended on Charlemagne's personality and determination to create a powerful state. After his death and the fragmentation of his empire, the revival ceased. When Eriguena produced his *On the Division of Nature* in the 860s, it was said that no one had the learning to understand it. Something more deep-rooted than the imposition of 'culture' from above was needed, and in the ninth century the European economy was too weak to provide it.

In 967 there was an isolated but significant breakthrough. A monk named Gerbert of Aurillac (later Pope Sylvester II) was sent by his abbot to Septimania in Spain, on the border between Christianity and Islam. Here he was able to study Aristotle, Ptolemy and other medical, scientific and mathematical authors from translated texts preserved by Arab scholars. While in the Christian world the Latin texts of classical authors had gradually vanished or become despised, Islam had valued ancient learning, and it would now be returned to the west, a process that was to reach its culmination in the thirteenth century. Gerbert mastered his sources to such effect that he was able to reintroduce knowledge of the abacus, the astrolabe, perfected by the Arabs from earlier Greek models, and the sphere into Christian Europe. There is only limited evidence of their use – as regards the astrolabe, there is no record of any star chart being made in medieval Europe, for instance, and there was no European observatory until the late sixteenth century – but the possibility of a revival of learning was established. In the twelfth century, Gerard of Cremona translated at least seventy-one, and probably more, works of astronomy alone from Arabic sources. No monastic library of the period is known to have had this number of pagan works.

The real upturn of the European economy took place between 1000 and 1300. In 1000 there were still only a tiny number of towns, perhaps a hundred in all in western Europe; by 1300 there were some 5,000. In his study of the rise of the northern Italian cities between 1000 and 1300, Philip Jones has shown how they gained self-confidence and a strong sense of their own identity, often drawing on their ancient Roman foundations. They evolved sophisticated systems of government, under which different social classes and economic groups collaborated in maintaining stability, even allowing a place for *il popolo*, the citizenry as a whole. Popular education was revived, and some 70 per cent of Florentine children (girls as well as boys) may have received a primary education in the fourteenth century from private schools. The first universities emerged because the major cities, Bologna, Padua, Siena, Modena, needed well-trained professionals, in law, rhetoric and medicine. The university itself, along with the town hall, market and public square, became a symbol of independence and status.[22]

With the revival of learning across a range of subjects – the medieval curriculum included a compulsory foundation in grammar, logic, rhetoric, music, mathematics and astronomy, from which students would progress to law, medicine, or theology – there was inevitably a renewed interest in rational thought. The political and economic needs of the period encouraged open-mindedness, planning and calculation. Faced with a disparate set of surviving texts, some ancient and some modern, students themselves were forced to be critical of contradictions. Thus debate and the mastery of logic became an important feature of education. The Church acquiesced in these developments. It needed administrators as much as the cities did, particularly in the papal curia, which had to communicate in sophisticated Latin with bishops and rulers throughout Europe. Yet there was also the potential for conflict. For the first time in 800 years, since Theodosius' decree of 381, the Church was exposed to the possibility of a clash between faith and reason. The logic taught in the medieval schools was formal and structured, but if it was applied to the teachings of the Church, it might well expose the philosophical weakness of their foundations.

XIV

FAITH, REASON AND THE TRINITY

WITH the conversion of the Arian kings in the fifth and sixth centuries and the spread of a Church that lacked effective central authority, heresy had ceased to be a major issue. There is no record in the west of any execution of a heretic (as against the intransigent 'pagans', whose deaths were recorded by Bede) until King Robert I of France ordered the burning of fourteen citizens from Orleans in 1022. Although these were accused of belonging to a heretical sect, it appears that they had become caught up in political infighting within the French court, and the charge of heresy was essentially opportunistic. However, the concept of heresy had been revived. Two years later, Bishop Gerard of Cambrai examined a group of virtually illiterate peasants whose 'heresy' centred on their determination to return to the teachings of the gospels. They preached abstinence, the abandonment of worldly desires, and charity towards their neighbours. Although there is evidence that these 'heretics' were tortured during their preliminary examination, it appears that the persecution of heretics was fairly restrained until the end of the twelfth century. The Jews suffered far worse fates. As the knights of the First Crusade, who set out in the spring of 1096, passed through towns in France and the Rhineland where there were Jewish populations, they carried out several massacres of those who refused to convert. It was part of a hardening of attitudes, as Jews, lepers and heretics were increasingly defined as part of a common threat to the Church and to society.[1] This development went hand in hand with a new determination by the papacy, initiated by the formidable Gregory VII (1073–85), to reassert its control over western Christianity, largely through claiming the right of the Church to intervene in every aspect of human behaviour. The relative freedom of Christians to adapt their faith to local circumstances was now under severe threat.

The most persistent of heresies were those that contrasted the opulence and worldly power of the Church with the teachings of the gospels. The Cathars, for instance, were dualists, rejecting the material world – with which they believed the Church had compromised – in favour of an original purity based on the teachings of Christ and the apostles. They became deeply rooted in southern France in the twelfth century and gained strength because of the continued uncertainty of the Church about how to treat them. In 1198, a vigorous young pope, Innocent III, launched a more determined response. He equated heretics with traitors – heresy was no less than treason against the person of Jesus Christ – and called on secular rulers to support him in what was now as much a political as a religious campaign. A crusade was launched against the Cathars, ending in indiscriminate slaughter of innocent and 'guilty' alike. Protests against the bloodshed were met with the bleak rejoinder that God would sort out good from evil when those massacred reached judgement. At the Fourth Lateran Council, held in Rome in 1215, it was decreed that there was no possibility of salvation for anyone who remained outside the Church, and that Church and state should collaborate in the extermination of heresy. The Council laid the foundations of an inquisition of suspected heretics, and over the next thirty years its structure was elaborated. Under the influence of the Dominicans, the inquisitors set about the burning of those found guilty of heresy – to the intense anger of many cities (such as Toulouse), which resented the intrusion of the Church into the affairs of their citizens.[2]

The heretics with which the Inquisition was concerned were often illiterate, vulnerable and thus scarcely aware of the gravity of the charges against them. Yet by now there was also a new educated elite attuned to the power structure of the Church and the subtleties of its teachings. Would it be possible for the most sophisticated minds of the age to teach freely and creatively without offending the Church? Medieval thought is often presented as scrutinising obscure elements of Christian belief, but if it can also be seen as a battle between intelligent and original minds and a naturally conservative institution embedded in the theology of Augustine, then it becomes more absorbing, not least for the variety of strategies adopted by the protagonists on either side. While the Church might execute heretics from the poorer classes, intellectuals who overstepped the mark were normally 'only' excommunicated (although this left them under the threat of eternal hell fire if they did not recant before their deaths).

It was the most brilliant logician of the twelfth century, Peter Abelard (1079–1142), who laid down the challenge. The moving story of Abelard's love affair with Heloise, which led to her pregnancy, their marriage and then the brutal end of their physical relationship when her uncle had Abelard castrated, tends to overshadow his achievements as a philosopher. From an early age, Abelard had shown enormous intellectual curiosity, and he moved from his native Brittany to Paris, where he began to teach. In the cathedral schools – of which Notre-Dame was the most prestigious – teachers would compete with each other for the best posts, and Abelard, who revelled in debate, became famous for the victories he effected over rival teachers. His primary interest was in logic, but after his separation from Heloise, he retreated to the monastic house at St Denis, where he developed his interest in theology.[3]

The issue that fascinated him was the Trinity. How could there be three divine persons, Father, Son and Holy Spirit, distinct from each other, each fully God, but without there being three gods? Could he produce a formula that would provide backing for the doctrine? It was a challenging task. As Michael Clanchy, author of a fine biography of Abelard, puts it: 'The perfect analogy for the Trinity seemed to be on the verge of discovery, rather like the discovery of a new drug in modern science, and then the most fundamental problem of Christian theology and belief would have been solved. The successful discoverer would achieve the reputation of a Father of the Church, like St Augustine. If the analogy failed, on the other hand, the discoverer might be condemned as a heretic and imprisoned or killed. The stakes were therefore high and Abelard, as the highest player of his time, gambled against his soul to solve the mystery of the Trinity.'[4]

Abelard's first efforts at solving the problem, the *Theologia*, were condemned and ordered to be burned in 1121. The reasons remain obscure but seem to have included the accusation that he taught that there were three gods (tritheism). It appears that the underlying philosophical problems of the Nicene Trinity were exposed as soon as an educated mind set to work on them. The doctrine was so carefully balanced between Sabellianism – Jesus as a temporary manifestation of God – and tritheism that any new view of the problem risked being accused of one or the other. But this did not deter Abelard. He caught the mood of the new breed of students, who wanted a defence of the Trinity based on 'human and logical reasons . . . something intelligible rather than mere words'. He became obsessed with finding a way in which a coherent defence of the doctrine could be made, and in his later works his arguments became ever more complex. He developed a sophisticated analysis of what was meant by the 'sameness' – as in 'the same substance', or, a word he was fond of using, 'essence' – of the three divine persons, and their 'difference'. He conceived of a 'difference in definition' or 'a difference in property', which, he argued, each of the three persons could hold without compromising their sameness. 'Although God the Father is entirely the same essence as God the Son or God the Holy Spirit, there is one feature proper to God the Father insofar as he is Father, another to God the Son, and yet another to the Holy Spirit.'[5] Scholars remain unconvinced that he ever provided a watertight argument. But, nevertheless, his approach to the issue had set up a model for critical thinking.

The imposition of orthodoxy meant that all teachers, particularly those with original minds, were exposed to possible accusations of heresy. As always, personal rivalries played their part, and Abelard had offended many by his arrogance and his success in building up an enthusiastic student following. His most prestigious opponent, Bernard of Clairvaux, a powerful Cistercian monk and a close friend of the pope, Innocent II, recounted in horror that as a result of Abelard's teachings, 'the Catholic Faith, the childbearing of the Virgin, the Sacrament of the Altar, the incomprehensible mystery [sic] of the Holy Trinity, are being discussed in the streets and the market places'. He accused Abelard of tending towards Arianism when he talked of the Trinity; of Pelagianism when he talked of the grace of God; and of Nestorianism when he talked of the person of Christ. Bernard also attacked Abelard's use of reason, in fact the process of reasoning itself. 'Let him who has scanned the heavens go down to the depths of hell and let the works of darkness that he has dared to bring forth be clearly revealed in the light of day.' In short, 'faith in God has no merit, if human reason provides proof for it'.[6] Bernard also challenged Abelard's view that intention was an essential element in sin (with the implication that, contra Augustine, a baby could not have any guilt as it was too young to be able to form an intention) and that faith could be a matter of private judgement. He drew up a list of Abelard's supposed heresies to be brought for judgement before the pope at a synod to be held at Sens (in France). Abelard sent his own defence to the pope, but he was outmanoeuvred by Bernard, who held a secret meeting of the bishops before the council had opened and persuaded them to condemn the list of 'heresies'. On 16 July 1141, Innocent declared Abelard to be excommunicated. Only the intervention of the Abbot of Cluny, who gave Abelard protection for the remaining year of his life, allowed the excommunication to be lifted, so saving, one hopes, Abelard's already mutilated body from eternal punishment.

In his *Collationes* (*c*.1130), a stimulating dialogue between a Christian, a philosopher and a Jew, Abelard bemoaned the intellectual sterility of his age. He expounded on how the bastions of 'faith' had become an impediment to rational thought. 'Human understanding increases as the years pass and one age succeeds another ... yet in faith – the area in which threat of error is most dangerous – there is no progress ... This is the sure result of the fact that one is never allowed to investigate what should be believed among one's own people, or to escape punishment for raising doubts about what is said by everyone ... People profess themselves to believe what they admit they cannot understand, as if faith consisted in uttering words rather than in mental understanding.' The problem could hardly be stated more clearly.[7]

One of the most interesting features of Abelard's thought was his determination to return to the classics. As yet the texts from classical authors available to him were pitifully few. Two works of logic by Aristotle, Plato's *Timaeus* and a couple of texts by Cicero made up the main sources. (There was no way of discovering what classical texts still existed at this time, and it needed determined scholars such as Petrarch (1304–74) to scour monastic libraries for survivors.) Abelard had to have recourse to Augustine's *City of God*, which had disparaged ancient philosophy, and recast Augustine's views to show the importance of what had been rejected. He even attempted to show that the pagan philosophers had grasped the concept of the Trinity. If he had lived a few decades later, he would have been delighted with the flood of classical texts now entering from the Arab world. The link between Islam and Christianity was sustained by the famous commentaries on Aristotle by the Muslim philosopher Averroes (Ibn Rushd, 1126–98), which were adopted by many Christian theologians of the

thirteenth century and helped bring Aristotle, and the reasoned thought
he championed, back into the European consciousness. By now, universities had developed from the medieval schools. While Bologna retained
its pre-eminence in law, it was the university of Paris (the successor
of the cathedral schools) that offered the most sophisticated school of
theology. Learning was boosted by the two mendicant orders, the
Dominicans and the Franciscans, who between them provided most
of the great thinkers of the age.

The challenge of Aristotle, with his emphasis on the primacy of
reason and empirical experience, could be met in three ways. One was
to adopt his philosophical insights independently of Christianity. This
was the response of some Parisian theologians such as Siger of Brabant,
who were dubbed the 'Latin Averroists' on account of their adulation
of the Muslim philosopher. Naturally such an approach, which might
have led to genuine intellectual freedom of thought, was abhorrent to
the Church, and a large number of specific propositions attributed to
Averroes and other rationalists were condemned officially by the Bishop
of Paris in 1277. 'The most significant outcome', writes the historian
of science Edward Grant, 'was an emphasis on the reality and importance of God's absolute power to do whatever he pleases short of
bringing about a logical contradiction.'[8] This was essentially an
Augustinian approach and did nothing to encourage the study of the
laws of the natural world. The second approach to the problem, the one
favoured by conservatives, was to reject Aristotle by re-emphasising
the teaching of Augustine that faith had primacy over reason and that
worldly, empirical knowledge was to be scorned.

The third reaction was perhaps the most challenging: to try and integrate Aristotle with Christianity. It was a path fraught with difficulties,
not only because it risked challenging the Church's responsibility for its
own teaching but because Aristotle offered interpretations of the creation
and the immortality of the soul that conflicted with orthodox belief. The
greatest of these Aristotelians, and certainly one of the greatest theologians of all time, was the Dominican Thomas Aquinas (1225–1274),
who spent much of his teaching career in Paris. Aquinas absorbed the
works of Aristotle through his teacher, another Dominican, Albert the
Great, and integrated them into his *Summa Theologiae*, a massive struc-
tural survey of Christian doctrine in which reasoned judgement was
placed at the core. Aquinas brought back the possibility of reason, and
rather than decrying the power of the human mind, he exults in it. While

Augustine had argued that human beings had been so corrupted by original sin that their power of reasoning had been almost extinguished, Aquinas sees reason as a gift from God. He uses it to the full to explain Christian doctrine, including the existence of God. Yet there remained an unresolved tension. What if a particular Christian doctrine could not be defended by reason? With the clarity of thought that was his hallmark, Aquinas knew that reason had its limits.[9] In this, as has already been seen, he was going no further than pagan philosophy, which fully accepted that there were matters the human mind could not grasp. The Greek philosophers could live with the idea that there are things we cannot know.[10] This was unacceptable to the Church, which could hardly sustain its authority if it had to accept that there were fundamental problems of existence to which there were no answers. The solution, already implicit in the works of Augustine, was to elevate some aspects of Church teaching as matters of 'faith'.

Abelard had done his best to bring the Trinity within the realm of reason, but he had suffered for it at the hands of those who wished to preserve 'the faith' as some kind of mystery that was sustained above the heads and minds of those 'in the streets and market place'. Aquinas was wise enough not to try to provide a reasoned defence of the Trinity and he made it an article of faith: 'The truth that God is three and one is altogether a matter of faith; and in no way can it be demonstratively proved.' He went on to argue that trying to prove the Trinity by reason would actually detract from faith. First, faith had in itself a dignity that required the mystery of the Trinity to be preserved as one of those 'invisible realities which were beyond the reach of human reason'. Secondly, Aquinas admitted that rational arguments for doctrines such as the Trinity were bound to be unconvincing and thus they made those who proposed them the laughing stock of unbelievers. This did not mean that Aquinas did not search for analogies to help our understanding of the concept, just as Augustine did, but he accepted that ultimately the human mind was incapable of grasping the full truth.[11] One has to admire Aquinas, not only for his extraordinary intellectual qualities but for his integration of reason in theology without destroying Church authority. It was a fine balancing act even if to groups such as the Averroists it would have been seen as a capitulation.

Aquinas himself was always under pressure from conservatives. Some of his writings are to be found in the propositions condemned in 1277, three years after his death, and it is known that other campaigns were launched against him. It took the determination of Pope John XXII to recognise his genius and proclaim him a saint in 1323. His eventual integration into Catholic theology as the greatest medieval scholar of them all confirmed the status of the Trinity as an article of faith, a mystery beyond the power of reason to comprehend. As Dante ascends into Paradise in his *Divine Comedy*, he experiences the Trinity essentially in mystical terms.[12]

The problem was that this attempt to close off discussion of the Trinity, and other articles of faith, had to call on the support of the authority of the Church and state to sustain it. This explains why Innocent III drew in the secular rulers to support his fight against heresy. The common front of Church and state was underpinned by the rediscovery of Roman law. A single sixth-century manuscript of the Digest of Justinian's law code had survived in the west and turned up in Padua in about 1070. The code included Justinian's and Theodosius' laws against paganism and in support of the Trinity, so those states that now absorbed Roman law, including the Holy Roman Empire, also took on the defence of Christian orthodoxy. Thus the Trinity, embedded at the core of Church doctrine, was upheld in secular and ecclesiastical courts alike. The threat of prosecution for denying the Trinity continued in legal systems for centuries. 'It is striking to note', writes the scholar Jaroslav Pelikan, 'that the unchallenged theological hegemony of the doctrine of the Trinity, beginning in the fourth century and ending in the eighteenth and nineteenth century, was basically coextensive with the willingness and ability of civil authorities to go on enforcing it.'[13] Even the Act of Toleration, passed by the English Parliament in defiance of the Anglican Church in 1689, did not extend to tolerating arguments against the Trinity. The scientist Isaac Newton worked assiduously to demolish the scriptural arguments for the Trinity, but he could never publish what he had written.

One must not exaggerate the power of the institutional Church. When Pope Boniface VIII (1295–1303) attempted to assert his power over secular rulers by forbidding them to tax clergy and by claiming that popes should be superior over kings, he was widely resisted and then imprisoned by the French king, Philip IV. The undignified exile of the papacy to Avignon followed, and political theorists such as Marsilius of Padua were able to revive Aristotle's works on the ideal city and mount a strong case for the supremacy of the state over the

Church. It was one of several important new forces, including the re-discovery of the importance of classical learning by Petrarch and the so-called humanists, that led to a rethinking of the fundamentals of intellectual life. When the authority of the Roman Catholic Church broke down in the sixteenth century, there was a revival of alternative formulations of the Trinity, including docetism and unitarianism (the belief that there is only one person in the Godhead rather than three). However, most of the Protestant Churches maintained the orthodox doctrine of the Trinity.[14] In the Thirty-Nine Articles of the Church of England, finalised in 1571 during the reign of Queen Elizabeth, the Nicene Creed, Athanasius' Creed and the Apostles' Creed are listed together in Article Eight as acceptable statements of the faith. Catholicism as such could be condemned, but the core doctrine of orthodox Catholicism was absorbed into Protestantism.

This common front forms the background to the sorry story of the sixteenth-century physician Michael Servetus (1511–53). In his native Navarre in Spain, Servetus encountered Muslims and Jews and became aware of how offensive the doctrine of the Trinity was to them on the grounds that it made a human being (Jesus) divine. If Christianity really was a universal religion, of appeal to all, he argued, then the Trinity could not be defended, and after a wide study of the relevant texts, Servetus published his *On the Errors of the Trinity* in 1531. One of his immediate concerns was to challenge the claim of Peter Lombard, the author of the most influential textbook of medieval theology, *The Sentences*, that the doctrine of the Trinity could be found on every page of scripture. Servetus responded: 'To me not only the syllables but all the letters and the mouths of babes and sucklings, even the very stones themselves, cry out there is one God the Father and [as a sepa-rate being] his Christ, the Lord Jesus ... Not one word is found in the whole Bible about the Trinity nor about its persons, nor about the essence nor the unity of substance nor of the one nature of the several beings nor about any of the rest of their ravings and logic chopping.'[15]

Servetus' occupation allowed him to travel freely. In Lyons he fell into the hands of the Catholic Inquisition, but the body did not have enough documentary evidence of his views at hand to prosecute him for heresy. The resourceful Servetus escaped over the French border and made for Geneva, which was then presided over by the Protestant reformer John Calvin. But Servetus had sent Calvin a copy of his works, and when he arrived, Calvin had him arrested for his views on the

Trinity. With the support of his fellow reformers and the approval of Lutheran leaders, he sentenced Servetus to be burnt as a heretic. The law under which Servetus was convicted had been adopted from the code of Justinian, and it prescribed the death penalty for the crime of the denial of the Trinity. The burning of Servetus was followed by a successful rooting out of the printed edition of his *On the Errors of the Trinity*; only three copies survive today.

Worse was to come. The inevitable result of having 'faiths' based on rival doctrines that could not be supported by reasoned thought was conflict between opposing churches, in this case Catholicism and Protestantism. The destruction caused to Europe by the Wars of Religion between 1618 and 1648 was unprecedented in the range and number of countries affected. In south-west Germany, for example, no other event in recorded history has had similarly devastating effects on the population, and in some areas of central Europe the population fell, under the accumulation of atrocities, epidemics and the breakdown of agriculture, to a third of pre-war levels. It was from sheer exhaustion and horror at the atrocities and counter-atrocities that by 1648, Europeans, in the words of Jonathan Israel, 'had to accept that the Almighty, for whatever reason, refused to signal which church teaches the true faith . . . and ordained general confessional deadlock reaching from the Americas and Ireland to Poland, Hungary-Transylvania, and the fringes of the Orthodox world, with many lands in between remaining deeply split'.[16] This 'profound spiritual crisis' led to the revival of an ideal that had been lost for well over a thousand years, that of religious toleration. The forces opposing it remained powerful, and the early Enlightenment philosophies of toleration – that of John Locke, for instance – were limited, but the moral bankruptcy of the old spiritual regime was obvious. Never had the loss of the fourth-century concept that 'God enjoys being worshipped in a variety of ways' been more keenly felt.

CONCLUSION

We must not see the fact of usurpation; law was once introduced without reason, and has become reasonable. We must make it regarded as authoritative, eternal, and conceal its origin, if we do not wish that it should soon come to an end.

Blaise Pascal, *Pensées*

THERE can be few more distinguished theologians than Thomas Torrance (born 1913). Over a long life he has penetrated most of the key issues of Christian theology with enormous erudition supported by a strong faith that suffuses his work. He is especially well known for his work on the relationship between science and theology. His particular contribution is to argue that each academic discipline has its own inherent rationality, which can be understood through 'scientific' exploration. The theologian and the natural scientist, he suggests, are engaged in an identical mission in their search for truth – a mission to explore and expound the internal structure of their chosen discipline. The contrast is with Aristotle, who applied a universal system of logic, deductive and inductive reasoning, to any body of knowledge.

Torrance is also known for his rejection of dualism, the idea, rooted in Platonism, that God exists on one plane and the material world far below it on another. Rather God as creator of the world *ex nihilo*, 'out of nothing', must infuse it with his own revelation. For Torrance, knowledge of God and knowledge of the natural world both come through God and cannot be separated as Plato required. Here Torrance appears to have been strongly influenced by the Swiss-German theologian Karl Barth (1886–1968), whom he helped introduce to English-speaking audiences. Barth had argued, and here Torrance followed him, that human beings can learn little by examining the world around them through their own senses and use of reason, but rather they must search for the revelation of God. As Torrance himself put it: 'Man is sought and found; he does not seek and find. We are concerned with a movement of God to man; not a movement of man to God.'

The Incarnation of Jesus is a symbol of God's readiness 'to assume our abject servile condition, our state under the slavery of sin, in order to act for us and on our behalf from within our actual existence'.[1] In this sense the Incarnation breaks down the barrier that Plato and the Neoplatonists maintain between the material and immaterial worlds (and Barth rejects Plato's dualism as does Torrance). Unlike many theologians who write about science, Torrance is immensely respected by natural scientists, and in 1978 he was awarded the prestigious Templeton Prize for Progress in Religion.

One of Torrance's major academic interests has been the Trinity, particularly the final formulation of the doctrine in the fourth century. So it was fitting for him to be asked to give the Warfield Lectures at Princeton Theological Seminary in 1981 on the sixteen hundredth anniversary of the Council of Constantinople of 381. Here was his chance in retirement to explore a subject close to his heart. The lectures were written up in an expanded form in *The Trinitarian Faith*, published in 1988.

Torrance's thesis is that the relationship between Father and Son, as expounded at Nicaea, 'is the supreme truth upon which everything else in the Gospel depends ... It is on the ground of what God has actually revealed of his own nature in him [Jesus Christ] as his only begotten Son that everything else to be known of God and of his relation to the world and to human beings is to be understood.'[2] The bishops meeting at Nicaea confirmed a doctrine that had always been inherent in the Church's teaching. Torrance is therefore one of those theologians who sees the Nicene Trinity not as a new concept hammered out in the specific context of the fourth century, but as an eternally living truth that needed defending from those who tried to subvert it.

In the debates that raged during the fourth century, Torrance's hero is Athanasius. While many scholars have tended to be more sympathetic to the intellectual Cappadocians, Torrance sees them as having taken a wrong path by implicitly given superiority to God the Father over Jesus the Son and the Holy Spirit.[3] For Torrance it is Athanasius who again and again gets things right, and Torrance accords him the accolade of 'a scientific theologian' who proceeds in theology in the same way that natural scientists would in their field. Even if Athanasius was let down by his successors, Torrance argues that enough of his teaching persisted, mediated in some of its aspects through Epiphanius, for it to triumph at the Council of Constantinople.[4] Despite the attempts by Arians and others to destroy God's revelation of himself through Christ, the bishops, meeting first at Nicaea and then, after much more thought on the Holy Spirit, at Constantinople, safeguard what God the Father has revealed through the Son and Holy Spirit.

Torrance's argument is presented with coherence and eloquence and gains further strength from the personal faith that underpins it. Yet it leaves a serious question. What has happened to the historical events of the fourth century? In the 340 pages of a book centred on the council of 381, there is not a single reference to Theodosius, or even, in the discussions of Nicaea, to Constantine. Although Torrance decries dualism, there is a sense that the revelation of God through Jesus Christ hovers at a different level, above the actual nitty-gritty of the imperial politics that pervaded the councils and the arguments of the Church fathers. For the historian fortunate enough to have a great deal of evidence from the period, it is hard to see how the Council of Constantinople can be seen as providing a harmonious reassertion of the Nicene truth. Even its own leading participants saw it as a shambles.

The case of Torrance highlights how an alternative theological tradition has come to supplant the historical reality. Augustine, the founder of this tradition, did not write about the Council of Constantinople because he simply did not know about it. Nor does Augustine say much more about Theodosius. In his accolade of the emperor in *The City of God*, he only describes Theodosius' victory over Eugenius at the Battle of the River Frigidus and his penance after the massacre at Thessalonika. By the time of Gregory the Great, 200 years later, Theodosius has disappeared completely from the Catholic Church's records. Gregory had spent some years in Constantinople as a papal ambassador in the 580s, and he would certainly have known more than Augustine about the council of 381. He included it at the core of the western theological tradition. When he became pope, he proclaimed that 'all the four holy synods of the holy universal church [i.e. Nicaea, 325, Constantinople, 381, Ephesus, 431, Chalcedon, 451] we receive as we do the four books of the holy Gospels'.[5] He added to the authority of the councils his own as the successor of Peter. 'Without the authority and consent of the apostolic see [Rome] none of the matters transacted [by a council] have any binding force.' This imprinted in the western Church the belief that the bishops meeting in the councils had themselves resolved the doctrinal issues, although the papacy should have ultimate authority over what was to be believed. In short, the emperors had had nothing to do with the development of doctrine. With memories of imperial rule fading in the west, there was no reason for any theologian or historian to challenge Gregory's version of events. Thus the 'theological' account of the fourth century became ever more remote from the historical reality. It affects the presentation of the subject in that histories of the Church still accord the Council of Constantinople responsibility for proclaiming the Nicene faith, rather than the imperial laws that accompanied it and that provided the framework without which it would never have been enforced.

In short, there are two different approaches to AD 381. The first is theological, rooted in the fifth and sixth centuries, articulated in the works of Augustine and preserved in the theology of both the Roman Catholic and Protestant traditions: that what happened at Nicaea and Constantinople was no less than a revelation of God and as such totally independent of any historical process. This approach is strengthened by the assertions that the bishops were in consensus and that there was no possible theological alternative to Nicaea as it was developed in 381. It is to be found in most standard introductions to theology and omits any reference to the role of Theodosius.

The second is that this is a historical issue like any other, in which the evidence, from the contemporary accounts of the council and the lawmaking of the emperor, and its interpretation must take central place. It is not clear from Torrance's approach how one should actually deal with this evidence: *The Trinitarian Faith* seems to suggest that it should be ignored altogether. Yet can one obliterate the historical factors that shaped the making of Christian doctrine, in favour of doctrine being 'revealed' by God? Torrance's approach appears to create a philosophical impasse.

It is the central argument of this book that the events of 381 cannot be airbrushed from the narrative. It is time to sum up, for a historical perspective, the consequences of Theodosius' imposition of the Nicene Trinity in 381.

It is impossible to believe that the Church would itself have come to an enforceable consensus on the Trinity if an emperor had not provided the legal framework within which the Nicenes could be privileged over the various groups of 'heretics' who opposed them. Theodosius' role was crucial. His powers and status as a quasi-divine figure transcended those of his rivals in any case, but the Church was beset by its own internal tensions, which would have precluded consensus. What Theodosius achieved was the championing of one Christian faction over another and the strengthening of its position by ostracising its rivals, both Christian and pagan. He was helped by the disunity of those who opposed the resurgent Nicenes and the immense patronage he could divert to those Nicenes who took over the bishoprics after the expulsion of the 'Arians'.

The theocracy of the emperor, initiated, of course, by Constantine some seventy years before Theodosius' edict, was sustained by the imperial intervention in the council of 451 at Chalcedon, which led to the Chalcedonian doctrine of the human and divine nature of Christ. Here the emperor Marcian's officials were instrumental in devising a formula that could then be imposed by the emperor independently of the corrosive debate of the bishops. When, in the west, some 150 years later, Pope Gregory claimed that the bishops themselves had achieved consensus at these councils, he was ignoring the historical record and the well-documented role of the emperors. This was understandable in view of his desperate need to assert his own papal authority at a time of social and economic breakdown, but his initiative allowed the essentially political aspects of the matter and the historical context to be submerged.

The fact that the emperors provided the framework within which a solution could be enforced did not mean that the theological debates of the fourth century were not highly sophisticated. One of the aims of this book is to show that theological thought operated at as high an intellectual level as other fields of enquiry for which Greek philosophy was famous. The problem – and here I would part company with many theologians – is that these issues did not seem capable of philosophical resolution (and those philosophers outside the tradition of Platonism would certainly have recognised this). The finding of certainty depends on incontrovertible axioms or empirical evidence from which an argument can begin. When the historian Socrates said that the Nicene debates were 'like a battle fought at night, for neither party

appeared to understand distinctly the grounds on which they calumniated one another', he was describing a debate that lacked any agreed
foundations. Although there were defined areas of conflict – over the
interpretation of specific verses from the scriptures, for instance –
the ground was always shifting as scripture and philosophy were
used to achieve different ends. There was never a moment when
the antagonists sat down and tried to set out the assumptions they
shared and their ultimate objectives. Personal and political antagonisms intruded all too easily. Inevitably there were some, such as
Athanasius and Ambrose, who used bullying tactics, which included
the denigration of their opponents. The bitter nature of the debate
overshadows the intellectual qualities of many of the participants,
such as the Cappadocian Fathers and the Eunomians. The high
standard of argument and analysis on both sides is what gives the
debate its importance.

The elimination of the different perspectives, above all those of the
subordinationists, from the Christian tradition is a major loss. For
centuries they were subject to routine denigrations by orthodox theologians. 'On the one side their doctrine was a mass of presumptuous
theorising supported by alternate scraps of obsolete traditionalism and
uncritical textmongering, on the other it was a lifeless system of unspir-
itual pride and hard unlovingness' runs one tirade against the 'Arians'
from a work regarded as the authoritative English study of the issue
for fifty years.[6] It is time that such narrow and prejudiced assessments
of the debates of the fourth century were rejected and the intellectual
achievements of the subordinationists accorded greater respect. It is
only then that the theological sophistication of the debate can be appreciated.

Perhaps the most extraordinary legacy of AD 381 lies in the definition of God it bequeathed to European thought, a definition that has
had an enormous impact on the way in which the philosophy of religion is approached even today. On my desk as I write is a well-received
volume, *Metaphysics: A Guide and Anthology*.[7] Part One is simply
entitled 'God'. Why not 'The Possibility of the Supernatural'? It is quite
acceptable to conceive, as the Greeks did, of other ways of conceptual-
ising an immaterial world that does not include a supreme creator who
maintains a continuing interest in one species in one tiny part of the
universe. The primary question in the philosophy of religion should
be, one might argue, that of how to define the supernatural and develop

methods to discover whether such a dimension exists at all. Instead, after AD 381, all the preliminary problems were ignored and the issue was discussed solely in terms of the existence or non-existence of a much more narrowly defined entity, 'God'. As Richard Hanson recognised (see p. 102), AD 381, followed by the suppression of pagan alternatives, was a decisive moment that led to the narrowing of perspectives on the supernatural.

Another result of the closing of the debate was the creation of the confrontation between science and Christianity. There is no attempt here to argue that science and religion (which covers an enormous variety of 'spiritual' activities) are necessarily in conflict. The problem only arises when religions begin proclaiming certainties. The Greeks had no trouble in differentiating between *logos* – a reasoned account, such as one might find in mathematics, the sciences or even history – and *mythos*, an imagined narrative as in a religious myth or a work of art. Any healthy mind needed *mythoi*: we cannot live without imagination and speculation, not least because speculation often provides the inspiration for reasoned thought. It was accepted that the truth of a myth could not be proved; its power operated at a different level and one could never assume any kind of certainty in its content. When the Church acquiesced in Theodosius' legislative programme, it replaced sophisticated speculation about the ways in which the relationships between God the Father and Jesus the Son might be expressed – this speculation was certainly in the realm of *mythos* – with the acceptance of a single dogmatic formula. There had always been debate over where the boundaries between *mythoi* and *logoi* lay,[8] but a philosophically coherent distinction between the two could be maintained. Now the Christians, by insisting that elements of what had always been accepted as unprovable speculation (*mythoi*) could be accorded the status of eternal truths, the 'leap of faith' replacing the long hard slog of reason, had destroyed that distinction.

This was hardly recognised at the time, but by the sixteenth and seventeenth centuries, the certainties of 'faith' were challenged as rational thought reasserted the status it had enjoyed in the ancient Greek world as a means of achieving knowledge.[9] A confrontation was inevitable. Since the seventeenth century, articles of faith have been continually eroded by the growth of scientific knowledge and Christianity has been split between those who cling to ancient beliefs, however impossible to defend rationally (creationism, for instance), and those who reinterpret their faith to fill the shrinking spaces where science cannot reach (and, in many cases, will never reach). Moreover, it is possible to argue that the remaining articles of faith that fill these spaces are not there because there is any rational support for them but often as a result of historical accident. This was certainly the case with Theodosius' programme of the 380s and 390s. This does not prevent the articles of faith being proclaimed as truths, but they can only be defended by 'revelation' or 'the authority of the Church'. It is a position that, of course, many scientists and philosophers cannot accept. While the scientific tradition relies on speculation and imaginative responses to problems, it also acknowledges just how hard certainty is to achieve and so is rightly suspicious of those who claim to know the answers to the major questions of existence.

The acceptance of Theodosius' law by the Church also consolidated a new approach to reward and punishment in the hereafter. Christian ethics can be derived from the teachings of Jesus in the gospels. Early Christian communities placed a strong emphasis on caring for their own, and this tradition was continued even in the opulent days of the fourth century by such impressive monk-bishops as Basil of Caesarea, who combined intellectual brilliance with a programme of building leper colonies. But increasingly access to heaven or hell seemed to depend on holding correct belief, so that the self-glorifying Nicene Ambrose of Milan is assumed to be destined for heaven while the 'Arian' missionary Ulfilas and the brilliant Origen are assumed not to be. In essence, sainthood had become politicised. The culmination of this approach is to be found in Augustine's belief as expressed in *The City of God* that good works cannot guarantee you a place in heaven. (Of course, as so often in Augustine's work, the influence of Paul is to be found here.) Hand in hand with this questionable development goes the elaboration of the horror of hell fire used by the religious authorities in their fight against potential dissidents.

The tragedy of Thoedosius' imposition and its aftermath lay in the elimination of discussion, not only of spiritual matters but across the whole spectrum of human knowledge. 'Pagan' thinkers shared with many Christians a belief that freedom of debate was an essential part of a healthy society. The Nicene debates themselves show that intellectual progress was being made, because the participants were continually revising their positions in response to each other. From 381 onwards, Theodosius and his successors eliminated the tradition of free speech.

By deriding the opponents of Nicaea as 'demented heretics' and threat-ening them with the weight of the law and eternal punishment, they destroyed the possibilities of continuing the debate. The legal process was adapted to deal with those defined as 'heretics'. It was a precedent from which there was to be no turning back. In the east, by the time of Justinian, the law code of the empire was promulgated jointly in the name of the emperor and a Nicene Jesus Christ: paganism, including the activities of the philosophers, was outlawed. In the west, Augustine devel-oped a rationale for the persecution of those who opposed what was now established as 'truth'. He went even further by denigrating intellec-tual curiosity and so casting a pall over the joy of learning. The Armenian bishop who noted, as early as the fifth century, that 'clever theologians soon become heretics' was proved right.

The conclusion that can be put forward is a radical one, but it seems to best fit the historical evidence. Through the intervention of the state, Theodosius brought to a premature end a debate that was still vital and full of possibilities. The Church was forced by the sheer weight of imperial power to acquiesce in a doctrine that had not come to fruition and that, if debate had been allowed to continue, might never have. No one can say whether the Greek tradition of free thought would have continued in either east or west, or how intellectual life would have evolved without Theodosius' intervention. There were many other pressures and events that led to the evolution of Byzantine autoc-racy and the emergence of an effective papacy (Gregory VII, Innocent III) centuries after the collapse of imperial authority in the west. What is certain is that, in the west, the historical reality, that the Nicene Trinity was imposed from above on the Church by an emperor, disap-peared from the record. A harmonised version of what happened at the Council of Constantinople, highlighting a consensus for which there is little historical evidence, concealed the enforcement of the doctrine of the Nicene Trinity through the medium of imperial legislation. The aim of this book has been to reveal what has been concealed. Arguably, the year AD 381 deserves to be seen as one of the most important moments in the history of European thought.

APPENDIX: THE CREEDS OF NICAEA (325), CONSTANTINOPLE (381) AND ATHANASIUS (c.430?)

THE following is the creed passed at Nicaea:

We believe in one God Father Almighty Maker of all things, seen and unseen:

And in one Lord Jesus Christ the Son of God, begotten as only-begotten of the Father, that is of the substance (*ousia*) of the Father, God from God, Light of Light, true God of true God, begotten not made, consubstantial (*homoousios*) with the Father, through whom all things came into existence, both things in heaven and things on earth: who for us men and for our salvation came down and was incarnate and became man, suffered and rose again on the third day, ascended into the heavens, is coming to judge the living and the dead:

And in the Holy Spirit.

But those who say 'there was a time when he did not exist' [e.g. Arius and his followers], and 'Before being begotten he did not exist', and that he came into being from non-existence, or who allege that the Son of God is of another *hypostasis* or *ousia*, or is alterable or changeable, these the Catholic and Apostolic Church condemns.

The creed passed at Constantinople in 381 runs as follows:

We believe in one God Father Almighty, maker of heaven and earth and all things, seen and unseen;

And in one Lord Jesus Christ the Son of God, the Only-begotten, begotten by his Father before all ages, Light from Light, true God from true God, begotten not made, consubstantial (*homoousios*) with the Father, through whom all things came into existence, who for us men and for our salvation came down from the heavens and became incarnate by the Holy Spirit and the Virgin Mary and became a man, and was crucified for us under Pontius Pilate and suffered and was buried and rose again on the third day in accordance with the Scriptures and ascended into the heavens and is seated at the right hand of the Father and will come again to judge the living and the dead, and there will be no end to his kingdom;

And in the Holy Spirit, the Lord and Life-Giver, who proceeds from the Father, who is worshipped and glorified together with the Father and the Son, who spoke through the prophets;

And in one holy, catholic and apostolic Church;

We confess one baptism for the forgiveness of sins;

We wait for the resurrection of the dead and the life of the coming age, Amen.

The Constantinople Creed is a slightly modified form of the Nicene Creed. It drops the anathemas against the Arians and enlarges the section on the Holy Spirit, raising the status of the Spirit without making it 'of one substance' with the Father and Son. This appears to follow the position taken by Basil of Caesarea and it effectively excludes the Macedonians, who wished to retain the lowly status of the Holy Spirit in the creed of 325. It omits 'that is of the substance (*ousia*) of the Father', surprisingly in view of the central position *homoousios* had taken in the debate, although 'consubstantial' is retained in its original position.

The Athanasian Creed was probably composed in the first half of the fifth century in southern Gaul, in other words near the time of Augustine's death in 430. Despite its title, no one has been able to link it directly to Athanasius and it seems that it was originally composed in Latin, which is why its origin is assumed to be in the west. It sets out a definition of the Trinity as follows:

We worship one God in the Trinity and the Trinity in unity, without either confusing the persons or dividing the substance; for the person of the Father is one, the Son's is another, the Holy Spirit's another; but the Godhead of Father, Son and Holy Spirit is one, their glory equal, their majesty equally eternal. Such as the Father is, such is the Son, such also the Holy Spirit; uncreated is the Father, uncreated the Son, uncreated the Holy Spirit; infinite is the Father, infinite the Son, infinite the Holy Spirit; eternal is the Father, eternal the Son, eternal the Holy Spirit; yet they are not three eternal beings, but one eternal, just as they are not three uncreated beings or three infinite beings, but one uncreated and one infinite . . . Thus the Father is God, the Son is God, the Holy Spirit is God; yet they are not three gods but one God . . .

The creed ends with the famous/notorious anathemas: 'And they that have done good shall go into life everlasting and they that have done evil into everlasting fire. This is the catholic faith which, except a man believe faithfully and firmly, he cannot be saved.'

NOTES

Preface

1. For details, see Select Bibliography.
2. Callahan shows how, in particular, Psalm 68, Verse 31: 'Ethiopia shall stretch out her hands under God' has inspired dreams of the return of black evangelicals to Africa.

Introduction

1. In 'Christian Accounts of the Religious Legislation of Theodosius I', R. Malcolm Errington carries out a meticulous analysis of Theodosius' legislation as it was recorded by contemporary historians. He suggests that its impact has been exaggerated by modern historians. The point is taken, but the cumulative effect of church and state policies against heretics and pagans does seem to mark a significant turning point, and this is the argument made in this book.

Chapter One: Disaster

1. For a standard comprehensive history of the empire, see Mackay.
2. A fine narrative overview of the fourth and fifth century crisis can be found in Peter Heather's *Fall of the Roman Empire*. Heather, who is an acknowledged expert on the Goths, sees the appearance of the Huns as the crucial factor that tipped the balance against the Romans. I have used Heather as my main background source for this chapter. See also Potter.

3.   For Ammianus Marcellinus' fuller assessment of Valens' character, see his *The Later Roman Empire*, tr. Walter Hamilton, London, 1986, Book 31:13.

4.   Potter (pp.536–7) specifically notes the remarkable stability of the upper echelons of the civil service of the two regimes.

5.   Ammianus Marcellinus, op.cit., Book 31:2, for his description of the Huns.

6.   Ibid., Book 31:6.

7.   Ibid., Book 31:12–13, for Ammianus Marcellinus' graphic description of the battle and the death of Valens.

8.   For Theodosius' background and early life see Friell and Williams, Chapter Two.

Chapter Two: The Divine Emperor

1.   I have drawn heavily on Sabine MacCormack's *Art and Ceremony in Late Antiquity*, for this chapter. On the accession of the members of the House of Valentinian, see Section II, Part One:5. Themistius' words come from his Oration 5:64 b–c and are quoted in Garnsey and Humfress, p.25.

2.   Quoted in MacCormack, pp.206–7. The quotation comes from Themistius' Oration 15.

3.   See Cameron and Hall. The quotation comes from 1:6 of this work. For the Oration in Praise of Constantine (often referred to as the *Laus Constantini*), see Drake, Chapter Ten, 'The Fine Print'. See also Van Dam, 'The Many Conversions of the Emperor Constantine', pp.127–51.

4.   Themistius is quoted in MacCormack, p.210. Themistius, Oration 15:189 b–c. For the quotation on rhetoric, see Cameron, p.132. Discussing the plea for clemency made by the Bishop of Antioch, Flavianus, to Theodosius when tax riots broke out in Antioch in 387, Cameron notes how one is surprised by 'the boldness of Christian writers, who unblushingly placed the emperor in the role of God himself'.

5.   Ammianus Marcellinus, *The Later Roman Empire*, tr. Walter Hamilton, London, 1986, Book 16:10.

6.   Quoted in Cameron, p.129. Synesius (died AD 413) is interesting because his surviving speeches show him as a sceptical Christian who remains deeply attracted to Greek philosophy. When asked

to become a bishop, for instance, he hesitates because he is uncertain whether the resurrection actually happened or not. See the opening chapters of Cameron and Long.

7. I was not the only one to be reminded of this famous quotation when President Bush was commenting on the Israeli invasion of Lebanon in July 2006. It comes from Tacitus' *Agricola*, as does the quotation about the Britons being seduced by bathhouses.

8. A long quotation from Aelius Aristides' panegyric to Rome can be found in Lewis and Reinhold, pp.135–8.

9. 600,000 is the figure given for the fourth-century Roman armies by Ward-Perkins, p.41.

10. The separation of Illyricum reflected moments when the security of the important Danube border was under particular threat, but it was an unwieldy administrative area as it was split between Latin- and Greek-speaking communities, and in 395 it was to be permanently divided along the linguistic boundary.

11. Garnsey and Humfress, Chapter Three, 'Emperors and Bureaucrats', provide a succinct introduction to the administration. See also Christopher Kelly, and Chapter Three, 'The Limits of Empire', of Heather. Specifically on law, see Matthews, *Laying Down the Law*, Chapter Two, 'Emperors, Laws and Jurists'; Errington, *Roman Imperial Policy from Julian to Theodosius*; and Honoré.

12. There are reconstructions in Friell and Williams, and in Chapters Two and Four of Heather.

13. Quoted in Heather, p.186.

14. Theodoret, *Ecclesiastical History*, Book 4:30. Available in the Select Library of Nicene and Post-Nicene Fathers of the Christian Church, second series, Volume Three, Oxford, 1892, or through the Internet.

15. Quoted in Friell and Williams, p.53. The original is found in the Theodosian Code, 16:1, 2.

16. Sozomen, *Ecclesiastical History*, 7:4:5.

17. For this see Matthews, *Western Aristocracies*, especially Chapter IV, 'The Accession of Theodosius', and Chapter VI, 'Provincial Upper Classes: Evangelism and Heresy'; and Sauer, especially, for the west, Chapters Five and Six.

Chapter Three: Free Speech in the Classical World

1. This is Themistius' Oration 5. It is to be found, with commentary, in Heather and Moncur, Chapter Three. The ancient post of consul, held by two men for a year, was the most senior of the magistracies, and emperors would use it to boost either their own status or that of senior officials they wished to honour.

2. The quotation comes from Book III:43 of Thucydides, *The Peloponnesian War*, Rex Warner translation, Harmondsworth, 1954.

3. Aristotle, the opening sentence of his *Metaphysics* (I.1.980a21–7). The opening paragraphs of the *Metaphysics* are often quoted as the direct opposite of the view put forward many centuries later by Augustine that curiosity is 'a disease'. Aristotle's view was championed by Thomas Aquinas, who sought to bring the power of reason and delight in learning back into European thought. See further Chapter Fourteen.

4. See Lloyd, *Magic, Reason and Experience* and *The Revolutions of Wisdom*, for studies in the evolution of Greek philosophy and science.

5. Geoffrey Lloyd. In one of his more recent studies, *Ancient Worlds, Modern Reflections*, Lloyd shows how in China in these same centuries, the state was, in the last resort, the only employer of intellectuals and thus there was a premium on conformity.

6. See 'Rhetoric' in Brunschwig and Lloyd, pp.465–85. The quotation from Gorgias is on p.474.

7. Aristotle, *Metaphysics* II. 1. 993a30–34.

8. See Bobzien for an excellent example of how debates within Stoicism remained at a high level.

9. Cicero, *Tusculanae disputationes*, 2.2.7. Quoted in Snyder, p.93. This is an excellent introduction to the issue discussed here.

10. These are well covered in Ehrman.

11. Quoted in Grafton and Williams, p.63.

12. For the following discussion of Porphyry and Lactantius I have drawn heavily on Digeser.

13. Ibid., p.110.

14. The decree is printed in full in Lewis and Reinhold, pp.602–4. For comment on its importance, see Drake, p.195.

15. Liebeschuetz, *Continuity and Change in Roman Religion*, p.300.

Chapter Four: The Coming of the Christian State

1. See Richard Norris, 'Articulating Identity', Chapter Eight in Young, Ayres and Louth. This is useful for many of the themes discussed in the early part of this chapter.
2. Quoted in Ehrman, p.141.
3. The concept of apostolic succession is well dealt with in Pelikan, *The Christian Tradition* pp.108–20.
4. Quoted in Markus, *Gregory the Great and his World*, p.7.
5. A good introduction to early Christian texts can be found in Ehrman.
6. The name Tanakh derives from the three parts of the Jewish scriptures: the Torah, the five books of Moses; the Nevi'im, the Prophets; and the Kethuvim, the Writings (which include the Psalms, the Book of Job, the Song of Songs and Ecclesiastes).
7. For Marcion, see Pelikan, *The Christian Tradition*, pp.72–81.
8. Quoted in MacMullen, *Christianising the Roman Empire*, p.40.
9. Quoted in Rives, pp.285–307 for this theme. The quotation is from Cyprian's *De Unitate*, 17.428.
10. Quoted in Ehrman, p.137.
11. Liebeschuetz, *The Decline and Fall of the Roman City*, p.140.
12. The quotation from Jerome's Letter XXII is to be found in *Select Letters of St Jerome*, translated by F. A. Wright, London, 1933. The quotation from Dante comes from the *Inferno*, Canto XIX, lines 115–117, translated by Barbara Reynolds. The degree to which European architecture was revolutionised by this building programme is still often unrecognised, but see Janes.
13. Cameron and Hall, Book One:38.
14. This is the central argument of Drake. The developments described below can be followed in this book.
15. For a balanced assessment of the dispute and Arius' ideas, see Williams.
16. Socrates, *Ecclesiastical History*, I.23.6. An English translation is to be found in the Select Library of Nicene and Post-Nicene Fathers of the Christian Church, second series, Oxford and New York, 1891.
17. For accounts of the Council, see Hanson, *The Search for the Christian Doctrine of God*, Chapter Six, and Drake, pp.251–8.

18. Hanson, *The Search for the Christian Doctrine of God*, p.168.
19. Quoted in Drake, p.311. It comes from a letter written in *c.* 335 to the bishops.
20. Potter, p.577.

Chapter Five: True God from True God?

1. See MacMullen, *Voting About God in Early Church Councils*, pp.30–1.
2. Origen, *On First Principles*, 2.6. Quoted in Ford and Higton, p.87.
3. *Catechetical Orations*, number 14.
4. For examples, see Vaggione, pp.107–8, and Hanson, *The Search for the Christian Doctrine of God*, pp.106–9.
5. Philo, *Quis Rerum Divinarum Heres Sit*, 205.
6. Quoted in Hanson, *The Search for the Christian Doctrine of God*, pp.344–5.
7. Ibid., p.346.
8. From Arius' *Thalia* (320s), quoted in Ford and Higton, pp.86–7.
9. Richard Vaggione provides full details of Eunomius' life and thought. Although it has been customary to denigrate Eunomius, he played a vital part in the debate by producing reasoned objections to the Nicenes that forced them to clarify their own views.
10. Ayres, p.160. 'We should be careful of assuming that this preference [for Nicaea] reveals a detailed understanding of Nicaea: it probably reflects a growing suspicion that those who pushed the Dated creed understood its somewhat vague terminology in subordinationist senses they found unacceptable. Nicaea was the obvious alternative, the most appropriate cipher for their own sensibilities.' Ayres' is a meticulous study of the process by which the Nicene Trinity achieved a broader acceptance. He is more sensitive than earlier commentators to the different paths ('trajectories' as he terms them), which coalesced to bring greater (but certainly not total) acceptance of Nicaea in the second half of the century.
11. Hanson, *The Search for the Christian Doctrine of God*, p.380.
12. Quoted in Wiles, p.28.
13. Ammianus Marcellinus, *The Later Roman Empire*, tr. Walter Hamilton, London, 1986, Book 22:5.

14. For the quotation from Ammianus Marcellinus, see ibid., Book 23:3. See MacMullen, *Voting about God in Early Church Councils*, Chapter Five, 'The Violent Element', for his thoughts about the high level of religious violence in these years.

15. An excellent introduction to Athanasius is to be found in David Brakke, 'Athanasius' in Philip Esler, Volume Two, pp.1102–27. The quotation comes from p.1120. Richard Hanson notes, on p.422 of *The Search for the Christian Doctrine of God*, that Athanasius 'is no favourer of Greek philosophy' and decries it in his work *Contra Gentes*. He preferred to root his theology specifically in the scriptures, although he was also a somewhat obsessive defender of *homoousios*, even though the word is unscriptural.

16. As David Potter puts it: 'As Athanasius' extensive discourse on his woes dominates the later historiographic traditions of the church, it is now very hard to see the history of the period in any way but his.' It is only recently that scholars have begun to recover the many tangled strands that made up the thinking of both Nicene and subordinationist groups. Potter, p.420. The quotation from Athanasius comes from his *Against the Arians*, discourse II, para. 58.

17. Quoted in Pelikan, *Christianity and Classical Culture*, p.175. For Gregory of Nazianzus' life, see McGluckin.

18. Online translation can be accessed at www.earlychristianwritings.com/fathers

19. McGluckin, p.57.

20. Quoted in Ayres, p.205.

21. It is discussed in ibid., Chapter Fourteen.

22. See McGrath, *Christian Theology*, p.331.

23. Ammianus Marcellinus, op.cit., Book 30:9.

24. Sozomen, *History of the Church*, VI:7:2. An English translation is to be found in the Select Library of Nicene and Post-Nicene Fathers of the Christian Church, second series, Oxford and New York, 1891.

25. A good summary of the relationships of Valentinian and Valens with the churches can be found in Errington, *Roman Imperial Policy from Julian to Theodosius*, Chapter VII.

26. MacMullen, *Voting About God in Early Church Councils*, p.32.

Chapter Six: The Swansong of Free Speech: the Theological Orations of Gregory of Nazianus

1. The transition is described in Limberis.
2. McGluckin, Chapter Five, 'An Invitation to Byzantium', and Chapter Six, 'Archbishop of Constantinople', cover the main events in this chapter and the next. Gregory's own account survives as well as two poems that describe his fears as he sets out for his appointment in Constantinople.
3. Quoted in Van Dam, *Kingdom of Snow*, p.139.
4. Lines 696 ff. in Carolinne White's translation of *De Vita Sua*, which contains the sad story of Gregory's time in Constantinople.
5. Oration 21 in the accepted numeration – this numeration does not necessarily follow the chronological sequence in which the orations were given. See McGluckin, pp.266–9, for a summary and analysis.
6. 'There were certainly Eunomian theologians, as well as Homoian clergy of Demophilus in attendance at these orations, and Gregory knew that he was expected to give the performance of his life.' Ibid., p.277. MacMullen, *Voting About God in Early Church Councils*, discusses how popular involvement in city assemblies was transferred into Church councils (Chapter Two, 'The Democratic Element'), and he has further comments, p.51 ff.
7. I have used Norris here. The translations of the orations are by F. Williams and I. Wickham.
8. See the discussion in Vaggione, beginning on p.234.
9. Norris, p.176.

Chapter Seven: Constantinople, 381: the Imposition of Orthodoxy

1. King has the full versions of the edicts/decrees with comment. I have also drawn on Errington, *Roman Imperial Policy from Julian to Theodosius*, from which this quotation is taken (p.222). Errington sees the decree as focused on Illyricum alone, where there were substantial Homoian populations.
2. White, lines 1514–17.
3. A full account is given by McGluckin, pp.350–69.
4. White, lines 1680–7.
5. Ibid., lines 1704–9. For the interference of the emperor, see Hanson, *The Search for the Christian Doctrine of God*, pp.814–15.

6. Epistle 130, quoted in Ruether, p.48.
7. Sozomen's comments are in his *History of the Church*, Book VII:8; Socrates' in his *Ecclesiastical History*, V:8.
8. Sozomen, op.cit., VII:9.
9. Flavian was consecrated but Paulinus' supporters refused to give in. Paulinus went off to a council in Rome in 382, where he was endorsed by the western bishops. The eastern bishops seem to have split over the issue, leaving an awkward void in this important part of the empire.
10. Socrates, op.cit., V:8.
11. Theodoret, *Ecclesiastical History*, Book V:9. Available in the Select Library of Nicene and Post-Nicene Fathers of the Christian Church, second series, Volume Three, Oxford, 1892, or through the Internet.
12. Sozomen, op.cit., VII:12.
13. Ibid., VII:12.
14. Hanson, *Studies in Christian Antiquity*, 'The Doctrine of the Trinity Achieved in 381'. The quotation is on pp.243–4.

Chapter Eight: Ambrose and the Politics of Control

1. Julian, *Contra Galilaeos*, 113D (Wilmer Wright translation, London, 1961).
2. Ayres, p.70.
3. Gregory of Nazianzus, Oration 21:35.
4. Ayres, p.60.
5. 'I never heard the Nicene creed until I was exiled', from Hilary's *De Synodis*, 91. See Hanson, *The Search for the Christian Doctrine of God*, Chapter Fifteen, for an account of Hilary's ideas.
6. Ibid., p.501.
7. Jerome, Epistle 69:9. Quoted in Chadwick, p.434.
8. A balanced biography of Ambrose is by N. McLynn. I have drawn heavily on it for this chapter.
9. *De Fide*, 2:13.
10. Hanson, *The Search for the Christian Doctrine of God*, pp.672–3.
11. J. N. D. Kelly, p.143. The metaphor originates in one of Aesop's Tales but is also found in the works of the poet Horace.
12. Quoted in McLynn, p.114.
13. Symmachus, *Relatio* ('Official Dispatch'), 3:5, 8, 10, to be found

in Croke and Harries, pp.37–8. See Matthews, *Western Aristocracies*, pp.203–11, for discussion of the conflict.

14. Croke and Harries, Chapter Two, for the text of Ambrose's reply.

Chapter Nine: The Assault on Paganism

1. McLynn, pp.298 ff. for the Callinicum affair.
2. Clark, p.112.
3. Eunapius of Sardis, *Vitae Sophistarium*, vi.11 (*c*.395); quoted in Rousseau, p.9.
4. Libanius, Oration 30: *Pro Templis*. A good discussion of this oration can be found in Sizgorich, pp.75–101. For the archaeological evidence, see Sauer.
5. Friell and Williams, pp.65–7.
6. The long-term results of the confrontation, if such it was, were important. A hundred years later, the imperial structure of the western empire collapsed with the abdication of the boy emperor Romulus Augustulus in 476. The Church hierarchy was, however, to survive, and under the papacies of Leo I (440–461) and Gregory the Great (590–604), the bishops emerged as secular rulers, defending Rome and dealing directly with kings and chieftains, both Christian and non-Christian. Ambrose's interpretation of the events of 390, that an emperor had recognised the supremacy of the Church, became embedded in Catholic ideology now that there was no alternative secular tradition left to challenge it. In the tortuous tussle for supremacy between Hildebrand, Pope Gregory VII (1073–85), and the Holy Roman Emperor Henry IV, Gregory was able to rely on the precedent of 390 with some success.
7. Friell and Williams, Chapter Six, '*Contra paganos*', for the outline of the measures against pagans. The law on the status of lapsed Christians is to be found in Salzman, p.196.
8. Quoted in Rousseau, p.119.
9. Theodoret, *Ecclesiastical History*, V:24, describes the battle, but he is already mythologising it as a Christian versus pagan conflict. See the comments of Errington in *Roman Imperial Policy from Julian to Theodosius*, pp.253–8. Augustine, *The City of God*, Book V, Chapter Twenty-Six, tells how 'Soldiers who took part in the battle have told us that the javelins were wrenched from

their hands as they aimed them when a violent wind blew from the side of Theodosius towards the enemy and not only whirled away with the utmost rapidity the missiles discharged against the emperor's forces but even turned them back on to the bodies of the foes.' It was accounts such as this that allowed stories of miracles to emerge and become consolidated.

10. Edward Gibbon, *The Decline and Fall of the Roman Empire*, Volume 3, Chapter 26.
11. Bede, *The Ecclesiastical History of the English People*, Book 2, Chapter Two.
12. Ehrman and Jacobs, pp.57–67, reprint the funeral oration.
13. Quoted in Cameron, p.136.
14. Errington, *Roman Imperial Policy from Julian to Theodosius*, p.249.

Chapter Ten: Epiphanius' Witchhunt

1. J. N. D. Kelly, p.197.
2. A succinct introduction to Origen can be found in Chapter Twenty-One of Chadwick. See also Chapter Eleven of Ayres, Young and Louth, 'The Alexandrians' by Ronald Heine.
3. McGluckin, p.37.
4. Chadwick, p.135.
5. Ibid., p.138.
6. Bynum is the place to start. Origen is dealt with in Chapter Two. Origen's later critics, who insisted on an actual material body being reconstituted, got themselves involved in absurd discussions as to how this body would be, whether it would still have sinful genitals or not, and so on.
7. Chadwick, p.137.
8. Jerome's respect for Origen was so widely known that even at the height of the controversy that followed, Augustine was able to write to Jerome from the west to ask for more translations of Greek works, 'especially that Origen you mention in your writings with particular pleasure'. J. N. D. Kelly provides a good narrative account of this controversy.
9. The scene is described in Jerome's letter *Against John*, which can easily be accessed in translation on the Internet.
10. Letter 82. The quotation is from J. N. D. Kelly, p.208.

11. Even though he had been declared a heretic, some of Origen's works survived, and they were to be championed in the sixteenth century by the great humanist scholar Erasmus. What attracted Erasmus to Origen was his belief in free will and reason. Origen's belief that one should be curious, sceptical and confident of the possibilities of human creativity appealed to Renaissance humanists. Erasmus saw Origen's approach to theology as far superior to the narrow pessimism of Augustine, who had openly derided what he called 'the disease of curiosity' and portrayed humanity as sunk in sin. Yet like their Catholic counterparts, the Protestant Reformers would later choose Augustine over Origen and warn their flocks of their sinfulness and the inevitability of their eternal damnation. See Diarmaid MacCulloch, pp.113–14.

12. For Greek and classical views on the afterlife, see Segal, Chapter Five. MacMullen provides an unusual overview of the contrast between pagan and Christian views of the afterlife in his *Voting About God in Early Church Councils*, p.47:

> Non-Christians in the Greco-Roman world, so far as we can enter their thoughts, evidently accepted the possibility of superhuman beings at work in great events, earthquakes or military disasters; but the possibility had little reality, it was little considered. Minor events causing loss or pain also might be blamed on superhuman agents, invoked by magic. That too was a reality off the side, so as to speak, a rare thing, forbidden, a resort for only wicked and credulous people. In fact, superhuman beings were beneficent. So the philosophers said, and common piety agreed . . . To blame evil on the gods was deeply impious and it made no sense.
>
> Into this Greco-Roman thought world, Christianity introduced an alternative view: one of opposing forces, God's and Satan's, alike able to smite and confound. It established itself in step with Christianity itself, and was as universally spread about as other Christian beliefs, through the preaching of the churches' leaders and the elaboration of stories about the church's heroes. They too were able to hurt as to heal.

13. Bremmer notes (p.57) that 'the New Testament has very little to say about the existence of heaven, hell or purgatory', although the apocalyptic sayings of Jesus in the synoptic gospels do suggest a division into saved and unsaved. I have used Bremmer's account

for the background material here unless otherwise cited. It is significant that *The Cambridge History of Christianity: Origins to Constantine* (ed. Margaret M. Mitchell and Frances Young, Cambridge, 2006) has no entry for 'hell' in its index.

14. See Lloyd, *In the Grip of Disease*, p.233.

15. See Augustine's *The City of God*, Book XXI, Chapter 12 (from which the quotation is taken) onwards. See also the entry on 'hell' in Fitzgerald.

16. This is perhaps one explanation why intellectual life in the pagan world was so much livelier and unrestrained than it was under Christianity in the years following Theodosius' law. It is hard to find anything positive to say about the doctrine of hell as it was developed in the fourth century and elaborated in increasingly extravagant language in the centuries to come. Perhaps the most eloquent sermon made on the subject is that by the American preacher Jonathan Edwards, in his 'Sinners in the Hands of an Angry God' (1741). The most notorious passage runs as follows (Marsden):

> The God that holds you over the pit of hell, much as one holds a spider, or some loathsome insect, over the fire, abhors you, and is dreadfully provoked; his wrath towards you burns like fire; he looks upon you as worthy of nothing else, but to be cast into the fire; he is of purer eyes than to bear to have you in his sight; you are ten thousand times so abominable in his eyes as the most hateful venomous serpent is in ours. You have offended him infinitely more than ever a stubborn rebel did his prince: and yet 'tis nothing but his hand that holds you from falling into the fire every moment: 'tis to be ascribed to nothing else, that you did not go to hell the last night ... but that God's hand has held you up; there is no other reason to be given why you haven't gone to hell since you have sat here in the house of God, provoking his pure eye by your sinful wicked manner of attending his solemn worship; yea, there is nothing else to be given as a reason why you don't this very moment drop down into hell.
>
> Oh sinner! Consider the fearful danger you are in.

Edwards implies that he himself will not suffer this dreadful fate, but it is unclear on what grounds he excludes himself. Contemporary accounts suggest that Edwards' congregation was very disturbed by this sermon.

Chapter Eleven: Enforcing the Law

1. See Vaggione, Chapter Eight, 'Troglodyte', and Chapter Nine, 'Heretic', for these events.
2. See Humfress.
3. Ibid., p.140. For the trial of Priscillian, see Matthews, *Western Aristocracies*, pp.160–71.
4. Quoted in Humfress.
5. Theodosian Code XVI.5.65. Quoted in Millar, *A Greek Roman Empire*, p.151.
6. Quoted in Chadwick, p.591.
7. Humfress, p.140. The *codex* first appears in the first century AD. About 1.5 per cent of the texts at the great rubbish dump of Oxyrynchus from this century are *codices* and the first literary reference to a text written on a *codex* is a work by the poet Martial at the end of the century. Christians favoured the *codex* over the scroll, perhaps to distance themselves from the scroll literature of the Jews, and by the fourth century it was the most popular method of producing texts.
8. Martin of Deacon's *Life of Porphyry* is most easily accessed at www.fordham.edu/halsall/basis/porphyry. This is an important source for showing the resilience of paganism and the violent means necessary to destroy the ancient buildings that housed pagan cults.
9. Quoted in Garnsey and Humfress, pp.152–3. The law is to be found in the Theodosian Code at XVI.10.24.
10. Theodosian Code XVI.10.25. Quoted in Millar, *A Greek Roman Empire*, p.122.
11. This comes from a fuller exposition of some of Theodosius' laws, the *Novellae*, and is quoted in ibid., p.121.
12. Ibid., p.128, for both quotes. See also Millar, *The Greek World*, pp.457–86, 'Christian Emperors, Christian Church and the Jews of the Diaspora in the Greek East, AD 379–450'.
13. Garnsey and Humfress, p.75. See also Rapp, pp.242–52, 'Episcopal Courts'. A good overview from which the Syrian example is taken is Dossey.
14. Rapp, p.245.
15. See Stead, Chapter Sixteen, 'Christ as God and Man'.
16. Quoted in Millar, *A Greek Roman Empire*, p.39, from Socrates' *Ecclesiastical History* VII.29.5.

17. Millar, *A Greek Roman Empire*, p.176. The law is to be found in the Theodosian Code XVI.5.66.

18. Quoted in ibid., p.180.

19. This is a point made by Gray. I have depended heavily on his account. See Wessel, which shows how Cyril skilfully exploited Athanasius to win support.

20. Quoted from varied original sources in Millar, *A Greek Roman Empire*, p.186.

21. Cameron, p.206.

22. In one of the most remarkable letters to survive from this period, Galla Placidia, the daughter of Theodosius I, who was now married to the emperor of the west, Constantius III, passed on Leo's concerns to Theodosius II's pious sister, Pulcheria, who exercised great influence in the eastern court: 'Therefore, may your clemency, in accordance with the Catholic faith, once again, now in this same way share in our objectives, so whatever was done at that disorderly and most wretched council [of Ephesus in 449] should by every effort be subverted.' She put in a special plea that the authority of the Bishop of Rome be respected in doctrinal matters. Millar, *A Greek Roman Empire*, p.38. It is to be found in the Letters of Leo, 58.

23. Stead, pp.193–4. This book provides an excellent introduction to some of the major philosophical issues exposed by the coming of orthodoxy.

24. Chadwick, pp.607–8.

25. Gray, p.222.

26. Quoted in MacMullen, *Voting About God in Early Church Councils*, p.32.

27. Quoted in Chuvin, p.133.

28. See Fouracre, pp.104–5.

29. Wildberg, p.316.

30. For the Council of Constantinople, see Davis, Chapter Six, with background discussion in Gray, Chadwick, etc.

31. For a discussion of the deteriorating position of Jews in this period, see Lange.

32. Quoted in McGinn, p.113.

33. Cameron, p.217.

34. Gray (p.235) sums up the results of Justinian's religious policy: 'Byzantine theology would never be the same. It would never

again have the range of inquiry possible in a church that accepted both Antiochene and Alexandrian interpretations of scripture. The affair of the Three Chapters had effectively consolidated control of exegesis in the hands of the one person whose job it was to represent the mind of the church (and an exceedingly single-minded church it had become) – the emperor. The often fallible and brawling bishops of history became the sainted and infallible authorities for a monolithic, unchanging Christian tradition. Thinking that departed from them in the area of dogma, especially on the Trinity and on Christology, became impossible.'

Chapter Twelve: Augustine Sets the Seal

1. It proved a profound shock when 'the unmediated urgency of the angular street-Greek' of Paul reached the west for the first time, after centuries in which Jerome's elegant translation had reigned supreme. MacCulloch, p.83. MacCulloch says of the discovery of Paul's original Greek text: 'if there is any one explanation why the Latin West experienced a Reformation and the Greek-speaking lands to the east did not, it lies in this experience of listening to a new voice in the New Testament text'.
2. I am indebted to Froehlich, pp.279–99.
3. Quoted in Ayres, Young, and Louth, Chapter Twenty-Seven, David Hunter, 'Fourth Century Latin Writers: Hilary, Victorinus, Ambrosiaster, Ambrose', p.305.
4. Hill, Introduction, p.39.
5. Sanders, p.2.
6. Froehlich, p.291.
7. Poem 'On the Providence of God', Gaul, 416. Quoted in Ward-Perkins, p.29.
8. See Betz.
9. Quoted in Fitzgerald, p.621 (article by Fredriksen on Paul).
10. For the debate with Pelagius, see any standard life of Augustine, such as Brown, *Augustine of Hippo*, or Lancel. Augustine's theology is covered in Harrison, and in Rist.
11. See the whole debate in *Arianism and Other Heresies*, Volume 18 of the Works of Saint Augustine, with introduction and notes by Roland Teske SJ, New York, 1995, pp.175–338.

12. Augustine, *The City of God*, Book XIX, Chapter 4.

13. Augustine, *Confessions*, Book XIII, 12.

14. Letter 169.1. Lancel, Chapter Thirty, is very good on the background to *De Trinitate*.

15. Gunton, p.39. It was argued by I. Chevalier in his *Saint Augustin and la Pensée Grecque: Les Relations Trinitaires*, Fribourg, 1940, that Augustine read Gregory of Nazianzus' *Theological Orations* around 413, when he was already deep in his work. However, recent scholarship has failed to confirm this – see the article on the Cappadocians in Fitzgerald, pp.121–3, especially p.123.

16. Lancel, p.385.

17. See the critique of Augustine's approach in David Brown, Chapter Seven, 'The Coherence of the Trinity'.

18. Hill, Augustine, *The Trinity*, Introduction, p.56.

19. McGrath, *Christian Theology*, pp.333–4.

20. Hill, Augustine, *The Trinity*, Introduction, p.19.

21. McGrath, *Christian Theology*, Chapter Ten, on the difficulties.

22. He writes in the introductory comments to *The Trinity* (London, 1970, pp.10–11): 'Despite their orthodox confession of the Trinity, Christians are, in their practical life, almost mere "monotheists". We must be willing to admit that, should the doctrine of the Trinity have to be dropped as false, the major part of religious literature could well remain virtually unchanged.'

23. *Catechism of the Catholic Church*, London, 1994, para. 237 (p.56).

24. *Soliloquia*, 1.2.7.

25. *Confessions*, Book X:35. See the article on 'Curiosity' by N. Joseph Torchia in Fitzgerald.

26. Hankinson, p.447.

27. Quoted in Drake, p.407.

28. Quoted in Rist, p.215.

29. Roach, p.138.

30. Augustine, *The City of God*, Book XIX, Chapter 13.1.

31. Ibid., Book XIX, Chapter 15.

32. Laurence Brockliss, 'The Age of Curiosity', Chapter Five in Bergin.

Chapter Thirteen: Collapse in the Christian West

1. I have relied heavily on Ward-Perkins for this chapter. It is particularly good on the archaeological evidence for the collapse of the Roman economy, and is supplemented by McCormick. There have been two recent general studies of the centuries after the collapse of the empire, both of which have received high acclaim. They are Smith and Wickham. Both stress the diversity of responses during the period. Smith, in particular, makes the point that the period is one between the two Romes, classical and papal, and this allowed greater expression than would have been otherwise the case. However, neither book dispels the picture of low living standards and dislocated trade that Ward-Perkins and McCormick detail.

2. See Moorhead for an assessment.

3. Markus, *Gregory the Great and his World*, p.4.

4. See Peter Brown's classic, *The World of Late Antiquity*, Chapters Nine and Ten.

5. See Jones, Chapter Two, for a survey of Italy after 500.

6. Ward-Perkins, p.145.

7. Quoted in Markus, *Gregory the Great and his World*, p.52.

8. Ibid., p.208.

9. Smith, p.238.

10. The text of Gregory's *Ecclesiastical History* together with Ernest Brehart's comments can most easily be accessed at www.fordham.edu/halsall/basis/gregory-hist

11. See Vauchez.

12. Markus, *Gregory the Great and his World*, pp.39–40.

13. Lapidge.

14. Ibid., p.127.

15. See Lapidge's conclusions, ibid., pp.126–32. To give a comparison with an eastern monastery at this period, one can cite the library on the Greek island of Patmos in 1201, where only sixteen of the 330 texts did not deal with theological issues.

16. For Reichenau, see the evocative visit made by Judith Herrin recorded in the 'Afterword' to her *The Formation of Christendom*.

17. See Thucydides' analysis of the Melian dialogue, Book V. 84–118 of his *The Peloponnesian War*, or Tacitus' report of the riposte of a British chieftain to a Roman general, 'You create a wasteland and call it peace', in his *Agricola*.

18. Thacker, p.463. Chris Wickham, the author of the widely acclaimed *Framing the Early Middle Ages*, puts it more vigorously (p.343): 'The faith of many historians in the reliability and importance of every line of Bede's account often seems excessive, given the degree to which he manipulated known sources such as the *Vita Wilfridi*.' It certainly has been a feature of Anglo-Saxon scholarship to give enormous prominence to Bede, understandably so perhaps as there is so little written material surviving. To be fair to the man, he might have achieved much more if he had lived in an age where he had had access to a wider variety of sources and been able to look beyond a purely Christian perspective.

19. Markus, *The End of Ancient Christianity*, p.149.

20. Van Dam, *Saints and their Miracles in Late Antique Gaul*, has both commentary and texts.

21. I have relied on McCormick. His analysis of the European slave trade is in Chapter Nine, 'Traders, Slaves and Politicos', especially pp.244–54.

22. Jones, *passim*. For the rise of the universities in these towns, see pp.449–53.

Chapter Fourteen: Faith, Reason and the Trinity

1. See Moore, especially Chapter One.

2. See Roach, especially Chapter Four.

3. Brower and Guilfoy reflects the renewed interest in Abelard's intellectual achievements. Chapter One, 'Life, milieu and intellectual contexts', by John Marenbon is especially useful.

4. Clanchy, p.110.

5. Abelard, *Theologica Christiana*, 3.164. Quoted in Chapter 7, 'Trinity', by Jeffrey E. Brower, in Brower and Guilfoy, p.226.

6. The first quotation is from Roach, p.53. See ibid., pp.52–6, for the conflict between Abelard and Bernard. The quotation of Bernard's about 'scanning the heavens' is to be found in Clanchy, p.25.

7. Quoted in David Luscombe, 'Thought and Learning', Chapter Twelve in Luscombe and Riley-Smith, p.496.

8. Grant, p.537.

9. An extract on this theme from Aquinas' first major theological work *Summa Contra Gentiles*, 1–47, is to be found in Helm, p.106.

10. It was the fifth century BC philosopher Protagoras who had said, 'Concerning the gods, I am unable to discover whether they exist or not, or what they are like in form: for there are many hindrances to knowledge, the obscurity of the subject and the brevity of human life.' The contrast with the orthodoxy that evolved in Christianity was obvious, notably in the rise of the concept of 'faith' as an accepted body of doctrine that could not be supported by human reason.

11. These ideas and quotations are drawn from Davies, Chapter Ten, 'The Eternal Triangle'.

12. Dante, *The Divine Comedy*, Paradise, Canto XXIV, lines 139–41 in the translation by Charles Sissons, Oxford, 1980.

13. Pelikan, *Credo*, p.227

14. Diarmaid MacCulloch, pp.184–8.

15. Quoted in Bainton, p.24.

16. Israel, p.63. For the revival of religious toleration, see in particular Chapter Six, 'Locke, Bayle, and Spinoza: A Contest of Three Toleration Doctrines'.

Conclusion

1. An excellent introduction to Torrance is McGrath, *T. F. Torrance*. The first quotation is from a lecture given by Torrance entitled 'The Christian Doctrine of Revelation' and quoted in ibid., p.135. The second quotation comes from Torrance, p.153.

2. Torrance, p.30.

3. See ibid., pp.236–42. In their attempts to rebut charges that they were teaching three gods, the Cappadocians created 'a damaging distinction between the Deity of the Father as wholly underived or "uncaused" and the deity of the Son and the Spirit as eternally derived or "caused"' (p.238).

4. Ibid., pp.244–7. As Athanasius died in 373 and there is no record that Epiphanius attended the Council of Constantinople, the process by which those meeting at Constantinople might have taken over Epiphanius' 'credal statement about the Holy Spirit' and incorporated it into their creed is not clear. Note also the view of many scholars that 'the credal statement' is a later insertion.

5. See 'Orthodox Catholicism in the West', pp.349–57 in Pelikan, *The Christian Tradition*.

6.   Gwatkin, p.266.

7.   Crane and Farkas.

8.   See, for instance, the essays in Buxton.

9.   Of course, one can take this challenge back to the re-emergence of Aristotle in the thirteenth century, but Aristotle was absorbed as one more form of authoritarian dogma while Galileo and Newton, inter alia, were genuinely able to extend the scope of what could be known. In his *Aristotelean Explorations*, Geoffrey Lloyd shows how Aristotle always accepted the provisionality of knowledge. New facts could always challenge old theories. While Aristotle would doubtless have been glad to have been brought back into the western intellectual tradition by Aquinas and others, he would have been disappointed by the way his thought had become dogmatic. Galileo got it right when he suggested that Aristotle would have welcomed the way he, Galileo, challenged some of Aristotle's assertions. This was the true spirit of scientific enquiry.

SELECT BIBLIOGRAPHY

Note: the easiest way to access the works of ancient authors is now through a search engine on the Internet.

Ayres, Lewis, *Nicaea and its Legacy; An Approach to Fourth Century Trinitarian Theology*, Oxford 2004.

Ayres, Lewis, Young, Frances, and Louth, Andrew (eds.), *The Cambridge History of Early Christian Literature*, Cambridge, 2004.

Bainton, Roland, *Hunted Heretic, The Life and Death of Michael Servetus, 1511–1553*, Boston, 1953.

Bergin, Joseph (ed.), *The Seventeenth Century: The Short Oxford History of Europe*, Oxford, 2001.

Betz, Otto, 'The Essenes', Chapter Fifteen in William Horbury, W. D. Davies, and John Sturdy, (eds.), *The Cambridge History of Judaism*, Volume Three, Cambridge, 1999.

Bobzien, Suzanne, *Determinism and Freedom in Stoic Philosophy*, Oxford, 1998.

Bremmer, Jan, *The Rise and Fall of the Afterlife*, London and New York, 2002.

Brower, Jeffrey E., and Guilfoy, Kevin (eds.), *The Cambridge Companion to Abelard*, Cambridge, 2004.

Brown, David, *The Divine Trinity*, London, 1985.

Brown, Peter, *Augustine of Hippo*, London, 1977.

Brown, Peter, *The World of Late Antiquity*, London, 1971.

Brunschwig, Jacques, and Lloyd, Geoffrey (eds.), *Greek Thought, A Guide to Classical Knowledge*, Cambridge, Mass., and London, 2000.

Buxton, Richard, *From Myth to Reason: Studies in the Development of Greek Thought*, Oxford, 1999.

Bynum, Caroline Walker, *The Resurrection of the Body in Western Christianity 200–1336*, New York, 1995.

Callahan, Allen Dwight, *The Talking Book: African Americans and the Bible*, New Haven and London, 2006.

Cameron, Alan, and Long, Jacqueline, *Barbarians and Politics at the Court of Arcadius*, Berkeley and Oxford, 1993.

Cameron, Averil, *Christianity and the Rhetoric of Empire: The Development of Christian Discourse*, Berkeley and London, 1991.

Cameron, Averil, and Hall, Stuart (eds.), *Eusebius: Life of Constantine*, Oxford,1999.

Chadwick, Henry, *The Church in Ancient Society, From Galilee to Gregory the Great*, Oxford, 2001.

Chuvin, P., *A Chronicle of the Last of the Pagans*, Cambridge, Mass., and London, 1990.

Clanchy, M. T., *Abelard, A Medieval Life*, Oxford, 1997.

Clark, Gillian, *Christianity and Roman Society*, Cambridge, 2004.

Crane, Tim, and Farkas, Katalin, *Metaphysics: A Guide and an Anthology*, Oxford, 2004.

Croke, Brian, and Harries, Jill, *Religious Conflict in Fourth Century Rome*, Sydney, 1982.

Davies, Brian, *The Thought of Thomas Aquinas*, Oxford, 1992.

Davis, Leo Donald, *The First Seven Ecumenical Councils: Their History and Theology*, Collegeville, Minnesota, 1983.

Digeser, Elizabeth, *The Making of a Christian Empire: Lactantius and Rome*, Ithaca and London, 2000.

Dossey, Leslie, 'Judicial Violence and the Ecclesiastical Courts', in Ralph Mathisen (ed.), *Law, Society and Authority in Late Antiquity*, Oxford, 2001.

Drake, H.A., *Constantine and the Bishops: The Politics of Intolerance*, Baltimore and London, 2003.

Ehrman, Bart, *Lost Christianities; The Battle for Scripture and the Faiths We Never Knew*, Oxford, 2003.

Ehrman, B., and Jacobs, A., *Christianity in Late Antiquity: A Reader*, New York and Oxford, 2004.

Errington, R. Malcolm, 'Christian Accounts of the Religious Legislation of Theodosius I', in *Klio, 79*, Berlin, pp.389–443.

Errington, R. Malcolm, 'Church and State in the First Years of Theodosius I', in *Chiron*, 27, Munich, 1997, pp.21–72.

Errington, R. Malcolm, *Roman Imperial Policy from Julian to Theodosius*, Chapel Hill, 2006.

Esler, Philip (ed.), *The Early Christian World*, London and New York, 2000.

Fitzgerald, Allan (ed.), *Augustine Through the Ages*, Grand Rapids, Mich., and Cambridge, 1999.

Ford, David, and Higton, Mike (eds.), *Jesus* (Oxford Readers Series), Oxford, 2002.

Fossier, Robert (ed.), *The Cambridge Illustrated History of the Middle Ages, Volume II, 950–1250*, Cambridge, 1997.

Fouracre, Paul (ed.), *The New Cambridge Medieval History, Volume I, c.500–c.700*, Cambridge, 2005.

Freeman, Charles, *The Closing of the Western Mind*, London, 2002, New York, 2004.

Friell, Gerard, and Williams, Stephen, *Theodosius: The Empire at Bay*, London, 1994.

Froehlich, Karlfried, 'Which Paul? Observations on the Image of the Apostle in the History of Biblical Exegesis', in Bradley Nassif (ed.), *New Perspectives in Historical Theology*, Grand Rapids, Mich., and Cambridge, 1996.

Garnsey, Peter, and Humfress, Caroline, *The Evolution of the Late Antique World*, Cambridge, 2001.

Gleick, James, *Isaac Newton*, London, 2003.

Grafton, Anthony, and Williams, Megan, *Christianity and the Transformation of the Book*, Cambridge, Mass., and London, 2006.

Grant, Edward, 'The effect of the condemnation of 1277', in Norman Kretzmann, Anthony Kenny and Jan Pinborg (eds.), *The Cambridge History of Later Medieval Philosophy*, Cambridge, 1982.

Gray, Patrick, 'The Legacy of Chalcedon: Christological Problems and their Significance', Chapter Nine in Michael Maas (ed.), *The Cambridge Companion to the Age of Justinian*, Cambridge, 2005.

Gunton, Colin, *The Promise of Trinitarian Theology*, Edinburgh, 1991.

Gwatkin, H. M., *Studies of Arianism*, Cambridge, 1882.

Hankinson, R. J., *Cause and Explanation in Ancient Greek Thought*, Oxford, 1998.

Hanson, Richard, *The Search for the Christian Doctrine of God*, Edinburgh, 1988.

Hanson, Richard, *Studies in Christian Antiquity*, Edinburgh 1985.

Harrison, Carol, *Augustine, Christian Truth and Fractured Humanity*, Oxford, 2000.

Heather, Peter, *The Fall of the Roman Empire: A New History*, London, 2005.

Heather, Peter, and Moncur, David, *Politics, Philosophy and Empire in the Fourth Century; Select Orations of Themistius*, Liverpool, 2001.

Helm, Paul (ed.), *Faith and Reason*, Oxford, 1999.

Herrin, Judith, *The Formation of Christendom*, Oxford, 1987.

Hill, Edmund (ed.), Augustine, *The Trinity*, New York, 1991.

Honoré, Tony, *Law in the Crisis of Empire, 379–455 AD: The Theodosian Dynasty and its Quaestors*, Oxford, 1998.

Humfress, Caroline, 'Roman Law, Forensic Argument and the Formation of Christian Orthodoxy', in S. Elm, E. Rebillard and A. Romano (eds.), *Orthodoxie, Christianisme, Histoire*, Rome, 2000.

Israel, Jonathan, *Enlightenment Contested*, Oxford, 2006.

Janes, D., *God and Gold in Late Antiquity*, Cambridge, 1998.

Jones, Philip, *The Italian City-State, From Commune to Signoria*, Oxford, 1997.

Kelly, Christopher, *Ruling the Later Roman Empire*, London, 2004.

Kelly, J. N. D., *Jerome*, London, 1975.

King, N., *The Emperor Theodosius and the Establishment of Christianity*, London, 1961.

LaCugna, Catherine, *God for Us: The Trinity and the Christian Life*, San Francisco, 1991.

Lancel, Serge, *St Augustine*, English translation, London, 2002.

Lange, Nicholas de, 'Jews in the Age of Justinian', Chapter Sixteen in M. Maas (ed.), *The Cambridge Companion to the Age of Justinian*, Cambridge, 2005.

Lapidge, Michael, *The Anglo-Saxon Library*, Oxford, 2006.

Lewis, Naphtali, and Reinhold, Meyer (eds.), *Roman Civilization: Sourcebook II: The Empire*, New York, 1955.

Liebeschuetz, J. W., *Continuity and Change in Roman Religion*, Oxford, 1979.

Liebeschuetz, J. W., *The Decline and Fall of the Roman City*, Oxford, 2001.

Limberis, Vasiliki, *Divine Heiress: The Virgin Mary and the Creation of Christian Constantinople*, London and New York, 1994.

Lloyd, Geoffrey, *Ancient Worlds, Modern Reflections*, Oxford, 2004.

Lloyd, Geoffrey, *Aristotelean Explorations*, Cambridge, 1996.

Lloyd, Geoffrey, *In the Grip of Disease, Studies in the Greek Imagination*, Oxford, 2003.

Lloyd, Geoffrey, *Magic, Reason and Experience*, Cambridge, 1979.

Lloyd, Geoffrey, *The Revolutions of Wisdom*, Berkeley and London, 1957.

Luscombe, David, and Riley-Smith, Jonathan (eds.), *The New Cambridge Medieval History, Volume IV (c.1024–c.1198), Part One*, Cambridge, 2004.

Maas, Michael (ed.), *The Cambridge Companion to the Age of Justinian*, Cambridge, 2005.

MacCormack, Sabine, *Art and Ceremony in Late Antiquity*, London 1981.

MacCulloch, Diarmaid, *Reformation, Europe's House Divided 1490–1700*, London, 2003.

Mackay, Christopher S., *Ancient Rome: A Military and Political History*, Cambridge, 2004.

MacMullen, Ramsay, *Christianising the Roman Empire (AD 100–400)*, New Haven and London, 1984.

MacMullen, Ramsay, *Voting about God in Early Church Councils*, New Haven and London, 2006.

Markus, R. A., *The End of Ancient Christianity*, Cambridge, 1990.

Markus, R. A., *Gregory the Great and his World*, Cambridge, 1977.

Marsden, George, *Jonathan Edwards, A Life*, New Haven and London, 2003.

Mathisen, Ralph (ed.), *Law, Society and Authority in Late Antiquity*, Oxford, 2001.

Matthews, John, *Laying Down the Law: The Making of the Theodosian Code*, New Haven and London, 2000.

Matthews, John, *Western Aristocracies and Imperial Court, AD 364–425*, Oxford, 1975.

McCormick, Michael, *Origins of the European Economy, Communications and Commerce, AD 300–900*, Cambridge, 2001.

McGinn, Bernard and Patricia, *Early Christian Mystics*, New York, 2001.

McGluckin, John, *Saint Gregory of Nazianzus: An Intellectual Biography*, Crestwood, New York, 2001.

McGrath, Alister, *Christian Theology: An Introduction*, Oxford, 2001.

McGrath, Alister, *T. F. Torrance: An Intellectual Biography*, Edinburgh, 1999.

McLynn, N., *Ambrose of Milan: Church and Court in a Christian Capital*, Berkeley, 1994.

Millar, Fergus, *A Greek Roman Empire: Power and Belief under Theodosius II, 408–450*, Berkeley and London, 2006.

Millar, Fergus, *The Greek World, the Jews and the East*, Chapel Hill, 2006.

Moore, R. I., *The Formation of a Persecuting Society*, Oxford, 1987.

Moorhead, John, *Theodoric in Italy*, Oxford, 1992.

Nassif, Bradley (ed.), *New Perspectives in Historical Theology*, Grand Rapids, Mich., and Cambridge, 1996.

Norris, F. W., *Faith Gives Fullness to Reasoning: The Five Theological Orations of Saint Gregory Nazianzen*, Leiden, 1991.

Pelikan, Jaroslav, *Christianity and Classical Culture*, New Haven and London, 1993.

Pelikan, Jaroslav, *The Christian Tradition, Volume I, The Emergence of the Catholic Tradition (100–600)*, Chicago and London, 1971.

Pelikan, Jaroslav, *Credo: Historical and Theological Guide to Creeds and Confessions of Faith in the Christian Tradition*, New Haven and London, 2003.

Pelikan, Jaroslav, *Whose Bible Is It?*, London and New York, 2005.

Potter, David, *The Roman Empire at Bay AD 180–395*, London and New York, 2004.

Rapp, Claudia, *Holy Bishops in Late Antiquity*, Berkeley and London, 2005.

Rist, John, *Augustine: Ancient Thought Baptised*, Cambridge, 1994.

Rives, J., *Religion and Authority in Roman Carthage from Augustus to Constantine*, Oxford, 1995.

Roach, Andrew, *The Devil's World, Heresy and Society 1100–1300*, Harlow, 2005.

Rousseau, P., *Ascetics, Authority and the Church in the Age of Jerome and Cassian*, Oxford, 1978.

Ruether, Rosemary Radford, *Gregory of Nazianzus, Rhetor and Philosopher*, Oxford, 1969.

Salzman, Michele, *The Making of a Christian Aristocracy: Social and Religious Change in the Western Roman Empire*, Cambridge, Mass., and London, 2002.

Sanders, E. P., *Paul*, Oxford, 1991.

Sauer, Eberhard, *The Archaeology of Religious Hatred in the Roman and Early Medieval World*, Stroud and Charleston, 2003.

Segal, Alan, *Life after Death: A History of the Afterlife in Western Religion*, New York and London, 2004.

Sizgorich, Thomas, '"Not Easily Were Stones Joined by the Strongest Bonds Pulled Asunder": Religious Violence and Imperial Order in the Later Roman World', in *The Journal of Early Christian Studies*, 15.1, (2007).

Smith, Julia, *Europe after Rome: a New Cultural History 500–1000*, Oxford, 2005.

Snyder, H. Gregory, *Teachers and Texts in the Ancient World*, London and New York, 2000.

Stead, Christopher, *Philosophy in Christian Antiquity*, Cambridge, 1994.

Thacker, Alan, 'England in the Seventh Century', Chapter Seventeen in Paul Fouracre (ed.), *The New Cambridge Medieval History, Volume I, c.500–c.700*, Cambridge, 2005.

Torrance, T. F., *The Trinitarian Faith*, Edinburgh, 1988.

Vaggione, Richard, *Eunomius of Cyzicus and the Nicene Revolution*, Oxford, 2000.

Van Dam, Raymond, *Kingdom of Snow, Roman and Greek Rule in Cappadocia*, Philadelphia, 2002.

Van Dam, Raymond, 'The Many Conversions of the Emperor Constantine', in Kenneth Mills and Anthony Grafton (eds.), *Conversion in Late Antiquity and the Early Middle Ages: Seeing and Believing*, New York and Woodbridge, 2003.

Van Dam, Raymond, *Saints and their Miracles in Late Antique Gaul*, Princeton and Chichester, 1993.

Vauchez, André, 'The Birth of Christian Europe: 950–1100', in Robert Fossier (ed.), *The Cambridge Illustrated History of the Middle Ages, Volume II, 950–1250*, Cambridge, 1997.

Ward-Perkins, Bryan, *The Fall of Rome and the End of Civilization*, Oxford, 2005.

Wessel, Susan, *Cyril of Alexandria and the Nestorian Controversy*, Oxford, 2004.

White, Carolinne (tr.), *De Vita Sua, Gregory of Nazianzus: Autobiographical Poems*, Cambridge, 1996.

Wickham, Chris, *Framing the Early Middle Ages, Europe and the Mediterranean, 400–800*, Oxford, 2005.

Wildberg, Christopher, 'Philosophy in the Age of Justinian', Chapter
   Thirteen in M. Maas (ed.), *The Cambridge Companion to the Age
   of Justinian*, Cambridge, 2005.
Wiles, Maurice, *Archetypal Heresy, Arianism Through the Centuries*,
   Oxford, 1996.
Williams, Rowan, *Arius*, second edition, London, 2001.

INDEX

Simon Magus, 149
Simplicianus of Milan, 162
sin, forgiveness, 134
Sirmium, 10, 20, 23, 112
Sirmium creed (357), 62–3, 64, 84
slavery, institution of, 171
Socrates (Athenian philosopher), 30, 31, 71
  (church historian), xvii, 53, 94, 98, 200–1
Soliloquia (Augustine), 169–70
Sol Invictus, 13, 47
soul
  independent existence, 31
  and *logos*, 71
Sozomen, xviii, 26, 98, 100, 101, 102
Spain
  Arab conquest, 177
  Maximus' rule, 173
  Roman rule, 3
  Vandal invasion (409), 174
Sparta, 30
spectabiles, 22
sphere, knowledge of, 184
state, relationship with Church, xvi, 9, 51,
  193–4
Stead, Christopher, 151
Stephan of Ripon, 182
Stoicism, 32–3
subordinationism, xix, 53, 60–6, 80
  and 'begetting', 84, 85
  demonised, 108
  as dominant belief, 132
  elimination from Christian tradition,
    201
  Eunomian, 63–4, 84–5
  and hierarchical Trinity, 68, 72
  Platonism and, 60–1
  scriptural support, 60
  Sirmium creed, 62, 63
Summa Theologiae (Aquinas), 191
Sutton Hoo, Suffolk, 175–6
Sylvester II, Pope, 184
Symmachus, Bishop of Rome, 152
Symmachus, prefect of Rome, 113–14,
  121, 126
Synesius of Cyrene, xi, 17
synoptic gospels, 60, 133
Syria
  and Chalcedonian settlement, 152, 154,
    155
  in Roman Empire, 46

Tacitus, 17, 18, 127, 181
Talking Book, The (Callahan), xv
Tanakh (Hebrew scriptures), 42, 43, 44
Tatianus, pretorian prefect, 120, 125
Tertullian, 44, 63, 67, 106, 158, 165

Tervingi tribe, 7
texts
  circulation, 74
  heretical, 150
  inclusion in canon, 42–4, 74
Thecla, Paul's companion, 158
Themistius, court orator, xvi, 12, 13, 14,
  15, 24, 27–8, 34, 73, 113–14, 171
Theodora, Empress, 153
Theodore of Mopsuestia, 154
Theodoret, historian, 25, 101, 127, 154
Theodoric, Ostrogoth, 174, 178
Theodosius, Bishop of Synnada, 142
Theodosius I, Roman Emperor
  abandons policy of toleration, 104
  accession, 16
  adoption of Nicene faith, 26
  and Ambrose, 117–18, 122, 124–5
  Athaneric, meeting, 23
  baptism, 23
  and bishops, 99
  Callinicum affair (388), 118, 121, 145
  campaign against Arbogast, 126–9
  campaigns against Goths, 22, 23
  as co-emperor, 11
  Council of Constantinople (381), 94,
    96–7, 109
  Council of Constantinople (383),
    101–2, 117, 140
  death, 129
  Demophilus, bans, 92, 94
  divine support, 14, 15, 16
  doctrine, influence, xvi, xvii
  early reign, 24
  as eastern emperor, 21, 22
  Edict (380), 25–6, 75, 76, 81, 106
  and enforcement of belief, 170
  entry to Constantinople (380), 23, 91
  epistula to Auxonius, 100
  epistula to Eutropius, 1, 92–4
  and Eugenius, 126
  Eunomians, decrees, 140–1
  forces Valentinian to renounce
    Homoian faith, 116
  as general, 10–11
  Gothic troops, 126, 127
  and Gratian, 112
  and Gregory of Nazianzus, 97
  heresies, laws against, xvi, 102, 140–1
  humilitas, 122, 198
  joint edict against 'heresy' (379), 25,
    108
  law-making, xviii, xix, 22, 156
  limits freedom of discussion, xii, 130
  marriage to Galla, 117
  and Maximus, 89, 95, 112, 173